AGE-FRIENDLY CITIES AND COMMUNITIES
A global perspective

Edited by
Tine Buffel, Sophie Handler and Chris Phillipson

First published in Great Britain in 2018 by

Policy Press
University of Bristol
1-9 Old Park Hill
Bristol
BS2 8BB
UK
t: +44 (0)117 954 5940
pp-info@bristol.ac.uk
www.policypress.co.uk

North America office:
Policy Press
c/o The University of Chicago Press
1427 East 60th Street
Chicago, IL 60637, USA
t: +1 773 702 7700
f: +1 773-702-9756
sales@press.uchicago.edu
www.press.uchicago.edu

© Policy Press 2018

British Library Cataloguing in Publication Data
A catalogue record for this book is available from the British Library

Library of Congress Cataloging-in-Publication Data
A catalog record for this book has been requested

ISBN 978-1-4473-3131-5 hardcover
ISBN 978-1-4473-3135-3 ePub
ISBN 978-1-4473-3136-0 Mobi
ISBN 978-1-4473-3132-2 ePdf

The right of Tine Buffel, Sophie Handler and Chris Phillipson to be identified as editors of this work has been asserted by them in accordance with the Copyright, Designs and Patents Act 1988.

Cover design by Policy Press
Front cover image: istock
Printed and bound in Great Britain by CPI Group (UK) Ltd, Croydon, CR0 4YY
Policy Press uses environmentally responsible print partners

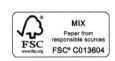

Contents

List of tables and figures

Tables

Figures

Acknowledgements

This book reflects the activities of a large number of organisations and individuals, and the editors are grateful for their generous support and assistance. The idea for the book arose from meetings of the International Network on Population Ageing and Urbanisation (INPAU), which were supported through a grant from the UK Economic and Social Research Council (ESRC) under their International Network and Partnership scheme (ES/JOI9631/2). The work was additionally supported through grants received by Dr Tine Buffel under the EU Intra-European Marie Curie Fellowship Scheme (330354) and the ESRC Future Leaders Scheme (ES/N002180/1).

A number of individuals were especially helpful in supporting work for this book. We would like to give particular mention to Jo Garsden, Rebecca Bromley and Jill Stevenson, all of whom provided valuable administrative support and advice. A range of organisations also gave assistance, including: Age Platform Europe, AgeUK, Manchester City Council, Manchester Institute for Collaborative Research on Ageing at the University of Manchester, Manchester Urban Ageing Research Group, Royal Institute of British Architects and the World Health Organization. The editors are grateful to the Vrije Universiteit Amsterdam; the Institute for Gerontological Research, Berlin; the Open University (UK); and Vrije Universiteit Brussel, for financial support for meetings of INPAU.

Finally, particular thanks must go to all our contributors, who have produced an exciting set of ideas and perspectives on age-friendly issues. We are indebted to their patience and dedication in supporting the work of INPAU and the development of this book.

Tine Buffel, Sophie Handler and Chris Phillipson
March 2017

List of abbreviations

AAA	Atelier d'Architecture Autogérée
ACT	Australian Capital Territory
AFCC	Age-friendly cities and communities
AFI	Age-Friendly Ireland
AFM	Age-Friendly Manchester
AMD	Age-related macular degeneration
BAME	Black and Asian minority ethnic
BGOP	Better Government for Older People
COTA	Council of the Ageing Australia
GM	Greater Manchester
GNAFCC	Global Network for Age-Friendly Cities and Communities
HKHS	Hong Kong Housing Society
HKJC	Hong Kong Jockey Club
HKSAR	Hong Kong Special Administrative Region of China
IAGG	International Association of Gerontology and Geriatrics
ICS	Institute of Community Studies
INPAU	International Network on Population Ageing and Urbanisation
MACA	Ministerial Advisory Council on Ageing
MICRA	Manchester Institute for Collaborative Research on Ageing
NAVIOP	Needs and Aspirations of Vision Impaired Older People
NGO	Non-governmental organisation
NSW	New South Wales
OECD	Organisation for Economic Cooperation and Development
OPC	Older people's council
P-E	Person–environment
RIBA	Royal Institute of British Architects
UN	United Nations
VOP	Valuing Older People
WHO	World Health Organization

Notes on contributors

Luma Issa Al Masarweh is a PhD researcher in the Department of Sociology at Case Western Reserve University, USA.

Tine Buffel is a Research Fellow in the School of Social Sciences at the University of Manchester, UK.

Lisa Cannon is a Research Assistant in the Centre for Research on Ageing, Health and Well-Being, Australian National University.

Pui Hing Chau is an Assistant Professor in the School of Nursing, University of Hong Kong, Hong Kong.

Francis Cheung is an Associate Professor in the Department of Applied Psychology, Lingnan University, Hong Kong.

Meredith Dale is a social geographer and freelance collaborator at the Institute for Gerontological Research, Berlin, Germany.

Dale Dannefer is Selah Chamberlain Professor of Sociology and Chair of the Department of Sociology, Case Western Reserve University, USA.

Liesbeth De Donder is Professor in Adult Educational Sciences at the Vrije Universiteit Brussel, Belgium.

Nico De Witte is Professor in Adult Educational Sciences at the Vrije Universiteit Brussel and lecturer at University College Ghent.

Daan Duppen is a PhD researcher within the D-SCOPE project at the Department of Educational Sciences of the Vrije Universiteit Brussel, Belgium.

Cathy Gong is a Research Fellow in the Centre for Research on Ageing, Health and Well-Being, Australian National University, Canberra, Australia.

Mark Hammond is a PhD researcher at Manchester School of Architecture, UK.

Sophie Handler is Research and Planning Officer for Age-friendly Cities at the University of Manchester, UK.

Josefine Heusinger is Professor of Social Work at the University of Applied Sciences Magdeburg, Germany.

Caroline Holland is a Senior Research Fellow at the Open University, UK.

Rebecca L. Jones is Senior Lecturer in Health at the Open University, UK.

Jeanne Katz is a medical sociologist who taught at the Open University, UK, until she retired in 2015.

Jessica A. Kelley is Associate Professor in the Department of Sociology at Case Western Reserve University, US.

Hal Kendig is Professor of Ageing and Public Policy at the Centre for Research on Ageing, Health and Well-Being, Australian National University, Canberra, Australia.

Bernard McDonald is a PhD researcher and a former Research Associate with the Irish Centre for Social Gerontology at the National University of Ireland Galway, Ireland.

Paul McGarry is Strategic Lead, Greater Manchester Ageing Hub.

Sheila Peace is Emeritus Professor of Social Gerontology at the Open University, UK.

David R. Phillips is Professor of Social Policy at Lingnan University, Hong Kong.

Chris Phillipson is Professor of Sociology and Social Gerontology at the University of Manchester, UK.

Samuèle Rémillard-Boilard is a PhD researcher in the School of Social Sciences at the University of Manchester, UK.

Thomas Scharf is Professor of Social Gerontology at Newcastle University, UK.

An-Sofie Smetcoren is a postdoctoral researcher at the Department of Educational Sciences of the Vrije Universiteit Brussel, Belgium.

Fleur Thomése is Associate Professor of Sociology at the Free University, Amsterdam, Netherlands.

Olivia Vanmechelen is the staff member responsible for care issues at the Kenniscentrum WWZ (Centre for Expertise in Wellbeing, Housing and Care) in Brussels, Belgium.

Dominique Verté is Professor Social Gerontology at the Vrije Universiteit Brussel, Belgium.

Kieran Walsh is Director of the Irish Centre for Social Gerontology and Director of Project Lifecourse at the National University of Ireland Galway, Ireland.

Stefan White is Professor and Director of the Centre for Spatial Inclusion Design, Manchester School of Architecture, UK.

Birgit Wolter is an architect and researcher at the Institute for Gerontological Research, Berlin, Germany.

Moses Wong is a Research Associate in the Department of Medicine and Therapeutics, Chinese University of Hong Kong, Hong Kong.

Jean Woo is Director of the Chinese University Jockey Club Institute of Ageing, Chinese University of Hong Kong, Hong Kong.

Series editors' preface

Chris Phillipson (University of Manchester, UK),
Toni Calasanti (Virginia Tech, USA) and
Thomas Scharf (Newcastle University, UK)

Demographic change and the growing proportions of older people across the world raise new issues and concerns for consideration by academics, policy makers and a wide range of professionals working with ageing adults worldwide. Ageing in a Global Context is a book series, published by Policy Press in association with the British Society of Gerontology, which aims to influence and transform debates in what has become a fast-moving field in research and policy. The series is seeking to achieve this in three main ways. First, it publishes books which rethink fundamental questions shaping debates in the study of ageing. This has become especially important given the restructuring of welfare states, alongside the complex nature of population change, both of these elements opening up the need to explore themes which go beyond traditional perspectives in social gerontology. Second, the series represents a response to the impact of globalisation and related processes, these contributing to the erosion of the national boundaries which once framed the study of ageing. From this have emerged the issues explored in various contributions to the series, for example: the impact of transnational migration, cultural diversity, new types of inequality, changing personal social relationships, and contrasting themes relating to ageing in rural and urban areas. Third, a key concern of the series is to explore interdisciplinary connections in gerontology. Contributions provide a critical assessment of the disciplinary boundaries and territories influencing the study of ageing, creating in the process new perspectives and approaches relevant to the 21st century.

Set within this context, we are delighted to include within the series a book which responds directly to major questions facing ageing societies across every world region. The global flourishing of age-friendly cities and communities initiatives provides fertile ground for critical thinking about what it is that makes places good places in which to age. The book's editors, Tine Buffel, Sophie Handler and Chris Phillipson, have been central to emerging scientific and policy debates about age-friendliness. In this book they have succeeded in bringing together an impressive cast of international scholars to explore multiple perspectives on the problems and the potential of designing age-friendly environments. Of particular importance is the focus on engaging directly with ageing adults in improving the environments in which they live. The book is essential reading for academics, policy makers and practitioners who share an interest in developing age-friendly societies.

Part 1
Age-friendly cities and communities: background, theory and development

ONE

Introduction

Tine Buffel, Sophie Handler and Chris Phillipson

The main purpose of this volume is to provide an assessment of the potential for developing environments responsive to the aspirations and needs of older people. Bringing together theories and empirical research, the book examines experiences of ageing in contrasting urban settings, drawing together a range of multi- and interdisciplinary perspectives. It provides a critical appraisal of what has been termed the development of 'age-friendly cities and communities', by exploring such policies in the context of urban change arising from globalisation, urban regeneration and austerity. Building on a range of international perspectives, the book develops new ways of approaching the issue of ageing and urbanisation. Crucially, it identifies age-friendly strategies designed to improve the lives of older people and ways in which older people themselves can be involved in the co-production of age-friendly policies and practices.

The discussion of how environmental complexity influences ageing is essential for all those involved in building and managing 'age-friendly' communities. The book is especially relevant to scholars in the field of social gerontology, social policy, housing, public health, urban studies, sociology and geography. It should also appeal to policymakers, urban planners, international organisations, service providers, practitioners and older people interested in improving the quality of life in cities. The volume was conceived as an attempt to draw together a fresh assessment of findings on the creation of age-friendly communities, drawing on insights from research, policy and (design) practice. It aims to stimulate discussion and consideration of new areas for theoretical and empirical development, and to raise aspirations of what is now a worldwide 'age-friendly' movement.

Background

Developing what has been termed 'age-friendly cities and communities' (AFCC) has become an important area of work in the field of public policy and ageing (WHO, 2015). This reflects, first, the complexity of demographic change, with the emergence of a wide spectrum of needs among different cohorts in the 50-plus age group; second, awareness of the importance of the physical and social environment in maintaining the quality of life of older people; and third, emphasis on community care and neighbourhood support as primary goals of health and social care.

Although the age-friendly movement has been in existence for over a decade, the research literature covering this topic remains sparse. Various studies have emerged, bringing together a combination of case studies and contributions to policy development (for notable examples see Caro and Fitzgerald, 2016; Moulaert and Garon, 2016). This book builds on and extends these existing studies, while bringing a distinctive approach grounded in acknowledgement of the strains affecting many communities in their attempts to develop support to groups such as older people. Such pressures include: widening economic inequalities within cities (Burdett and Sudjic, 2008; Harvey, 2008); the impact of rural migration on urban environments and the displacement of traditional sources of support (Lloyd-Sherlock et al, 2012); the influence of economic globalisation and the rise of 'world cities' (Phillipson, 2010; Sassen, 2012); increasing inequality between cities affected by either rapid industrialisation or de-industrialisation (Hall, 2013); and, finally, the impact of economic austerity following the global financial crisis of 2008 (Walsh et al, 2015).

Developments such as these have received limited acknowledgement within the age-friendly movement (Buffel and Phillipson, 2016). While the dominant approach in public policy has been towards encouraging what has come to be termed 'ageing in place' (Golant, 2009), the places in which older people experience ageing have often proved to be hostile and challenging environments (Buffel et al, 2013; Buffel, 2015). The different contributions to this book explore this theme in various ways: through examining the theoretical assumptions underpinning the idea of an 'age-friendly community'; through case studies of age-friendly work in contrasting environments in Asia, Australia and Europe; and through assessing different design and policy interventions aimed at improving the physical and social environments in which people live.

Aims and key research questions

Based on the context sketched out, this book has the following principal aims: first, to bring together theories and empirical research examining the experiences of older people in contrasting urban settings; second, to provide a critical perspective on developing age-friendly communities and to assess new ways of approaching the issue of ageing and urbanisation; third, to identify age-friendly strategies and initiatives designed to improve the lives of older people; and fourth, to identify ways in which older people themselves can be involved in the co-production of age-friendly policies and practices. These aims are reflected in the following questions examined in the various chapters in the book:

- How are different cities responding to population ageing? What kind of age-friendly strategies do they have? Who are the key actors? To what extent do older people influence these strategies?
- How do older people experience daily life in cities? How do older people utilise and benefit from their urban environment? To what extent are their experiences affected by differential access to resources (for example, material, social and cultural)?
- What is the impact of growing spatial inequalities on older people living in cities and neighbourhoods?
- How can cities be developed to improve the lives of older people? How can older people participate in urban governance structures? How should professionals engaged in the planning and design of cities respond to population ageing? What policies, programmes and processes would allow cities to develop as age-friendly communities?

The idea of promoting age-friendly environments embraces the full range of spatial forms – from densely populated urban areas to isolated rural communities. The focus of this volume is predominantly on the former (reflecting the work of the contributors) but many of the themes discussed will have relevance for many other types of communities, and reference has been made to these where appropriate. The book also has a strong interdisciplinary perspective, drawing on disciplines as diverse as architecture, environmental gerontology, human geography, sociology, social policy and urban design.

Origins of the book

The origins of the book stem from contributions and discussions in the International Network on Population Ageing and Urbanisation (INPAU). INPAU was a global network of major research groups, local authorities, NGOs and charitable foundations committed to studying the impact of population ageing on urban environments. The network had core funding from the UK Economic and Social Research Council International Partnership and Networking Scheme, as well as from partner universities in Asia, Europe and the United States, Manchester City Council and third sector organisations. INPAU brought together a range of disciplinary interests and research groups, with meetings combining the presentation of papers with site visits to urban areas of particular interest in respect of supporting ageing populations. In between regular meetings, the group organised numerous symposia at international conferences, and contributed to research proposals on age-friendly issues.

All of the chapters that follow have been specially commissioned but they build on and reflect the work of INPAU – the majority of contributors having been members of the network. In this context, the book does reflect discussions that have been carried on over a period of some five years, examining the theoretical and empirical challenges attached to understanding the relationship between population ageing and the complexity of urban development.

Structure of the book

The book is divided into three parts. **Part 1**, consisting of three main chapters, examines the origins and implementation of age-friendly policies, linking these to theoretical questions surrounding changes in the nature of community life in the 21st century. A key argument developed in this part concerns the need to incorporate issues relating to social inequalities and exclusion as an integral part of the debate around developing AFCCs. Following this introduction, Samuèle Rémillard-Boilard provides an overview of the contributing factors that have led to the development of AFCCs in Chapter Two. This focuses on the influence of the WHO AFCC model, and explores a number of issues associated with the implementation of age-friendly policies and initiatives. The chapter further locates discussions about AFCC in the context of theoretical debates within environmental gerontology, emphasising the importance of such perspectives and related disciplines in advancing knowledge about 'what works' in respect of age-friendly interventions.

In Chapter Three, Fleur Thomése, Tine Buffel and Chris Phillipson place the debate about AFCCs within a sociological context and explore the links between 'community' on the one side, and the idea of 'age-friendliness' on the other. The chapter draws on a range of theoretical perspectives in sociological and community studies to assess current pressures facing communities, especially those linked with neighbourhood inequalities and the impact of globalisation. It concludes by discussing strategies for strengthening the community dimension of AFCCs and develops key principles for a critical social policy strategy that promotes age-friendliness.

Building on this, Jessica A. Kelley, Dale Dannefer and Luma Issa Al Marsarweh, in Chapter Four, argue for a greater awareness and understanding of how *macro-level* developments, such as gentrification and transnational migration, influence the creation of AFCCs. The authors identify two key challenges that limit the success and effectiveness of both age-friendly initiatives and the scholarly field of environmental gerontology: first, **microfication**, or the tendency to focus on immediate aspects of everyday life while overlooking broader, overarching aspects of the social context that define and set key parameters of daily experience; and second, **erasure**, referring to the issue that certain groups of people remain 'unseen' in policy, research, or institutional practices. Remedying the limiting effects of these tendencies will be essential to increase the value and effectiveness of both of these enterprises, the authors conclude.

Part 2 consists of five chapters, each of which presents empirical research drawn from case studies demonstrating the challenges and opportunities for developing age-friendly policies in communities undergoing pressures from gentrification, migration and related forms of change. In Chapter Five, Meredith Dale, Josefine Heusinger and Birgit Wolter examine the impact of gentrification processes in Berlin, Germany, on the distribution of older people across the city as well as the everyday experiences of ageing in socially disadvantaged neighbourhoods. The chapter concludes with an overview of developments in the context of political processes, where urban transformation driven by economic interests generates growing conflict and contradiction with the needs of an ageing and increasingly less affluent population.

In Chapter Six, An-Sofie Smetcoren, Liesbeth De Donder, Daan Duppen, Nico De Witte, Olivia Vanmechelen and Dominique Verté turn to the question of how an age-friendly urban environment can support frail older people to 'age in place'. To address this issue, the chapter presents findings from a study that assessed the value of an Active Caring Community project in supporting frail older adults living in disadvantaged neighbourhoods in Brussels, Belgium. The project was aimed at creating a community that supports the process of ageing in place; where residents of the community know and help each other; where meeting opportunities are developed; and where individuals and their informal caregivers receive care and support from motivated professionals. The authors highlight the importance of the social dimension of the environment, and discuss a range of related opportunities and constraints that may affect older people's frailty.

In Chapter Seven, David R. Phillips, Jean Woo, Francis Cheung, Moses Wong and Pui Hing Chau provide a comprehensive overview of age-friendly approaches and developments in Hong Kong. The chapter first considers learning lessons from other large Asia-Pacific cities, including those in Japan, Korea, Thailand, Singapore and China, in terms of developing AFCCs. It then reviews a range of initiatives in Hong Kong, focusing in particular on those concerned with the domains of social participation and those involving housing and accommodation initiatives. The chapter concludes by discussing some of the positive achievements of the approach and some of the negative factors that might hinder future achievement of age-friendliness locally, including the pressing issue of elderly poverty in a rich city.

In Chapter Eight, Bernard McDonald, Thomas Scharf and Kieran Walsh examine the dynamics of the implementation process of an age-friendly county programme in one of the participating counties in Ireland, County Fingal. The chapter integrates the views of local, national and international stakeholders to explore the complex interplay of forces at these various levels that have influenced the development and impact of Fingal's local programme. Findings from empirical research are used to explore the key stakeholders' motivations and actions that were influential in developing and implementing the programme, and the attitudes, understandings and actions of these same stakeholders that underpin, and are reflected in, the processes established to involve older people in the programme. The chapter concludes by highlighting key issues that need to be addressed to enhance the potential impact of age-friendly community programmes on older adults' lives.

Chapter Nine focuses on the challenges and opportunities associated with implementing age-friendly approaches in Australia. In this chapter, Hal Kendig, Cathy Gong and Lisa Cannon review the evolution of Australia's ageing population, including its increasing diversity, and consider evidence on the liveability of Australian cities, especially for disadvantaged older people. The chapter provides a review of AFCC initiatives, comparing Sydney, Melbourne, and Canberra in a state and national context. It concludes with a critical assessment of both challenges and achievements associated with age-friendly work, and suggests a number of ways forward for developing and evaluating the AFCC approach in Australia.

Part 3 consists of five chapters that identify a range of design strategies and policy initiatives aimed at improving the environment in which older people live. In Chapter Ten, Stefan White and Mark Hammond explore what it means to use a 'capability' approach to designing an age-friendly city, including its potential for offering new ways of producing and occupying physical and social environments that respond directly to the lived experiences of older people. Drawing on an interdisciplinary community-engaged research/urban design project in Manchester, UK, the chapter examines the applicability of AFCC design guidance within a specific urban neighbourhood, and explores how the process of discovering and sharing information about the lived experience of older residents translates into the development and implementation of age-friendly activities focused around urban design.

Developing this 'design' perspective further, Sophie Handler, in Chapter Eleven, identifies new and creative ways in which architects, artists and designers might be drawn into debates around age-friendly urban practice. The chapter describes the way in which current understandings of age-friendly design are limited and how an emerging field of socially engaged design practice can be harnessed to reinvigorate the terms of age-friendly debate and practice – drawing a new generation of designers into conversation with age-friendly policy. By redefining what we mean by age-friendly design, it becomes possible, this chapter argues, to expand and invigorate the field of age-friendly practice, enabling creative practitioners to engage with and creatively inform age-friendly policymaking.

In Chapter Twelve, Paul McGarry charts the evolution of the Age-Friendly Manchester (AFM) programme and, more broadly, explores how the UK government's ageing policies and strategies have developed since the late 1990s, highlighting four distinctive periods of nationally led activity relating to older people. It goes on to consider how the subsequent development of the age-friendly approach in Manchester has enabled a range of actors, notably local government agencies, to develop ageing programmes in the absence of national leadership. It discusses the city's involvement in expanding its programme into an ambitious city-regional approach to age-friendly urban development, the first of its kind in the UK. The chapter demonstrates the potential for stimulating age-friendly initiatives at a local and regional level while at the same time highlighting the pressures facing urban authorities at a time of economic austerity.

In Chapter Thirteen, Sheila Peace, Jeanne Katz, Caroline Holland and Rebecca L. Jones test the inclusivity of age-friendliness for the lives of older people with sight loss living within English urban and rural communities. The chapter presents findings from an in-depth study with diverse groups of older people with vision impairment to consider how their needs and aspirations can be or are being met in relation to the development of age-friendly cities and communities. The study identifies transport and the built environment as two important areas for vision-impaired older people, emphasising the significance of more inclusive design, including assistive technology and accessible street design, in facilitating social inclusion.

In order to move AFCCs policies forward, the authors conclude, the approach requires recognition of the heterogeneity of the ageing population and the importance of involving people in co-design and co-production of living spaces.

Finally, in Chapter Fourteen, Tine Buffel, Sophie Handler and Chris Phillipson present a 10-point Manifesto for Change, drawing on arguments and perspectives developed by the contributors to this book. Despite the expansion of the WHO Global Network of Age-Friendly Cities and Communities, the chapter argues, challenges remain in responding to the growth of inequality and the impact of economic austerity on policies targeted at older people. Given this context, it becomes especially important to develop a framework for action that strengthens commitment to the primary goal of making environments responsive to the diverse needs of people as they age. The aim of the manifesto is to sharpen debate in the age-friendly field as well as encourage new approaches among the various stakeholders, including urban planners, community developers, health and social care professionals, policymakers, NGOs, voluntary workers, and not least, older people themselves.

References

Buffel, T. (2015) 'Ageing migrants and the creation of home: mobility and the maintenance of transnational ties', *Population, Space and Place*. Article first published online: 27 October 2015, DOI: 10.1002/psp.1994.

Buffel, T. and Phillipson, C. (2016) 'Can global cities be "age-friendly cities"? Urban development and ageing populations', *Cities*, 55: 94-100.

Buffel, T., Phillipson, C. and Scharf, T. (2013) 'Experiences of neighbourhood exclusion and inclusion among older people living in deprived inner-city areas in Belgium and England', *Ageing & Society*, 33(1): 89-109.

Burdett, R. and Sudjic, D. (eds) (2008) *The endless city*, London: Phaidon.

Caro, F.G. and Fitzgerald, K.G. (eds) (2016) *International perspectives on age-friendly cities*, New York, NY: Routledge.

Golant, S. (2009) 'Aging in place: solution for older Americans: Groupthink responses not always in their best interests', *Public Policy & Aging Report*, 19(1): 33-9.

Hall, P. (2013) *Good cities, better lives: How Europe discovered the lost art of urbanism*, London: Routledge.

Harvey, D. (2008) 'The capitalist city', *New Left Review*, 53: 23-42.

Lloyd-Sherlock, P., Barrientos, A. and Mase, J. (2012) 'Social inclusion of older people in developing countries: relationships and resources', in T. Scharf and N. Keating (eds) *From exclusion to inclusion in old age*, Bristol: Policy Press.

Moulaert, T. and Garon, S. (eds) (2016) *Age-friendly cities and communities in international comparison*, Cham: Springer.

Phillipson, C. (2010) 'Ageing and urban society: growing old in the "century of the city"', in D. Dannefer and C. Phillipson (eds) *The Sage handbook of social gerontology*, London: Sage Publications.

Sassen, S. (2012) *Cities in a world economy*, London: Sage Publications.

Walsh, K., Carney, G. and Léime, A. (2015) (eds) *Ageing through austerity: Critical perspectives from Ireland*, Bristol: Policy Press.

WHO (World Health Organization) (2015) *World report on ageing and health*, Geneva: WHO.

TWO

The development of age-friendly cities and communities

Samuèle Rémillard-Boilard

Introduction

Two dominant forces are shaping social and economic life in the 21st century – population ageing on the one side and urbanisation on the other. Population ageing is taking place across all countries of the world, albeit at varying levels of intensity. The proportion of those 60 years and over in the global north increased from 12% in 1950 to 23% in 2013, and is expected to reach 32% in 2050. In the global south, the share of older persons increased slowly between 1950 and 2013, from 6% to 9%, but is expected to accelerate in the coming decades, reaching 19% in 2050 (UN, 2014a). Of equal importance has been the spread of urbanisation, with over half of the world's population (54%) now living in urban areas, with this expected to increase to around two-thirds by 2050 (UN, 2014b). Understanding the relationship between population ageing and urban change has become a major issue for public policy. The case for such work is especially strong given that cities are where the majority of people (of all ages) now live and where they will spend their old age. A report from the Organisation for Economic Cooperation and Development (OECD, 2015, p 18) makes the point that:

> Designing policies that address ageing issues requires a deep understanding of local circumstances, including communities' economic assets, history and culture. The spatially heterogeneous nature of ageing trends makes it important to *approach ageing from an urban perspective*. Cities need to pay more attention to local circumstances to understand ageing, and its impact. They are especially well equipped to address the issue, given their long experience of working with local communities and profound understanding of local problems. (Emphasis added.)

This argument raises an important challenge for policies relating to ageing and their impact on communities across the world. One significant policy response has come from the World Health Organization (WHO), through its approach to developing what has been termed 'age-friendly cities and communities' (AFCCs). This chapter aims to provide an overview of the contributing factors that have led to the development of AFCCs. The chapter is structured in three parts. The first part addresses the development of the age-friendly movement, focusing on the influence of the WHO AFCC model, followed by an assessment of key issues associated with the implementation of age-friendly policies and initiatives. The second part highlights research findings from environmental gerontology, emphasising the importance of the physical and social environment in the lives of older people. Finally, the chapter considers success factors and challenges associated with implementing the AFCC approach.

Development of the WHO age-friendly programme

The origins of the AFCC movement can be traced back to the United Nations (UN) First World Assembly on Ageing, held in Vienna in 1982. Convened by the General Assembly of the UN, the assembly marked a significant milestone in the development of ageing strategies. The conference event highlighted increased international focus on issues arising from population ageing, illustrated in the adoption of the first international instrument on ageing: the Vienna International Plan of Action on Ageing. This called for an international response to the needs of a rapidly ageing world population, and invited governments to act on multiple issues affecting older people's wellbeing (for example, employment, income, health and nutrition, housing, education, environment and social welfare) (UN, 1983). While this instrument provided a significant advance in formulating ageing policies and programmes, its development was rooted in medical and epidemiological perspectives. As Kalache (2016, p 67) argues, at that time 'the preoccupation [in work with older people] was almost entirely disease-oriented ... conveying the firm message that health in older age was synonymous with disease, decline and disability'.

A second milestone came with the development of the 1986 WHO Ottawa Charter for Health Promotion, which stimulated a shift towards a more socio-ecological approach to health. The charter was adopted following the First International Conference on Health Promotion, held in Ottawa (Canada) in 1986, and became a key document for health promotion strategies. Kickbusch (2003, p 383) suggests that:

> The Ottawa Charter for Health Promotion ... exerted significant influence – both directly and indirectly – on the public health debate, on health policy formulation and on health promotion practices in many countries.... [It] initiated a redefinition and repositioning of institutions, epistemic communities, and actors at the 'health' end of the disease-health continuum ...

Although the Ottawa Charter did not specifically target older people, its adoption encouraged governments and local authorities to become partners in health promotion strategies. The charter stressed the importance of involving multiple actors (such as governments, social and economic sectors, voluntary organisations, communities) in the promotion of health, and proposed different strategies to achieve this goal. The Ottawa conference led to the launch in 1986 by the WHO of what became known as the Healthy Cities movement (Leeuw et al, 2014). This network – which has spread across cities in the global north and south – developed what was to become an influential focus on the social determinants of health and the impact of health inequalities on life chances in urban environments. It also initiated approaches that became central to the development of the age-friendly approach: first, the importance of reorienting health and social services towards the perspectives of users; second, strengthening community action; and, third, creating supportive environments throughout the life course (WHO, 1986, 2015a).

Twenty years after the First World Assembly on Ageing, the UN General Assembly met to review the outcomes of the Vienna International Plan of Action on Ageing. Held in Madrid, in 2002, the Second World Assembly on Ageing focused on three specific topics: older persons and development; advancing health and wellbeing into old age; and ensuring supportive and enabling environments (UN, 2002). This event led to the adoption of two major policies – the Madrid International Plan of Action on Ageing and the WHO Active Ageing Policy Framework – both of which provided the foundation for the AFCC programme. The Madrid plan identified the creation of enabling and supportive environments as a major priority for work in the field of ageing. The WHO (2002) defined an age-friendly city as one that could promote active ageing, defined as '... the process of optimizing opportunities for health, participation and security in order to enhance quality of life as people age' (WHO, 2002, p 12).

Global Age-Friendly Cities project

The age-friendly city programme was introduced for the first time in 2005 during the International Association of Gerontology and Geriatrics (IAGG) World Congress of Gerontology and Geriatrics held in Rio de Janeiro (Brazil). The idea was formalised with the launch of the WHO Global Age-Friendly Cities project in 2006, carried out in 33 cities across the global north and south. The aim of this study was to identify the core features of an age-friendly city from the perspective of older people, caregivers and local service providers (WHO, 2007a). A total of 1,485 older adults (60 years old and over), 250 caregivers and 515 service providers (drawn from the public and the private sectors) took part in more than 158 focus groups conducted in various cities around the world (Plouffe and Kalache, 2010).

All focus groups and community assessments were developed using the same research protocol (known as the Vancouver Protocol) (WHO, 2007b). This recommended that each city should conduct a minimum of five focus groups: four with older residents and one with informal caregivers representing older people with disabilities. Researchers were encouraged to recruit people from different backgrounds (for example, different age groups, gender, levels of autonomy and ethnic groups), but with two main criteria guiding the formation of the groups: the age of the participants and their socioeconomic status. The Vancouver Protocol recommended that participants be first divided into different age groups (60-74 years old, or 75 and over) and then divided a second time according to their socioeconomic status (low or middle), forming a total of four groups. Older residents who agreed to take part in the study would then be asked to describe how they experienced their city and to identify features that impeded or contributed to its age-friendliness. Parallel to these interviews, researchers were invited to talk to service providers and other groups, with contact made with professional staff in public municipal or regional services, representatives from the business sector, and voluntary organisations.

Findings from the focus groups identified eight domains that needed to be addressed in order to increase the age-friendliness of cities: housing; transportation; respect and social inclusion; social participation; social and civic engagement; outdoor spaces and buildings; community support and health services; and communication and information (WHO, 2007a, p 9) (see Figure 1). Each of these domains was further defined and presented under the form of a 'checklist of core features'. Results were published in a guide entitled *Global age-friendly cities*, also known as the WHO checklist (WHO, 2007a). This guide has since become one of the most frequently used tools to assess levels of age-friendliness of cities and communities in contrasting environments across the world (Plouffe et al, 2016).

Figure 2.1: Themes explored in the WHO global age-friendly cities guide 2007

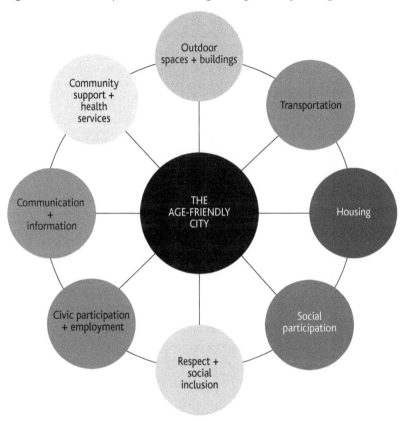

Source: Handler (2014, p 15).

Global Network for Age-Friendly Cities and Communities

To encourage implementation of recommendations from the 2007 project, the WHO launched the Global Network for Age-Friendly Cities and Communities (GNAFCC). Since its launch in 2010, the GNAFCC has had a rapid increase in membership, reaching over 500 cities and communities across 37 countries in the global north and south by 2017. In addition, there are 13 affiliated programmes associated with the GNAFCC, including networks of AFCCs at regional or national levels working directly with local communities, and organisations that promote the AFCCs framework through knowledge generation and information sharing. They play a significant role in supporting AFCC worldwide and serve as catalysts at the national and regional level by promoting an age-friendly approach and providing guidance and support to cities and communities who wish to become more age-friendly – in the local language, within the local policy context, and by providing opportunities for face-to-face meetings in the local area (WHO, 2017b).

By providing (via its website: www.agefriendlyworld.com) a platform for discussion and document sharing, the GNAFCC aims to 'foster the exchange of experience and mutual learning between cities and communities worldwide' (WHO, 2017b). Once membership has been approved, members are invited to use the network's website to share their experience and present successful initiatives brought about in their region. In return, the network supports members by connecting cities and communities, and providing research and policy tools and access to various publications.

Further iteration of the WHO approach came in the *World report on ageing and health* (WHO, 2015a), which provided a range of illustrations from the global north and south of age-friendly policies and interventions. These focus on the role of age-friendly environments in promoting functional ability in later life, in two main ways:

> [First] … building and maintaining intrinsic capacity, by reducing risks (such as high levels of pollution, encouraging healthy behaviours … or removing barriers to them (for example, high crime rates …), or by providing services that foster capacity….
>
> [Second] … by enabling greater functional capacity – in other words, by filling the gap between what people can do given their level of capacity and what they could do in an enabling environment (for example, by providing appropriate assistive technologies … or developing safer neighbourhoods …). (p 160)

European and North American age-friendly initiatives

The GNAFCC has been supported by a range of other age-friendly groupings, including international NGOs such as the International Federation on Ageing[1] (IFA) and various other organisations. In North America, these include the American Association of Retired Persons

(AARP) Livable Communities initiative, and similar work supported by the Livable Communities initiative sponsored by the National Association of Area Agencies on Aging. In the case of Europe, Age Platform Europe has occupied a leadership position in supporting age-friendly activities. In 2012, there was the launch of the campaign Towards an Age-Friendly European Union by 2020, driven by the 'goal to shape a fair and sustainable society for all ages'.[2] Arising from this work was the identification of the need for a network that would bring together a variety of stakeholders across Europe to exchange knowledge and good practice. This was advanced initially through the AFE-INNOVNET Thematic Network on Innovation for Age-Friendly Environments (2014-16), an EU-funded group that brought together a range of countries and cities across Europe. The work of the network led to the launch (in 2015) of the Covenant on Demographic Change, an EU-wide association of stakeholders committed to implementing 'evidence-based solutions to support active and health ageing as a comprehensive answer to Europe's demographic challenge'.[3]

Implementation of age-friendly policies and initiatives

Given the wide range of contexts in which age-friendly policies can be implemented, the WHO encourages cities and communities to tailor the model to their own needs and to develop their mechanisms in order to increase their level of age-friendliness. Local actors are nevertheless invited to follow certain guidelines when implementing their approach. Drawing on some of these guidelines, this section examines five key steps in the implementation process: identifying areas of action; developing partnerships and working in collaboration; involving older people in the decision-making process; monitoring the evolution of the approach; and evaluating the results (see, further, Warth, 2016).

Identifying areas of action

Identifying areas of action represents a key step in the implementation of age-friendly policies. The WHO encourages cities and communities to implement 'evidence-informed' planning (Warth, 2016, p 41), recommending that each city starts by conducting a baseline assessment of their age-friendliness (WHO, 2017c). Conducting focus groups with older people or consulting organisations and stakeholders, for example, has helped cities to identify and prioritise areas of action (Plouffe et al, 2016). Innovative methodologies have also been promoted to gather knowledge and evaluate the age-friendliness of communities, including: community audits; walking interviews; and co-research and participatory approaches with older people (De Donder et al, 2013; Handler, 2014; Buffel, 2015). Once their priorities and goals have been identified, participating cities are encouraged to write an action plan and monitor their progress as activities develop.

Developing partnerships and working in collaboration

The WHO also emphasises the importance of promoting collaborative thinking and coordination in the development of age-friendly cities. These mechanisms are essential, Beard and Warth (2016, p xvii) argue, 'to ensure that improvements are coherent, equitable, sustainable and centred on older people'. Building partnerships with stakeholders from various levels and disciplines (both from the public and private sector) has been identified as a key success factor for the development of AFCCs (Garon et al, 2014; Buffel et al, 2016). Comparing two case studies from the province of Quebec (Canada), Garon and colleagues (2014) described how the formation of a heterogeneous (and complementary) steering committee and the development of a collaborative partnership between stakeholders facilitated the implementation process in one municipality. The collaboration allowed this municipality 'to accomplish much more through its age-friendly city initiative than [the second case], which relied on a homogeneous partnership' (Garon et al, 2014, p 84). Research comparing age-friendly approaches in Manchester (UK) and Brussels (Belgium) similarly emphasised the importance of 'building synergies' and creating partnerships among various stakeholders. In both cities, Buffel and colleagues (2016) identified the importance of a multidisciplinary team as a key facilitator for the implementation of age-friendly initiatives.

Involving older people in the decision-making process

When joining the GNAFCC, cities are encouraged to involve older people in the assessment, planning and implementation of age-friendly developments (Warth, 2016). A variety of approaches have been adopted in recent years to support the participation of older people. These have ranged from consulting older residents (for example, by distributing surveys or conducting focus groups) to involving them in photovoice activities, working groups and steering committees (see, for example, Novek and Menec, 2014; Garon et al, 2016; Plouffe et al, 2016).

Research conducted in Manchester promoted the idea of involving older people as research partners in assessing the characteristics of age-friendly neighbourhoods (Buffel, 2015; Buffel et al, 2017). Working with targeted groups in three areas of south Manchester, a diverse group of 18 older volunteers were trained to become co-investigators in a research project assessing the age-friendliness of their community. Older residents acted as co-researchers at all stages of the process, including the planning, design and implementation. The co-researchers conducted 68 in-depth interviews with older residents, many of whom experienced multiple forms of social exclusion, health problems, social isolation and poverty (Buffel, 2015). Such attempts at involving older people as key actors represent an important challenge for the age-friendly movement. Commenting on the co-production approach of the Manchester study, the WHO (2015a, p 222), in the *World report on ageing and health,* stated that:

> ... this study represents a significant methodological step forward in developing new models for community engagement. Interventions such as those used in the study represent excellent sources of data, valuable exercises in community engagement for all participants, and cost-effective mechanisms for producing informed policy in times of austerity.

Monitoring the progress of the approach

The age-friendly model encourages cities to monitor and regularly review the development of their approach. The GNAFCC invites participating cities to 'assess, plan, implement, monitor and evaluate their progress in a continual cycle of improvement' (Warth, 2016, p 38). Providing space to reflect both on the achievement and challenges of developing age-friendly environments has been identified as an important dimension of the age-friendly process. In particular, it is recommended that cities reassess their level of age-friendliness on a regular basis in order to 'build knowledge on the situation of older persons' and document 'their (changing) needs over time' (Warth, 2016, p 41). Cities and communities that wish to join the network are therefore encouraged to develop their action plan using a three-year perspective (WHO, 2017c).

Evaluating the results

Members of the GNAFCC are encouraged to continuously assess, evaluate and improve their approaches to age-friendliness. This is reflected in concern with promoting evidence-based research and the development of indicators for measuring age-friendliness (Public Health Agency of Canada, 2015; WHO, 2015b). Frameworks and indicators can be instrumental in establishing a common understanding about the key dimensions of age-friendliness, and set goals and objectives in relation to them. Indicators may also be used to measure the baseline level of age-friendliness of the city and monitor changes over time as relevant interventions are implemented (WHO, 2015b). However, given the diversity of cities and communities involved in the network, the development of a common framework for evaluating the results of age-friendly policies may be difficult to achieve (see the following section).

To assist this work, the WHO (2015b) published a guide entitled *Measuring the age-friendliness of cities: A guide to using core indicators*. This document proposes a list of 'core and supplementary indicators' that cities can select and adapt to their local context. The core indicators are organised around three key principles: equity (measuring the level of inequality across subgroups); accessibility (measuring, for example, the neighbourhood's walkability, accessibility of public spaces and buildings and affordability of housing); and inclusivity (measuring, for example, engagement in volunteer activity, paid employment and socio-cultural activity, availability of social and health services, and participation in local decision making). Supplementary indicators, such as engagement in lifelong learning, internet access and emergency preparedness, are those that could be considered for inclusion in a local indicator set, allowing for a broader assessment of age-friendliness. The WHO (2015b, p 7) recommends that these indicators are not 'meant to be a prescriptive set of guidelines to be strictly followed but rather something to be adapted as necessary and appropriate'.

Developing age-friendly cities and communities: from policy to research

Despite progress in many areas of age-friendly work, research and evaluation of programmes has been relatively limited. A significant cause of this has been the extent to which work on age-friendly issues on the one side, and research in the field of 'environmental gerontology' (Wahl and Oswald, 2010) on the other, have run along parallel tracks with limited connections made between the two areas of activity. However, the application of research will be central to achieving a better understanding of the benefits and potential of the age-friendly model. Initial research in environmental gerontology examined the extent to which some physical contexts achieved a better 'fit' with the needs and abilities of older residents compared with others. This argument – developed as the 'press-competence model' (Lawton and Nahemow, 1973; Lawton, 1982) – emerged as a dominant framework for understanding person–environment relationships. The assumption of this approach was that individual behaviour was a product of congruence between the demand character of the environment (**environmental press**) and the capabilities of the person to deal with that demand (**personal competence**).

The person-environment (P-E) model became the dominant paradigm in environmental gerontology in the 1970s and 1980s, and has retained its influence (Wahl and Lang, 2010) (see, further, Chapters Four and Five). Through the 1980s and 1990s, however, new approaches emerged focusing on experiential dimensions to ageing and the environment (Rowles, 1978, 1983; Rubinstein and Parmelee, 1992). These raised issues both about the meanings associated with, and attachments to, places such as the (residential) home or neighbourhood. In contrast to the P-E model, research concerned with place attachment addresses the range of processes in operation when older people form affective, cognitive and behavioural ties to their physical surroundings (Peace et al, 2007).

Work in environmental gerontology has also raised issues about the global changes affecting communities, these undermining the strategies identified by Rowles (1978, 1983) by which older people maintained a sense of identity in later life (see, further, Chapter Three). This observation indicates challenges for the age-friendly approach and its aspirations to improve the quality of the environments in which older people live. Golant (2014, p 13), for example, suggests that such ambitions raise questions such as '… whether communities have acquired the structural capacity – that is the resources and opportunities – to accommodate the needs and goals of their aging populations …'. Resources may be especially limited in economically deprived urban neighbourhoods that may experience a variety of environmental pressures arising from the closure of local services and amenities, crime-related problems, poor housing and population turnover – all of which may mitigate against the development of age-friendly communities (Smith, 2009; Buffel et al, 2014; see, further, Chapters Three and Fourteen).

The application of work in environmental gerontology and related disciplines will be especially important in learning more about 'what works' in respect of age-friendly interventions. The importance of research has already been confirmed in knowledge acquired in examining progress with existing programmes. This aspect is now reviewed in the penultimate section of this chapter.

Age-friendly cities and communities: findings from research

From the launch of the original WHO project in 2006, what has been learnt about what makes for success in establishing AFCCs? Conversely, what are the obstacles and challenges that face those attempting to implement the WHO approach? This section considers the evidence to date, drawing on available research and case study material (see, further, Caro and Fitzgerald, 2016; Moulaert and Garon, 2016).

Success factors assisting the age-friendly model

In the introduction to their edited collection *International perspectives on age-friendly cities*, Fitzgerald and Caro (2016, pp 4-6) identify various preconditions that can influence the development of age-friendly policies, including a large and growing **concentration** of older people; a strong network of **social and civic organisations**; the availability of **health and social services**; and a variety of **housing options**. Other factors supporting age-friendliness include first, the extent to which cities and communities can mobilise a wide range of stakeholders, built around partnerships with public, private and third sector and non-governmental organisations (NGOs) (Garon et al, 2014; Buffel et al, 2016). Associated with this is the need for strong political leadership in gaining support for age-friendly policies at local and regional levels of government (Neal et al, 2014; Moulaert and Garon, 2015). Drawing on the example of Portland in the US, Neal and colleagues (2014, p 96) cite 'existing relationships between the university and local city planning and other government agencies' as a strength of the age-friendly programme developed in the city.

Second, the ability of cities and communities to develop their own interpretation of the age-friendly model has often been described as a feature of the WHO approach. Various researchers have advocated the need for the movement to remain flexible in order to adapt the specific needs of each local context (Menec et al, 2011; Liddle et al, 2014; Plouffe et al, 2016). The notion of 'flexibility' has been envisaged in various ways in the age-friendly literature. Liddle and colleagues (2014), for example, have stressed the importance for the age-friendly movement of extending its focus 'beyond cities' and questioned the ability of the WHO 'age-friendly' definition to be applied to 'non-city' settings (for example, rural areas, retirement communities, communities of interest). The flexibility of the WHO checklist has also been subject to discussion, with work from Menec and colleagues (2011) defending the need for the 'age-friendly' model to be dynamic and not necessarily limited to eight dimensions. As they explain, '[fewer dimensions] would be more parsimonious, however including more domains can emphasize aspects of the community environment that otherwise might not be considered' (Menec et al, 2011, p 482).

Third, an important factor in contributing to success is linked to the extent to which policies for older people are integrated into those focusing on urban (re)development and the management of cities. Social policies can promote older people's participation in community redevelopment in several ways, notably by ensuring greater use of the different resources that accompany urban living. Urban regeneration policies can benefit from the skills and experience of older people and the attachments they bring to their communities. However, they often tend to be 'invisible' in the implementation of such programmes. 'Mainstreaming ageing issues' within community and urban (re) development therefore represents major opportunities for social and public policy as well as for community organisations and older people to ensure that the needs of all age groups are met in urban policy fields (Buffel et al, 2016).

Challenges facing the implementation of the age-friendly approach

Several challenges have emerged with attempts to implement the age-friendly approach.

First, the success of AFCCs may be compromised by public policies arising from economic austerity. Taking the city of Brussels (Belgium) as an example, Buffel and colleagues (2016, p 41) showed in their research how reductions in public expenditure would force local authorities to reduce investments in social programmes, despite a growing demand for community health and social care services. A similar issue was also observed in Manchester (UK), where budget cuts threatened to 'reduce public services such as libraries, information and advice centres, and day-care facilities for older people' (Buffel et al, 2016, p 41). Although economic considerations have been raised in multiple studies (Walsh, 2015; Buffel and Phillipson, 2016), few research projects have explored the evolution of age-friendly policies in a context of economic austerity. This issue will be important to explore in the years ahead to better understand ways of ensuring the sustainability of age-friendly programmes.

Second, issues might be raised about the 'inclusivity' of the age-friendly approach. While the notion of 'active ageing', as noted earlier, has marked an important shift towards a more comprehensive and positive vision of ageing (WHO, 2002), concerns have also been raised regarding the extent to which it marginalises the most vulnerable groups of the older population. As Moulaert and Paris (2013, p 120) argue, an 'emphasis on [active ageing] can paradoxically undermine the value of or reject certain individual experiences associated with old age, such as disease, infirmity, impotence, frailty or vulnerability (Cardona, 2008)'. Ensuring that age-friendly policies and initiatives are able to address a wide range of ageing experiences may be especially important in a context of globalisation, international migration and economic recession. Phillipson (2012, p 28) argues that the combination of these forces has created the basis for new forms of exclusion and deepened disparities within the older population. While some groups have the resources to protect themselves from insecurities affecting communities, others may find themselves at higher risk of exclusion (see also Buffel and Phillipson, 2016).

Third, problems have been encountered with the evaluation of age-friendly policies and initiatives. Given the flexibility of the age-friendly model, cities and communities have developed an array of initiatives to increase their level of age-friendliness. As Warth (2016, p 39) emphasises, 'just as there is no one-size-fits-all solution to meeting the needs of older people, there is no one-size-fits-all recipe for creating age-friendly environments'. Evaluating their 'success' may therefore prove to be a complex task. In addition to selecting indicators and monitoring the results (outputs) of their efforts, Garon and colleagues (2016) recommend that cities and communities should also pay attention evaluating the implementation *process*. According to the authors, evaluating the 'mechanisms' and 'logic' behind the development of age-friendly initiatives is essential for understanding how the approach produces the observed results, so that necessary adjustments can be made (Garon et al, 2016, p 116).

Finally, it might be argued that AFCC policies are unlikely to be successful unless embedded in the various bureaucracies and networks of power that control community life. However, a range of initiatives will need to be taken forward to achieve this goal. The first of these concerns developing a more coherent link between research and policies on age-friendly issues. Research on environmental aspects of ageing has an impressive literature to its name, yet it remains detached from analysis of the impact of powerful global and economic forces transforming the physical and social context of cities and communities (Buffel and Phillipson, 2016). Remedying this will require close integration with insights from a range of disciplines, including social policy, urban sociology, gerontology, design and human geography. Understanding optimum environments for ageing must be viewed as an interdisciplinary enterprise requiring understanding of the impact of developments such as the changing dynamics of urban poverty on older people, the consequences of urban renewal and regeneration, and the impact of transnational migration (see further Chapter Fourteen).

Conclusion

The creation of AFCCs has become an important concern for public policy, as evidenced by the rapid expansion of the Global Network for Age-Friendly Cities and Communities, and the building of networks in Europe and North America. The movement has been able to achieve significant progress within a relatively short space of time. It has been able to develop a broad, global policy response to the forces of urbanisation and ageing, encouraging and enabling cities and communities worldwide to develop and adapt age-friendly programmes within their local neighbourhoods and communities. The WHO has provided a global network of support and dialogue between different communities, cities and regions, in association with other partners such as Age Platform Europe. Importantly, the WHO has developed a framework for action through its eight domains that ensures that the global policy response to ageing and urbanisation represents an integrated response (from housing and the built environment to issues around participation, respect and social inclusion), not one that is confined to health and social care programmes alone.

But while the age-friendly cities project has made significant progress as a global movement, important issues remain unaddressed. Most urgently, there is the question as to how the GNAFCC can develop and sustain itself within a context of austerity and budget cuts that continue to have a severe impact on the services on which older people rely. Unless this issue is addressed directly at a global and national level, the sustainability of the age-friendly programme must be placed in some doubt (Buffel and Phillipson, 2016).

There is, moreover, a broader issue surrounding the inclusivity of the age-friendly cities project. Although the movement has placed older people at the centre of various initiatives, there has been a failure within the movement to acknowledge the full diversity of ageing experiences. Examples include the marginalisation of many black and minority ethnic groups and those within the lesbian, gay, bisexual, transsexual and queer community (see further Chapter Fourteen). More generally, the social exclusion experienced by many groups in urban areas – notably migrants, refugees and those living in communities with high levels of deprivation – has been largely ignored within the age-friendly movement. Given the pressures associated with globalisation and economic recession, addressing social exclusion will be crucial to the successful development of the age-friendly cities project. This theme is addressed in various chapters in this book, with the remaining chapters in Part 1 examining economic and social changes affecting the communities in which people live.

Notes

[1] www.ifa-fiv.org/age-friendly (accessed 23 January 2017)
[2] www.age-platform.eu/articles/towards-age-friendly-eu (accessed 23 January 2017)
[3] www.age-platform.eu/special-briefing/covenant-demographic-change-officially-launched (accessed 22 January 2017)

References

Beard, J.R. and Warth, L. (2016) 'Foreword: international perspectives on age-friendly cities', in F.G. Caro and K.G. Fitzgerald (eds) *International perspectives on age-friendly cities*, New York, NY: Routledge, pp xvii–xviii.

Buffel, T. (ed) (2015) *Researching age-friendly communities: Stories from older people as co-investigators*, Manchester: The University of Manchester Library.

Buffel, T. and Phillipson, C. (2016) 'Can global cities be "age-friendly cities"? Urban development and ageing populations', *Cities*, 55: 94–100.

Buffel, T., De Donder, L., Phillipson, C., De Witte, N., Dury, S. and Verté, D. (2014) 'Place attachment among older adults living in four communities in Flanders, Belgium', *Housing Studies*, 29(6): 800–22.

Buffel, T., McGarry, P., Phillipson, C., De Donder, L., Dury, S., De Witte, N., Smetcoren, A.-S. and Verté, D. (2016) 'Developing age-friendly cities: case studies from Brussels and Manchester and implications for policy and practice', in F.G. Caro and K.G. Fitzgerald (eds) *International perspectives on age-friendly cities*, New York, NY: Routledge, pp 27–45.

Buffel, T., Skyrme, J. and Phillipson, C. (2017) 'Connecting research with social responsibility. Developing "age-friendly" communities in Manchester, UK', in D. Shek and R. Hollister (eds) *University social responsibility and quality of life. Concepts and experiences in the global world*, Singapore: Springer, pp 99-120.

Caro, F.G. and Fitzgerald, K.G. (eds) (2016) *International perspectives on age-friendly cities*, New York, NY: Routledge.

De Donder, L., De Witte, N., Verté, D., Dury, S., Buffel, T., Smetcoren, A., Brosens, D. and Verté, E. (2013) 'Developing evidence-based age-friendly policies: a participatory research project', in *Sage research methods cases*, London: Sage Publications.

Fitzgerald, K.G. and Caro, F.G. (2016) 'Introduction: international perspectives on age-friendly cities', in F.G. Caro and K.G. Fitzgerald (eds) *International perspectives on age-friendly cities*, New York, NY: Routledge, pp 1-21.

Garon, S., Paris, M., Beaulieu, M., Veil, A. and Laliberté, A. (2014) 'Collaborative partnership in age-friendly cities: two case studies from Quebec, Canada', *Journal of Aging & Social Policy*, 26(1-2): 73-87.

Garon, S., Veil, A., Paris, M. and Rémillard-Boilard, S. (2016) 'How can a research program enhance a policy? AFC-Quebec governance and evaluation opportunities', in T. Moulaert and S. Garon (eds) *Age-friendly cities and communities in international comparison. Political lessons, scientific avenues and democratic issues*, Cham: Springer, pp 99-120.

Golant, S.M. (2014) *Age-friendly communities: Are we expecting too much?*, IRPP Insight, February, No 5, Montreal: Institute for Research on Public Policy, available at http://irpp.org/wp-content/uploads/assets/research/faces-of-aging/age-friendly/golant-feb-2014.pdf.

Handler, S. (2014) *An alternative age-friendly handbook for the socially engaged practitioner*, Manchester: The University of Manchester Library.

Kalache, A. (2016) 'Active ageing and age-friendly cities – a personal account', in T. Moulaert and S. Garon (eds) *Age-friendly cities and communities in international comparison. Political lessons, scientific avenues and democratic issues*, Cham: Springer, pp 65-77.

Kickbusch, I. (2003) 'The contribution of the World Health Organization to a new public health and health promotion', *American Journal of Public Health*, 93(3): 383-8.

Lawton, M.P. (1982) 'Competence, environmental press, and the adaptation of older people', in M.P. Lawton, P.G. Windley and T.O. Byerts (eds) *Aging and the environment: Theoretical approaches*, New York: Springer, pp 33-59.

Lawton, M.P. and Nahemow, L. (1973) 'Ecology and the aging process', in C. Eisdorfer and M.P. Lawton (eds) *Psychology of adult development and aging*, Washington, DC: American Psychological Association, pp 619-24.

Leeuw, E., Tsouras, A., Dyakova, M. and Green, G. (2014) *Summary evaluation of Phase V of the WHO European Healthy City Network*, Copenhagen: WHO Regional Office.

Liddle, J., Scharf, T., Bartlam, B., Bernard, M. and Sim, J. (2014) 'Exploring the age-friendliness of purpose-built retirement communities: wvidence from England', *Ageing & Society*, 34(9): 1601-29.

Menec, V.H., Means, R., Keating, N., Parkhurst, G. and Eales, J. (2011) 'Conceptualizing age-friendly communities', *Canadian Journal on Aging*, 30(3): 479-93.

Moulaert, T. and Garon, S. (eds) (2016) *Age-friendly cities and communities in international comparison. Political lessons, scientific avenues and democratic issues*, Cham: Springer.

Moulaert, T. and Paris, M. (2013) 'Social policy on ageing: the case of "active ageing" as a theatrical metaphor', *International Journal of Social Science Studies*, 1(2): 113-23.

Neal, M.B., DeLaTorre, A.K. and Carder, P.C. (2014) 'Age-friendly Portland: a university–city–community partnership', *Journal of Aging & Social Policy*, 26(1-2): 88-101.

Novek, S. and Menec, V.H. (2014) 'Older adults' perceptions of age-friendly communities in Canada: a photovoice study', *Ageing and Society*, 34(6): 1052-72.

OECD (Organisation for Economic Co-operation and Development) (2015) *Ageing in cities*, Paris: OECD, available at http://dx.doi.org/10.1787/9789264231160-en.

Peace, M., Wahl, H.W., Mollenkopf, H. and Oswald F. (2007) 'Environment and ageing', in J. Bond, S. Peace, F. Dittmann-Kohli and G. Westerhof (eds) *Ageing in society*, London: Sage Publications, pp 209-34.

Phillipson, C. (2012) 'Globalisation, economic recession and social exclusion: policy challenges and responses', in T. Scharf and N.C. Keating (eds) *From exclusion to inclusion in old age: A global challenge*, Bristol: Policy Press, pp 17-32.

Plouffe, L. and Kalache, A. (2010) 'Towards global age-friendly cities: determining urban features that promote active aging', *Journal of Urban Health*, 87(5): 733-9.

Plouffe, L., Kalache, A. and Voelcker, I. (2016) 'A critical review of the WHO age-friendly cities methodology and its implementation', in T. Moulaert and S. Garon (eds) *Age-friendly cities and communities in international comparison. Political lessons, scientific avenues and democratic issues*, Cham: Springer, pp 37-46.

Public Health Agency of Canada (2015) *Age-friendly communities evaluation guide. Using indicators to measure progress*, Ottawa: Public Health Agency of Canada, available at www.phac-aspc.gc.ca/seniors-aines/alt-formats/pdf/indicators-indicateurs-v2-eng.pdf.

Rowles, G.D. (1978) *Prisoners of space? Exploring the geographical experience of older people*, Boulder, CO: Westview.

Rowles, G.D. (1983) 'Place and personal identity in old age: observations from Appalachia', *Journal of Environmental Psychology*, 3(4): 299-313.

Rubinstein, R.L. and Parmelee, P.A. (1992) 'Attachment to place and the representation of the life course by the elderly', in I. Altman and S.M. Low (eds) *Handbook of the sociology of aging, place Attachment*, New York, NY: Plenum Press, pp 139-64.

Smith, A. (2009) *Ageing in urban neighbourhoods*, Bristol: Policy Press.

UN (United Nations) (1983) *Vienna International Plan of Action on Ageing*, New York, NY: UN.

UN (2002) *Political declaration and Madrid International Plan of Action on Ageing*, New York, NY: UN.

UN (2014a) *Concise report on the world population situation in 2014*, New York, NY: UN.

UN (2014b) *World urbanization prospects. The 2014 revision*, New York: UN.

UN (2015) *World population ageing 2015*, New York, NY: UN.

Wahl, H.-W. and Oswald, F. (2010) 'Environmental perspectives on ageing', in D. Dannefer, and C. Phillipson (eds) *The Sage handbook of social gerontology*, London: Sage Publications, pp 111-24.

Walsh, K. (2015) 'Interrogating the "age-friendly community" in austerity: myths, realities and the influence of place context', in K. Walsh, G.M. Carney and Á. Ní Léime (eds) *Ageing through austerity. Critical perspectives from Ireland*, Bristol: Policy Press, pp 79-96.

Warth, L. (2016) 'The WHO Global Network for Age-Friendly Cities and Communities: origins, developments and challenges', in T. Moulaert and S. Garon (eds) *Age-friendly cities and communities in international comparison. Political lessons, scientific avenues and democratic issues*, Cham: Springer, pp 37-46.

WHO (World Health Organization) (1986) *The Ottawa Charter for Health Promotion*, Geneva: WHO.

WHO (2002) *Active ageing: A policy framework*, Geneva: WHO.

WHO (2007a) *Global age-friendly cities: A guide*, Geneva: WHO.

WHO (2007b) *WHO Age-friendly cities project methodology. Vancouver Protocol*, Geneva: WHO.

WHO (2015a) *World report on ageing and health*, Geneva: WHO.

WHO (2015b) *Measuring the age-friendliness of cities: A guide to using core indicators*, Geneva: WHO.

WHO (2017a) 'Affiliated Programmes' available at https://extranet. who.int/agefriendlyworld/affiliated-programmes/

WHO (2017b) 'WHO Global Network for Age-friendly Cities and Communities', available at www.who.int/ageing/projects/ age_friendly_cities_network/en.

WHO (2017c) 'Application form to join the WHO Global Network for Age-friendly Cities and Communities', available at www.who. int/ageing/application_form/en.

THREE

Neighbourhood change, social inequalities and age-friendly communities

Fleur Thomése, Tine Buffel, Chris Phillipson

Introduction

The background to the development of 'age-friendly cities and communities' (AFCCs) was reviewed in Chapter Two. AFCCs were among a number of initiatives taken during the 1990s and early 2000s aimed at developing more cohesive communities (Vanderbeck and Worth, 2015). The impetus to develop AFCCs was also linked with the promotion of 'ageing in place' in health and social care, a policy that emphasised the role of community networks in providing support to groups such as older people. But the development of AFCCs and related approaches coincided with new pressures affecting community life, notably those associated with the impact of globalisation and widening inequalities within and between cities (Buffel and Phillipson, 2016a). Thus, the virtue of community – for providing support for vulnerable groups – was being 'rediscovered' at a time of increasing social divisions affecting many urban neighbourhoods (Wacquant, 2008).

The purpose of this chapter is to place the debate about AFCCs within a sociological context, exploring links between 'community' on the one side, and the idea of 'age-friendliness' on the other. Much has been written about the latter, especially following the publication by the World Health Organization (WHO) of a guide to developing age-friendly cities (see Chapter Two), and the founding (in 2010) of the global network of AFCCs. However, much less has been said about the 'community' dimension to developing age-friendly activities. Gardner (2011) makes the point that much research examining the issue of 'ageing in place' has focused on the desire of older adults to remain in their own homes and the means by which they can best receive support (Wiles et al, 2011). But she argues that: 'Public places of aging – and in

33

particular neighbourhoods – have received less attention yet represent key locales in the lives (and well-being) of older people ageing in place' (Gardner, 2011, p 263). Relevant questions here include: what sort of 'communities' is the age-friendly movement trying to develop? Are terms such as 'neighbourhood' and 'community' still meaningful given the divisions and inequalities affecting social life? How or to what extent has the idea of community changed given a context of globalisation and transnational migration? And how (if change has occurred) has this affected the capacity of communities to support ideas associated with 'age-friendliness'?

To examine these points, the chapter will first explore how concepts relating to neighbourhood and locality have developed in sociological and community studies; second, assess current challenges facing communities, especially those linked with neighbourhood inequalities and the impact of globablisation; and finally, consider strategies for strengthening the community dimension of age-friendly cities.

Changing views of community

Research on the theme of 'community' has been a core element in the sociological tradition, in the UK and many other countries (Nisbet, 1953; Crow, 2002). The development of sociology as a discipline was itself closely aligned with research on the impact of urbanisation and industrialisation on social life, a theme pursued in different ways by Comte, Tönnies, Le Play, Marx and Durkheim (Crow and Allan, 1994). Yet despite the historical importance of the idea of community to sociology, definitions have proved elusive. Bell and Newby (1971, p 21), in their classic textbook *Community studies*, make the point that:

> The concept of community has been the concern of sociologists for more than two hundred years, yet a satisfactory definition of it in sociological terms appears as remote as ever. Most sociologists seem to have weighed in with their own idea of what a community consists of ... [and they] have not always been immune to the emotive overtones that the word consistently carries with it. Everyone – even sociologists – has wanted to live in a community ... [but] ... the term frequently lead[s] to a confusion between what it *is* (empirical description) and what the sociologist feels it should be (normative description).

Notwithstanding these difficulties, community studies have contributed to a considerable extent to our understanding of the dynamics of social life at a neighbourhood level, with important implications for the development of AFCCs. In spite of reservations expressed by many researchers about the concept, Crow and Allan (1994, p 1) make the point that much of what we do in everyday life: '... is engaged in through the interlocking social networks of neighbourhood, kinship and friendship, networks which together make up "community life" as it is conventionally understood'. They further suggest that: '"Community" stands as a convenient shorthand term for the broad realm of local social arrangements beyond the private sphere of home and family but more familiar to us than the wider society' (p 1).

The 1950s and 1960s have been defined (for example, by Crow, 2002; see also, Crow and Allan, 1994) as a period when 'traditional' community studies flourished, with research characterised by detailed descriptions of the way in which community life was reproduced through family and neighbourhood-based institutions or activities. In the UK, research based at the Institute of Community Studies (ICS) carried out by Young and Willmott (1957), Townsend (1957) and Willmott and Young (1960), reflected concerns in the 1950s that the development of the welfare state would encourage families to leave groups such as older people to fend for themselves, with a possible weakening in neighbourhood solidarity and cohesion. Yet the findings from research at the ICS emphasised the extent to which familial and neighbourhood-based ties continued to flourish, in central (inner-city) as well as suburban localities (see also Gans, 1962). This theme was further developed in the work of Fischer in the 1970s and 1980s in the US (see, eg, Fischer, 1982), where the researcher found that, contrary to views emphasising the ephemeral nature of urban ties, intimate social networks could be sustained in the varied 'subcultures' operating in city environments.

Personal communities and social networks

The scientific debate on the 'community question' was given fresh impetus by research in the 1980s and 1990s in Toronto, Canada, by Wellman (1979, 1996). Their emphasis on **'personal communities'** – the collection of significant personal ties in which people are embedded – builds on an approach that seeks to map the network of relationships that individuals sustain beyond the household. A key argument was that exploring the structure of individuals' relationships would generate a clearer understanding of the diverse character of social integration than previous community studies with their focus on geographic location had achieved. Wellman's (1979, 1996) research among over 800 adults residing in the upper-working/lower-middle class Toronto borough of East York suggested that primary ties tend to form *sparsely knit*, spatially dispersed, structures. This was in contrast with the *local, densely-knit* solidarities highlighted in earlier community studies. Indeed, based on their research findings, few East Yorkers appeared to depend on their neighbourhood for maintaining close and intimate ties. The implications of the research were that community networks had been 'liberated' from immediate geographical ties. Because of processes associated with urbanisation, geographical mobility and new forms telecommunication, close ties were often sustained beyond the immediate neighbourhood. Instead, they existed at a range of distances and levels – virtual as well as physical (Wellman, 1979, 1996).

Limitations of a network-analytical approach

While network analysis seemed to offer an advance on previous community studies, the limitations of this approach have also been noted (Milardo and Allan, 2000; Blokland, 2003; Allan and Phillipson, 2008). Two issues main have been highlighted: first, because data are generated on the direct relationships in which the central *individual* is involved, network approaches appear less able to explain *collective* patterns of social action that link different members of a network to one another (Milardo and Allan, 2000). Thus, relationships are treated as individual rather than collective constructs, disconnected from the contextual factors (such as macro-social forces) that shape the ties around which networks are built. Second, although a network approach can generate more representative data on people's various relationships as compared with traditional community studies, this may be at the expense of a more detailed understanding of the solidarities such relationships entail (Allan and Phillipson, 2008). At times, the emphasis in network analysis is simply on the existence of a relationship and/or how well someone is known. Even when more detailed data are collected, this information is generally used in a predominantly descriptive fashion, with limited attention to the subtleties that often underpin social and community-based ties (Clark, 2009).

Networks, of different kinds, can be said to be of great importance for all age groups (see the following section). At the same time, local ties constructed within neighbourhoods still have considerable relevance for understanding the character and quality of everyday life. Personal communities may be geographically dispersed and maintained in a variety of ways – increasingly through various forms of social media. But in later life, the immediate locality is often vital in terms of contributing resources, as a backdrop for memories of the past, and as a source of identity and meaningful ties (Rowles and Bernard, 2013). The argument here is that there is still much to be gained from a focus on people's attachment to neighbourhood, including the networks of which they are a part. Following this, the next section of this chapter reviews research findings examining the role of neighbourhood ties in the daily lives of older people.

The relevance of the neighbourhood for older people

Sociological research has identified a range of factors that underpin the significance of locality in later life. First, the built environment has a significant influence on the quality of life for all age groups, but may be especially important for the old, the young, and those with a disability of some kind. People in late old age may be especially dependent on the character of their immediate environment given the length of time spent within the home and surrounding locality – 80% of the time of those aged 70 and above based on research by Horgas and colleagues (1998). Indeed, neighbourhoods with good facilities, accessible public spaces and places to rest, as well as measures that promote pedestrian walkability, have been shown to play an important role in promoting older people's social participation as well as a sense of safety and wellbeing (De Donder et al, 2013; Buffel et al, 2014).

Second, the neighbourhood may be especially important where support beyond the immediate locality is absent, in circumstances of limited social ties, financial constraints and problems with physical mobility (Völker et al, 2007). Given such conditions, a heightened need for continuity and belonging in one's locality may be the result. Fischer (1982, p 175) makes the point that '... nearby associates are preferred when nearness is critical'. Meeting opportunities and interaction possibilities in the vicinity become relatively more important for those who are more dependent on their locality. In the Netherlands, 60% of the most important relationships in the networks of older people have been found to be located in the neighbourhood (Thomése and van Tilburg, 2000). Similar results have been reported in research from the Belgian Ageing Studies (Buffel et al, 2012). Another important finding is that older people with fewer economic resources and a decreased activities of daily living capacity seem to be more dependent on their neighbourhood as a source of social contact. Moreover, older people who feel a greater need for support not only appeal more often to their neighbours but also receive more support from the neighbourhood (Thomése et al, 2003).

Third, the emphasis on promoting 'ageing in place' highlights the role of the neighbourhood in the provision of informal sources of support (see, further, Chapter Six). This approach has been reinforced by an extensive academic literature on the preferences and priorities of older people (Means, 2007). Ageing at home appears to be the residential strategy most older people prefer, even when they have economic difficulties, or when they are in need of care (Gilleard et al, 2007; Buffel et al, 2012). Moreover, 'ageing in place' is often associated with **'attachment to place'** as an important dimension of later life (Krause, 2004; Oswald et al, 2011). Gilleard and colleagues (2007) found that both age and ageing in place positively affect older adult's 'place attachment'. The longer older people have lived in an area, the more likely they have developed strong emotional feelings and an affective bond towards their neighbourhood (Buffel et al, 2014; Smetcoren, 2015).

Finally, an important consideration concerns the extent to which neighbourhood change can promote social *exclusion* in older age as well as social *inclusion*. This theme reflects the impact of globalisation on communities, notably those in areas affected by rapid industrial change (Buffel and Phillipson, 2016a). The argument here is that the impact of globalisation on neighbourhood life may be especially important for older people, given the length of time they are likely to have resided in the same area. The significance of changes associated with globalisation (for example, new types of movement in old age, the emergence of transnational ties) raises questions about older people's integration with and sense of belonging to their neighbourhood. Globalisation may also result in greater variation in the communities and environments experienced in old age. As Phillipson (2007) argues, such processes have the potential to generate new social divisions between **'the elected'** and **'the excluded'**, or between those able to choose residential locations consistent with their biographies and life histories and those who experience rejection or marginalisation from their neighbourhood. The next section of this chapter explores this distinction in more detail, with a particular focus on the impact of deprivation and inequality affecting neighbourhood life, as well as the emergence of new relationships associated with transnational migration.

The impact of global change

Neigbourhood inequality and spatial segregation

Research in urban sociology on the changes affecting cities has been characterised by two distinctive views about the nature of globalisation and its impact on communities. The first points to what Delanty (2010) refers to as the 'displacement of urban communities and [the] re-organisation of space' (p 43), following the rise of what Sassen (1992) and others term 'global cities' (see, further, Buffel and Phillipson, 2016a). Here, globalisation is seen to produce the fragmentation and individualisation of communities through processes associated with gentrification, the rise of gated communities, and widening inequalities between the 'winners' (such as mobile professionals) and 'losers' from globalisation (such as those in casual/low-paid employment) (Standing, 2011; Hern, 2016).

Tammaru and colleagues (2016), in a study of 11 European capital cities, found spatial segregation in urban areas to be associated with increasing social inequality and cuts in government support to vulnerable groups. Such spatial segregation raises issues about the ability of communities to support groups with particular health or social care needs. Not all local communites present ideal environments in which to age in place (Menec et al, 2011). Resources may in fact be especially limited in economically deprived urban neighbourhoods that may experience a variety of environmental pressures arising from the closure of local services and amenities, crime-related problems, poor housing and social polarisation (Rodwin and Gusmano, 2006; Smith, 2009; Buffel and Phillipson, 2016a). These problems are often reflected in a deterioration both in the quality of local relationships and the street-level environment (Smith, 2009) (see, further, Chapters Four and Five).

The impact of global change, and resulting area-based, or geographic, inequality, also highlights differences in the way 'community' is experienced by older people. Buffel and colleagues (2013) explored experiences of neighbourhood exclusion and inclusion among older people living in a number of deprived inner-city areas in Belgium and England. The study suggested more similarities than differences between the neighbourhoods. For example, experiences of population turnover and changing economic and social structures appeared to translate into desires for a 'lost community', this finding equal expression from respondents in both countries (see also Blokland, 2003). Such views partly reflect the considerable investments older people have made in their locality, and a sense of disillusion that the changes affecting their neighbourhoods seem beyond their control.

At the same time, efforts made by older people to counter social exclusion are important to note. Lager and colleagues (2013) studied the impact of neighbourhood transitions on older adults' sense of belonging in a former working-class neighbourhood in the Netherlands. They found that older residents negotiated a sense of belonging in relation to everyday places and interactions within the neighbourhood. In spite of the urban renewal taking place, they created a sense of continuity by transferring specific routines and behaviours typical of their working-class identity to the present. Byrnes (2011) demonstrated how a group of poor, non-white, central-city residents in Detroit, Michigan appropriated a new age-segregated home. She suggests that participants cultivated a distinctive space within the facility to compensate for the deficiencies of a deteriorated inner-city neighbourhood.

Neighbourhoods and transnational communities

A second perspective on globalisation points to its potentially more constructive role in the maintenance of community life. Whereas the earlier examples refer to localities undermined by globalisation, other research has identified new connections formed between people and places. An important area where this plays out concerns the transnational relationships of migrant communities (Buffel, 2015b). Transnational communities may themselves be said to reflect both the growth of a global economy and instabilities associated with civil wars and political conflicts, and the impact of both on the maintenance of family and community ties. This development indicates the need for rethinking the approach to a number of age-friendly issues, especially given the importance of migration flows across Europe (Kingsley, 2016). The consequences of global trends associated with intensified international migration have spawned a substantial literature illustrating the activities of different ethnic groups in maintaining social, economic and cultural ties across transnational borders (Buffel, 2015b; Torres, 2015).

Older people (from a range of ethnic groups) may experience migration in different ways: as first-generation migrants growing old in their second homeland (Burholt, 2004); as migrants moving 'back and forth' between families living across different continents (Victor et al, 2012; Lager et al, 2013); as a group left behind coping with the loss of younger generations (Vullnetari and King, 2008); as one involved with the management of transnational caregiving (Baldasser, 2007); or as 'return migrants' moving back to their 'first homeland' (Barratt and Mosca, 2013; Percival, 2013). Buffel and Phillipson (2011) focus on the way in which communities are constructed through the activities of migrant groups, drawing on an account of the activities of Somali and Pakistani older people in Manchester and Moroccan and Turkish elders in Brussels (see, further, Buffel and Phillipson, 2016b). A sense of 'attachment to place' was a strong element in people's narratives about memories and experiences that had accumulated from living in their neighbourhood, with two recurring themes emerging in the various accounts: first, the proximity of members to their cultural community, which offered opportunities for developing social networks and realising common social bonds; and, second, the proximity of ethnic amenities. Both these elements were illustrated by the way in which the transnational ties and practices of older migrants had helped to transform their neighbourhoods into what could be described as a 'transnational social space' (Faist, 2000). For example, the establishment and use of ethnic business and communal places such as tea houses, and activities such as watching satellite TV, all reflect transnational practice, but at the same time, they are also part of what has been termed 'the creation of new places of belonging' (Ehrkamp, 2005). Such processes of producing and investing in the neighbourhood also reveal how the construction or reconstruction of identities occurs through the interconnections developed between global and local ties.

The changes to neighbourhood life highlighted in this chapter underline the need for new approaches to building age-friendly communities. Locality has retained its importance in the lives older people, but neigbourhoods are also being transformed by spatial inequalities, and the impact of deprivation, globalisation and transnational migration (see, further, Chapter Four). The penultimate section of this chapter examines some responses in terms of developing new forms of engagement in attempts to construct age-friendly environments.

Engaging older adults in age-friendly communities

The argument of this chapter is that while neighbourhoods have retained their importance in the lives of older people, changes have occurred that are of considerable relevance to the age-friendly debate. The places in which ageing is experienced may be affected by pressures arising from social exclusion, spatial inequality, transnational migration, or the impact of geographical and social mobility. But research also suggests a different approach to how we might view 'age-friendliness' developing within communities. Thus, reflecting on community studies in the 1950s and early 1960s, Elias and Scotson (1965, pp 146-7) argued that: 'It is difficult to imagine communities without women and children, though one can imagine communities almost without men.' But one might now add to this that: 'It is now impossible to imagine communities without older women and men.' However, the nature of how we view communities and older people is very different from earlier research. The first community studies viewed older residents largely as dependants, supported by an army of informal carers – notably their daughters (see, for example, Isaacs et al, 1972). Later research in urban sociology has tended to view older people as 'victims' in the face of urban change (Minton, 2009). However, a different view is now evident, one that emphasises the role of older people as carers, volunteers and community activists. Following this, Buffel and colleagues (2009) make the case for recognising older people as actors in 'placemaking'. Drawing on the work of Whyte (1943), Buffel (2012, p 24) argues that '… the concept of "placemaking" may be understood not just as an act of building or maintaining the neighbourhood, but as a whole process that fosters the creation of vital urban space' (see also Lager et al, 2013).

Policy strategies to promote age-friendliness

Policy strategies should be alerted to divergent tendencies influencing age-friendliness: on the one hand, structural dynamics behind inequalities and diversity in local and translocal communities; on the other hand, the need to support older adults in *appropriating* and constructing their own communities. Here, we would suggest a number of policy strategies that could contribute to the goal of creating age-friendly neighbourhoods.

First, addressing spatial diversity is important for the AFC approach. One strength of the AFCC framework is that it recognises the multiple domains of the neighbourhood environment, including both the social and built environments. However, its weakness is that the AFCC framework is largely prescriptive and fails to acknowledge the pressures that exist in many urban areas. Thus the development of AFCCs must give greater emphasis to an understanding of the strains facing communities and neighbourhoods, notably the spatial differences and inequalities that determine the quality of life of people ageing in place. This will require exerting direct influence on the spatial frameworks developed by urban planners, the integration of age-friendly policies with urban regeneration, and a closer relationship between those working on age-friendly issues on the one side, and those leading the development of urban areas – central and suburban – on the other.

Second, policies should aim at decreasing social exclusion. The exclusion of disadvantaged groups, such as those on low incomes or from ethnic backgrounds, will almost certainly be aggravated by spatial segregation (Burns et al, 2012). The relationship between community and individual exclusion is complex. Lehning and colleagues (2015) found that all income groups in a sample of older adults had lower expectations of ageing in place when they perceived problems within their neighbourhood. At the same time, low-income elders were more likely to expect to age in place than their higher-income counterparts. This could indicate that the former feel less able to make other arrangements despite difficulties with the quality of their environment. This suggests that neighbourhood problems at both an aggregate and individual level need to be accounted for in social policies. Housing policies can play a major role, with the affordability of housing (or lack of it) having a strong impact on spatial segregation (Tammaru et al, 2016). Health and mobility may also influence the extent of inclusion/exclusion in later life, with issues relating to mobility, safety and walkability of particular importance to older people experiencing chronic conditions such as frailty and dementia. Such themes have begun to receive attention in the existing AFCC literature (for example, Scharlach and Lehning, 2016), but they are not always linked to the resources necessary to support vulnerable older people in specific local contexts.

Third, recognising older people as actors in the social environment is key to creating age-friendly communities. The fundamentally subjective nature of communities, and the particular importance of negotiating one's local enviroment in deprived localities, make empowerment and recognition of older residents paramount to achieving age-friendliness. A relational and inclusive view of citizenship-as-practice (Buffel et al, 2012) supports such a strategy. This means a strong investment in involving older residents in the design of policies, especially for vulnerable and isolated groups within the community. Methods of co-research/co-investigation have been proven useful in engaging such groups (Buffel, 2015a), and have gained ground in the development of health and welfare services (Voorberg et al, 2015). Information and communication technologies may also support the involvement of older residents in navigating and designing their environment (López-de-Ipiña et al, 2013; Righi et al, 2015).

Fourth, the range of issues introduced by migration suggests a need for reframing age-friendly questions to reflect the different experiences of groups moving into and around urban areas. For example, although the impact of age-based discrimination remains an important dimension, **racism and ethnic-based discrimination** needs to have a stronger profile in age-friendly work, with greater understanding of their impact on health and wellbeing across the life course. The idea that urban life is now '**networked**' rather than conducted along traditional '**face-to-face**' lines also has implications for an age-friendly approach. A focus on developing age-friendly neighbourhoods *per se* may be advantageous in the majority of cases. But Clark (2009, p 1570) makes the point that for localities with more fragmented social ties a different approach may be needed, one that looks at supporting relationships that are sustained beyond the immediate community. This sugests that there is a need to consider the intersecting processes of building age-friendly communities at the local, national and transnational levels, building on an approach that moves beyond both geographical fixity and disciplinary boundaries (Buffel, 2015b).

Conclusion

This chapter has reviewed a variety of perspectives on the concept of 'community', focusing in particular on the consequences of spatial inequality and globalisation for ageing in place and AFCCs. Community has been presented as a multifaceted concept, pointing to various relationships between people and places at different geographical scales. On the one hand, community extends beyond local confines, into dispersed (translocal and transnational) networks and imagined belongings. On the other hand, proximity remains an important dimension of community. For older people in particular, the local setting has been identified as an important focal point for communities that support ageing in place. The diversity in meanings of 'community', and the inequalities that exist between and within neighbourhoods and places, are likely to mean that the process of developing age-friendly communities will involve reconciling conflicting interests and concerns. In this context, there is a need for developing new models of community development and engagement that will work with the range of concerns identified within and between different age groups. Such an approach faces particular challenges in terms of involving older people experiencing intense forms of exclusion, notably those associated with extreme poverty, racism and discrimination. A key role for social policy and community development will be to enhance the 'agency' of these particular groups, expanding opportunities to assist their engagement while recognising changing conditions within neighbourhoods and divergent views of what represents 'community'.

References

Allan, G. and Phillipson, C. (2008) 'Aging and the life course', in Scott, J., Treas, J and Richards, M. (eds) *The Blackwell companion to the sociology of families*, Oxford: Blackwell Publishing, pp 126-141.

Baldassar, L. (2007) 'Transnational families and aged care: the mobility of care and migrancy of ageing', *Journal of Ethnic and Migration Studies*, 33(2): 275-97.

Barrett, A. and Mosca, I. (2013) 'Social isolation, loneliness and return migration: evidence from older Irish adults', *Journal of Ethnic and Migration Studies*, 39(13): 1659–77.

Bell, C. and Newby, H. (1971) *Community studies*, London: Allen & Unwin.

Blokland, T. (2003) *Urban bonds*, Cambridge: Polity Press.

Buffel, T. (2012) *Experiences of place and neighbourhood in later life: developing age-friendly communities*, Brussels: VUB Press.

Buffel, T. (2015a) *Researching age-friendly communities: Stories from older people as co-investigators*, Manchester: The University of Manchester Library.

Buffel, T. (2015b) 'Ageing migrants and the creation of home: mobility and the maintenance of transnational ties', *Population, Space and Place*. Article first published online: 27 October 2015, DOI: 10.1002/psp.1994.

Buffel, T. and Phillipson, C. (2011) 'Experiences of place among older migrants living in inner-city neighbourhoods in Belgium and England', *Diversité Urbaine*, 11: 13-37.

Buffel, T. and Phillipson, C. (2016a) 'Can global cities be "age-friendly cities"? Urban development and ageing populations', *Cities*, 55: 94-100.

Buffel, T. and Phillipson, C. (2016b) 'Constructions of "home" among first generation migrants living in Belgium and England', in K. Walsh and L. Nare (eds) *Transnational migration and home in older age*, London: Routledge, pp 63-74.

Buffel, T., De Donder, L., Phillipson, C., Dury, S., De Witte, N. and Verté, D. (2014) 'Social participation among older adults living in medium-sized cities in Belgium: the role of neighbourhood perceptions', *Health Promotion International*, 29(4): 655-68.

Buffel, T., Phillipson, C. and Scharf, T. (2013) 'Experiences of neighbourhood exclusion and inclusion among older people living in deprived inner-city areas in Belgium and England', *Ageing & Society*, 33(1): 89-109.

Buffel, T., Verté, D., De Donder, L. and De Witte, N. (2009) 'Conceptualizing the neighbourhood as a dynamic social space: recognizing older people as actors in placemaking', *Proceedings of ESA 2009, 9th Conference of European Sociological Association*, Lisbon, Portugal.

Buffel, T., Verté, D., De Donder, L., De Witte, N., Dury, S., Vanwing, T. and Bolsenbroek, A. (2012) 'Theorising the relationship between older people and their immediate social living environment', *International Journal of Lifelong Education*, 31(1): 13-32.

Burholt, V. (2004) 'The settlement patterns and residential histories of older Gujaratis, Punjabis and Sylhetis in Birmingham', *Ageing & Society*, 24(3): 383-409.

Burns, V.F., Lavoie, J.-P. and Rose, D. (2012) 'Revisiting the role of neighbourhood change in social exclusion and inclusion of older people', *Journal of Aging Research*, 2012: 148287.

Byrnes, M.E. (2011) 'A city within a city: A "snapshot" of aging in a HUD 202 in Detroit, Michigan', *Journal of Aging Studies*, 25(3): 253-62.

Clark, A. (2009) 'From neighbourhood to network: a review of the significance of neighbourhood in studies of social relations', *Geography Compass*, 3(4): 1559-78.

Crow, G. (2002) 'Community studies: fifty years of theorization', *Sociological Research Online*, 7, available at www.socresonline.org.uk/7/3/crow.html.

Crow, G. and Allan, G. (1994) *Community life*, Harvester Wheatsheaf: Hemel Hempstead.

De Donder, L., Buffel, T., De Witte, N., Dury, S. and Verté, D. (2013) 'Perceptual quality of neighbourhood design and feelings of unsafety', *Ageing & Society*, 33(6): 917-37.

Delanty, G. (2010) *Community*, London: Routledge.

Elias, N. and Scotson, J. (1965) *The established and the outsiders*, London: Frank Cass.

Erkhamp, P. (2005) 'Placing identities: transnational practices and local attachments of Turkish migrants', *Journal of Ethnic and Migration Studies*, 31(2): 345-64.

Faust, T. (2000) 'Transnationalization in international migration: implications for the study of citizenship and culture', *Ethnic and Racial Studies*, 23(2): 189-222.

Fischer, C.S. (1982) *To dwell amongst friends: Personal networks in town and city*, Chicago, IL: University of Chicago Press.

Gans, H. (1962) *The urban villagers: Group and class in the life of Italian-Americans*, New York, NY: Free Press.

Gardner, P. (2011) 'Natural neighbourhood networks: important social networks in the lives of older adults living in place', *Journal of Aging Studies*, 25(3): 263-71.

Gilleard, C., Hyde, M. and Higgs, P. (2007) 'The impact of age, place, aging in place, and attachment to place on the well-being of the over 50s in England', *Research on Aging*, 29(6): 590-605.

OTJR: Occupation, Participation and Health, 32(3): 95-109.

Hern, M. (2016) *What a city is for: Remaking the politics of deplacement*, Cambridge, MA: The MIT Press.

Horgas, A.L., Wilms, H.U. and Baltes, M.M. (1998) 'Daily life in very old age: everyday activities as expressions of daily life', *Gerontologist*, 38(5): 556-68.

Isaacs, B., Livingstone, M. and Neville, Y. (1972) *The survival of the unfittest: A study of geriatric patients in Glasgow*, London: Routledge & Kegan Paul.

Kingsley, P. (2016) *The new odyssey: The story of Europe's refugee crisis*, London: Faber & Faber.

Krause, N. (2004) 'Neighbourhoods, health and well-being in later life', in Wahl, H.W., Scheidt, R. and Windley, P. (eds) *Focus on Aging in Context: Socio-Physical Environments. Annual Review of Gerontology and Geriatrics*, New York: Springer Publishing Company, pp 223-49.

Lager, D., van Hoven, B. and Huigen, P.P.P. (2013) 'Dealing with change in old age: negotiating working-class belonging in a neighbourhood in the process of urban renewal in the Netherlands', *Geoforum*, 50: 54-61.

Lehning, A.J., Smith, R.J. and Dunkle, R.E. (2015) 'Do age-friendly characteristics influence the expectation to age in place? A comparison of low-income and higher income Detroit elders', *Journal of Applied Gerontology*, 34(2): 158-80.

López-de-Ipiña, D., Klein, B., Vanhecke, S. and Perez-Velasco, J. (2013) 'Towards ambient assisted cities and citizens', *Proceedings of the 27th International Conference on Advanced Information Networking and Applications Workshops (WAINA)*, pp 1343-8, doi: 10.1109/WAINA.2013.203.

Means, R. (2007) 'Safe as houses? Ageing in place and vulnerable older people in the UK', *Social Policy & Administration*, 41(1): 65-85.

Menec, V., Means, R., Keating, N. and Parkhurst, G. (2011) 'Conceptualizing agefriendly communities', *Canadian Journal on Aging*, 30(3): 479-93.

Milardo, R. and Allan, G. (2000) 'Social networks and marital relationships', in R. Milardo and S. Duck (eds) *Families as relationships*, Chichester: John Wiley.

Minton, A. (2009) *Ground control: Fear and happiness in the twenty-first-century city*, London: Penguin Books.

Nisbet, R. (1953) *The quest for community*, New York, NY: Oxford University Press.

Oswald, F., Jopp, D., Rott, C. and Wahl, H.W. (2011) 'Is aging in place a resource for or risk to life satisfaction?', *The Gerontologist*, 51(2): 238-50.

Percival, J. (ed) *Return migration in later life*, Bristol: Policy Press.

Phillipson, C. (2007) 'The "elected" and the "excluded": sociological perspectives on the experience of place and community in old age', *Ageing & Society*, 27(3): 321-42.

Righi, V., Sayago, S. and Blat, J. (2015) 'Urban ageing: technology, agency and community in smarter cities for older people', *Proceedings of the 7th International Conference on Communities and Technologies*, New York, pp 119-28.

Rodwin, V. and Gusmano, M. (2006) *Growing older in world cities*, Nashville, TN: University of Vanderbilt Press.

Rowles, G. and Bernard, M. (2013) *Environmental gerontology: Making meaningful places in old age*, New York, NY: Springer.

Sassen, S. (1992) The Global City. Princeton, NJ: Princeton University Press.

Scharlach, A. and Lehning, A. (2016) *Creating age-friendly communities*, Oxford: Oxford University Press.

Smetcoren, A.-S. (2015) *I'm not leaving: Critical perspectives on ageing in place*, Brussels: Vrije Universiteit Brussel.

Smith, A. (2009) *Ageing in urban neighbourhoods*, Bristol: Policy Press.

Standing, G. (2011) *The precariat*, London: Bloomsbury.

Tammaru, T., Marciñek, S., van Ham, M and Mesterd, S. (2016) (eds) *Socio-economic segregation in European cities*, London: Routledge.

Thomése, G.C.F. and van Tilburg, T.G. (2000) 'Neighbouring networks and environmental dependency: differential effects of neighbourhood characteristics on the relative size and composition of neighbouring networks of older adults in the Netherlands', *Ageing & Society*, 20(1): 55-78.

Thomése, G.C.F., van Tilburg, T.G. and Knipscheer, C.P.M. (2003) 'Continuation of exchange with neighbors in later life: the importance of the neighborhood context', *Personal Relationships*, 10(4): 535–50.

Torres, S. (2015) 'Expanding the gerontological imagination on ethnicity: conceptual and theoretical perspectives', *Ageing & Society*, 35(5): 935–960

Townsend, P. (1957) *The family life of old people*, London: Routledge & Kegan Paul.

Vanderbeck, R. and Worth, N. (2015) *Intergenerational space*, London: Routledge.

Victor, C., Martin, W. and Zubair, M. (2012) 'Families and caring among older people in South Asian communities', *European Journal of Social Work*, 15(1): 81–96.

Völker, B., Flap, H. and Lindenberg, S. (2007) 'When are neighbourhoods communities?', *European Sociological Review*, 23(1): 99–114.

Voorberg, W.H., Bekkers, V.J.J.M. and Tummers, L.G. (2015) 'A systematic review of co-creation and co-production: embarking on the social innovation journey', *Public Management Review*, 17(9): 1333–57.

Vullnetari, J. and King. R. (2008) '"Does your granny eat grass?" On mass migration, care drain and the fate of older people in rural Albania', *Global Networks* 8(2): 139–71.

Wacquant (2008) *Urban outcasts: A comparative sociology of advanced marginality*, Cambridge: Polity.

Wellman, B. (1979) 'The community question: the intimate networks of East Yorkers', *American Journal of Sociology*, 84(5): 1201–31.

Wellman, B. (1996) 'Are personal communities local? A dumptarian consideration', *Social Networks*, 18(4): 347–54.

Whyte, W.F. (1943) *Street corner society*, Chicago, IL: University of Chicago Press.

Wiles, J., Leibing, A., Guberman, N., Reeve, J. and Allen, R. (2011) 'The meaning of "ageing in place" to older people', *Gerontologist*, 52(3): 357–66.

Willmott, P. and Young, M (1960) *Family and class in a London suburb*, London: Routledge & Kegan Paul.

Young, M. and Willmott, P. (1957) *Family and kinship in East London*, London: Routledge and Kegan Paul.

FOUR

Addressing erasure, microfication and social change: age-friendly initiatives and environmental gerontology in the 21st century

Jessica A. Kelley, Dale Dannefer, Luma Issa Al Masarweh

Introduction

The age-friendly cities movement has gained global enthusiasm for its efforts to address the multiple, interacting layers of the social world that influence the degree to which older adults are integrated in their communities (WHO, 2007). Many of the age-friendly initiatives implemented around the world have developed and occurred in parallel with the continued elaboration of academic research in environmental gerontology and related fields. Although these two streams have not always cross-fertilised, emergent and intersecting processes in the 21st century such as increasing globalisation, urban renewal and gentrification, and population ageing highlight the fact that both enterprises share common concerns and objectives, and they also share some common limitations. In this chapter, we articulate two key challenges, shared by prevailing paradigms in both age-friendly initiatives and the scholarly field of environmental gerontology: **microfication** and **erasure**. Then, using examples of two current issues facing many older people globally, we demonstrate how rapid social change in population processes underscores the need for concerted, multi-level consideration of the forces affecting the wellbeing of older adults.

The development of environmental gerontology

From its beginnings, environmental gerontology has been concerned with focusing on how environment and context may be arranged to enable older people to optimise and sustain high levels of physical, mental and social functioning. For example, early work such as Lewin's 'living space model' (1951), Lawton and Nahemow's (1973) 'ecological theory of aging' and Lawton's (1986) 'press-competence model' were developed as part of efforts to understand the interactions between older individuals and their environments. Studies in environmental gerontology have examined the socio-spatial implications of ageing and its complex relationship with the environment at the micro-level (for example, home and family) and at more encompassing levels of social organisation (such as neighbourhood, city, region – see, for example, Wahl et al, 2004). In doing so, scholars of environmental gerontology have pushed the agenda of social and environmental planning and policies to improve the experience of ageing. They have sought to advance 'ageing in place' and awareness of the importance of place attachment and spatial experience to older individuals and their conceptualisation of place as a home (Andrews and Phillips, 2005). They have further sought to understand the relevant dimensions of context and to contribute to specifying the mechanisms through which external forces shape individual wellbeing.

Thus, environmental gerontology is justifiably viewed as a positive and progressive sub-field by those concerned with identifying and advancing the interests of elders. Yet, the impact of such work must be judged not only by what it has contributed, but also by its aspirations and its potentials. By and large, the objectives of environmental gerontology include identifying the relevant dimensions of environment and the mechanisms through which environment shapes individual ageing, and how such mechanisms may be addressed through policy and practice. Yet its prevailing approach is incomplete, because its ability to respond to the challenge of rapid social change in the 21st century is limited. Similarly, age-friendly initiatives that attempt to identify the key barriers to ageing well in one's community must necessarily acknowledge that individuals can change all the while their environments – on multiple levels – are changing simultaneously. As Mahmood and Keating (2012, p 148) elaborate: 'Neither person nor place is static; at different points in the ageing process, the "same" home in the "same" neighborhood can foster or impede access to other material resources or social relationships.'

As a starting point for our arguments, we thus note that both environmental gerontology and age-friendly initiatives have focused heavily on the micro-level realities that are part of daily experiences. We acknowledge that such factors are important in influencing both quality of life and the ability to function in everyday life. Yet such processes, like processes of individual ageing more generally, do not exist in a vacuum, and cannot be adequately understood if viewed as circumstances that themselves have no broader context. If we are to understand the scope of the actual environmental mechanisms that influence both ageing and age-friendliness, attention must be paid not only to the conditions, risks and opportunities that ageing individuals encounter in the immediacy of everyday experience, but also to the factors that shape those immediate conditions. These factors, some close and some far removed, appear in many consequential forms, whether in the nature of accessible public services, in the state or national laws and policies that shape those services, or in the response to demographic shifts. In sum, to understand the causal processes behind individual outcomes, the macro-environment, no less than the micro-environment, requires attention.

The term 'macro-environment' has of course been an explicit part of the vocabulary of environmental gerontology from its beginnings, but its meaning has often been quite limited – referring mainly to basic characteristics of proximate contexts, such as the neighbourhood itself. This limited conceptualisation of the 'macro-environment' harkens back to Lawton's foundational work, in which 30 pages devoted to the macro approach refer mainly to neighborhoods (for example, Lawton, 1986, pp 21-52). However, neighbourhoods are themselves hardly free-standing realities. Neighbourhood conditions in general, and the age-friendliness of neighbourhood circumstances in particular, are subject to the vicissitudes of political, economic and other forces that lie beyond the neighbourhood, yet nevertheless affect crucial issues of daily life (such as food access, safety, transportation, communication) through factors such as migration and mobility, employment opportunities and policy developments. Such externally imposed influences and changes may also produce shifts in the experience of everyday social life and local culture.

Despite calls for integrating multiple levels of social organisation, from immediate home environments to policy, into age-friendly initiatives (Fitzgerald and Caro, 2014), many scholars continue to draw predominantly from the individual-level perspective espoused in environmental gerontology literatures in their approaches to policy as well as practical needs. Identification of problems and their analysis are both largely focused at the individual level, heavily drawn from the presumptive goal of ageing in place (compare Scharlach, 2016). While not unimportant, this focus by itself is inadequate to capture the full scope of influences and power dynamics that affect the lives of ageing individuals and their communities. To that end, in this chapter, we focus on two specific problems that follow from the neglect of the connection of local circumstances to macro-level dynamics. The first is microfication, or the tendency for scientists and policymakers to focus on the characteristics of ageing individuals and their immediate milieu, while paying little attention to the interaction between the micro-individual traits and the macro-level workings. The second is erasure, which is an extreme form of social exclusion where groups of people are simply 'unseen' in policy, practice, or science. In the next section, we describe both of these problems. Then we present two examples where we have observed rapid social change in the 21st century, exposing the lag in the paradigms of both environmental gerontology and age-friendly initiatives globally: urban renewal and gentrification; and transnational migration of older adults.

Challenge 1: microfication

According to Hagestad and Dannefer (2001), **microfication** refers to the tendency to focus on immediate aspects of everyday life (the details of daily experience, face-to-face interaction, interpersonal relationships and so on), while overlooking broader, overarching aspects of the social context that define and set key parameters of daily experience. Theoretical concerns in gerontology regarding the microfication of challenges of ageing (for example, Hagestad and Dannefer, 2001; Estes and Phillipson, 2002) should not be taken to imply that the micro-level of social reality is unimportant. Rather, we argue that an understanding of the fine-grained micro-realities of human experience comprises the beginning, not the endpoint, of an adequate analysis of how to understand and proceed to intervene in a given local situation. The layers of the social world in everyday life – the household, the apartment building, the street – are nested within one another, and the social worlds that one experiences at work or in other daily routines exist alongside those of family or household relations.

One such example of microfication in environmental gerontology is the tendency to look for solutions to mobility problems associated with limitations in activities of daily living in devices such as call-button lanyards or grab bars (for example, Iezzoni, 2003; Gooberman-Hill and Ebrahim, 2007; Resnik et al, 2009). Such discussions need to be accompanied by an interrogation of the broader, externally imposed dimensions of reality and institutional arrangements that serve to sort older adults into their current circumstances and living arrangements, as well as their states of health and functioning (Holstein and Gubrium, 2000; Abramson, 2015). Thus, attention to the constitutive mechanisms and dynamics present in everyday life, and to the risks and the opportunities that they afford, is essential to gain understanding of the mechanisms through which the conditions and state of a given individual are constituted, and these remain relevant throughout the life course (Dannefer and Kelley-Moore, 2009; Browning et al, 2016).

A second example involves older adults who choose to remain in sub-optimal housing, such as single-room occupancy (SRO) buildings, to live in or near city areas with desired features (Crystal and Beck, 1992). While the prevailing paradigm in environmental gerontology may indicate that such arrangements comprise a housing mismatch for older, co-morbid or functionally limited adults, the adults themselves may not see it this way. For them, importance of proximity to familiar spaces and resources outweighs the challenges of the immediate home environment for these seniors. A feature in *The New York Times* (Nagourney, 2016) profiling the greying homeless population in the United States detailed myriad cases of older adults who navigate precarious housing arrangements, including living in tents, in order to remain close to the services and charities that help support their existence.

For both examples, the immediate home environment is not the operant explanatory feature of the older adult's environment. In this way, such findings make clear that trying to understand an individual's situation solely by looking at characteristics of the individual, or even of the household, leaves us short of understanding. Of course, both individuals and neighborhoods can be seen as located within yet more encompassing social realities, with broader economic, political and cultural dimensions, an issue we discuss later in the chapter.

Analogous to the spatial aspects of microfication (focused on the immediate physical surroundings), microfication can also be seen as having a *temporal* aspect. For example, temporality describes the tendency to focus on current circumstances and assumes that an individual's needs and capacities can be read from current location, apart from considering the biographical and historical location of one's present situation. Here, the danger is in the neglect of cultural forces that are integral to the life experience and community life of residents. Such neglect risks the reduction of a lifetime of generative action to narrow 'prescriptions' for ageing well by gerontological specialists. Several key elements of such temporal dimensions of neighbourhood life – all potentially relevant to age-friendliness – involve temporal dimensions such as neighbourhood stability versus turnover, cohort replacement and neighbourhood composition, and the longevity of a given individual's or family's residence in the same neighbourhood

(Kelley-Moore and Thorpe, 2012; Woldoff, 2014). One type of situation in which the relevance of such factors is dramatically in evidence is that in which the arrival of new immigrants is part of the neighbourhood cohort replacement process. Immigrants in general and older immigrants in particular may appear as unremarkable, yet they bring with them, individually and collectively, experiences that have inevitably shaped their own sense of the aspects of everyday life that are required for meaning making and a sense of wholeness and integrity in an unfamiliar/alien context.

Challenge 2: erasure

The second problem deriving from a predominant focus on micro-level realities for older adults in age-friendly initiatives is the potential for **erasure**. Cultural erasure has its roots in the problem of **exclusion** – an absence of key voices and groups from the conversation. Erasure is a concept used as social critique of the ways certain groups of people are simply 'unseen' in policy, research, or institutional practices. It is a form of social exclusion so embedded in the cultural assumptions of a society that the absence of these groups is not even recognised. Some recent examples from other fields are: exclusion of sexual minority groups from public health research by focusing on behaviour and not identity (Young and Meyer, 2005); lack of legal protections from discrimination against Mexican Americans compared with 'real' races such as Black or White (Haney-López, 1998); and suburban development initiatives for predominantly White homeowners that overrun culturally important spaces for Black communities (Greason, 2013).

A poignant example of the erasure of vulnerable older adults in urban space is offered by Klinenberg's (2002) study *Heat wave*. In 1995, a severe weather event in Chicago resulted in 521 deaths, 73% of which were among adults aged 65 or older. More than 90% lived alone. The modal victim were poor, elderly, Black adults, disproportionately located in the most violent neighbourhoods of the city. Sadly, 170 of the victims' bodies were never claimed by family or friends from the morgue. Yet the study of the disaster, commissioned by the mayor, ultimately characterised the heat wave as a 'unique meteorological event caused by a rare convergence of critical factors'. The report focused on the epidemiology of heat exposure (that is, what happens when bodies are exposed to excessively high temperatures) and paid virtually no attention to the social patterning of the victims. In reaction to the complete absence of discussion regarding the preventability of the deaths of these disadvantaged older adults, Klinenberg concludes:

> Silent and invisible killers of silenced and invisible people, the social conditions that make heat waves so deadly do not so much disappear from view as *fail to register* with newsmakers and their audiences – including social scientific experts on disasters. (2002, pp 16-17; emphasis added)

While the concept of erasure has appeared in other work, such as critical race discourse (Gilborn, 2005) and disability studies (Campbell, 2008), to our knowledge it has had limited, if any, application in the study of older adults. Interestingly, resource debates cite the 'war between generations' or 'greedy geezers' (Williamson et al, 1999; Peterson, 2004; Williamson and Watts-Roy, 2009) when discussing the tension between investing in our youth or supporting our older citizens. Implicit in the characterisation of these debates is that older adults are recognised and considered, perhaps even actively working against the interests of younger people. For example, the housing debate tends to frame older adults as 'sitting on' good property, while young people are 'forced' to rent in less desirable areas (McKee, 2012).

Cultural erasure, however, is a more extreme form of social exclusion, because the social group is invisible to the mainstream culture. The substantial literature on the social exclusion of older people grounds the unequal treatment and devaluation of old and very old groups in the pervasive force of societal ageism (compare Scharf and Keating, 2012; Stuckelberger et al, 2012), a feature of which would be the complete erasure of older adults from the cultural gaze. Thus the poignancy in the findings of the Klinenberg study described earlier is that researchers and policymakers could not even see the glaring age disparity in the victims, effectively rendering their preventable deaths to an ageless accident.

In sum, the dual challenges of microfication and erasure can be found to operate across a diverse array of domains and experiences. A delimited focus on individual-level and micro-level characteristics of older adults' living environments, as well as invoking some degree of temporal suspension at all levels of consideration, can potentially obscure the influence of larger-scale factors that have implications for age-friendliness. Emerging trends in the 21st century, largely at the nexus of increasing globalisation and urbanisation, accompanied by population ageing, provide an opportunity to observe how the immediate milieu of older adults can be couched within social change and macro-level trends, and how the neglect of consideration at these levels can result in microfication and erasure. We first discuss urban renewal and gentrification. Then we turn to the emerging patterns of transnational migration among older adults.

Social change and emergent macro-level forces

Urban renewal and gentrification

An overriding narrative in the urban redevelopment/gentrification discourse is the effort to make city spaces 'family-friendly' again. Indeed, many urban redevelopment initiatives are grounded in the assumption that **familification** (Goodsell, 2013) – prioritising the housing and service needs of working-age residents and their children – is the formula for economic growth and stability in previously declining urban spaces. The return and settlement of 'families' in gentrifying areas are frequently touted as indicators that a neighborhood has succeeded in addressing issues related to social disorder, safety and economic desolation (Goodsell, 2013). Older adults, however, are effectively erased from urban renewal discourse that is grounded in **familism**, since these older persons do not figure in the constellation of families or neighbourhood age structure. As a result, economic and policy initiatives designed to support gentrification typically focus on the neighbourhood features of most value for families with children, such as the schools, day-care centres and playgrounds (DeSena, 2012). A complementary process in gentrifying neighbourhoods arises where the housing stock is increasingly occupied/rented by university students (Smith, 2008). Older residents, who are frequently home owners, can be faced with new neighbourhood social dynamics that no longer include them, or could even be overtly unwelcoming. In these circumstances, older adults are effectively erased from the vision of urban renewal – making clear the implicit cultural bias towards age-segregated residential landscapes (Hagestad and Uhlenberg, 2007) .

In addition to the erasure of older adults from definitions of safe, thriving neighbourhoods, the bias towards families in urban renewal is also the effective obliteration of older adults from the valued cultural and economic dynamics of neighbourhood life. Research shows that displacement is not as high a risk for older residents as is the potential to be erased, or rendered invisible, in their own neighbourhoods (Burns et al, 2012). One reason for this is that gentrification creates new partnerships and/or alters the social contract between community institutions and its residents (Hankins, 2007). As such, long-time older residents may lose influence or power in their own communities as other partnerships gain primacy. Further, these new stakeholders in the redevelopment of these neighborhoods may disinvest in activities and spaces that are long-standing and socially important for older adults (such as bingo halls, coffee shops and other traditional gathering places). Since these same older residents may not participate in the new activities (for example, kick boxing) or use spaces (such as gyms) for meeting friends, once-integrated seniors are more likely to remain home alone (Burns et al, 2012). This often carries an added irony when, as taxpaying homeowners, they may continue to contribute disproportionately to the community tax base relative to young renters.

The bias towards families in urban renewal is not just a free-market phenomenon. State-generated urban revitalisation efforts use this framework as well, effectively erasing poor older adults from their communities through policy and investment of public money in urban renewal. Public housing initiatives, such as HOPE IV (Home Ownership and Housing Opportunities for People Everywhere) and the Moving to Opportunity programme in the United States, are two such large-scale political and economic efforts to decentralise poverty in urban spaces (Chaskin and Joseph, 2010; Gennetian et al, 2011). While the intent is to replace concentrated low-income housing with new, low-density, mixed-income housing, such efforts can displace many older residents to make room for the younger replacement residents (Davidson and Lees, 2010). In the quest to accommodate children and working-age adults in these communities, seniors who qualify for public housing are increasingly concentrated in high-density buildings located further away from resource-rich areas or left behind in their deteriorating neighbourhoods (Kelley-Moore and Thorpe, 2012; Chaskin et al, 2013).

One argument for these programme choices is that seniors, who 'need' more accessible housing, should be congregated into one large-scale building, rather than scattered throughout the public housing communities across counties and cities (Van Hoffman, 1996). Such corralling of older adults – a deliberate form of age-segregation – is also justified because of claims of lower levels of crime and potential for disorder than would be likely if younger populations lived in such high-density environments (Newman, 1972; Normoyle and Foley, 1988). In the US, even the federal eligibility criteria for living in senior public housing includes a restriction that no one in the household can be under the age of 50, effectively excluding persons who are part-time or full-time caregivers of their grandchildren. In these ways, public housing policies effectively view the 'problem' of being old and poor as an individual rather than a structural issue.

In sum, the erasure of older adults from the discourse about urban renewal persists, either through free-market discrimination or through exclusion from residential priority in federal or state housing programmes. The economic or programmatic forces that serve to erase older adults from neighbourhoods with young families run counter to sociological work on the benefits of neighbourhood collective efficacy on child wellbeing. Such literature argues that intergenerational closure – or the degree to which non-household adults and children in a community are linked – is a mechanism contributing to positive outcomes for all residents (Coleman, 1988; Sampson et al, 1999). The concept of the 'urban village' is based, in some part, on the idea that the social dynamics of a diverse neighborhood can transcend individual social networks with regard to benefits and social control (Campbell and Lee, 1992). Further, other work shows that the degree of social capital decreases sharply as neighbourhoods become more age-homogeneous (Marshall et al, 2001).

Transnational migration trends and older immigrants

A second area in which the dual problems of microfication and erasure may challenge efforts toward age-friendliness is found within the 21st-century trend towards increasingly global and fluid migration patterns (see, further, Chapter Three). Coupled with population ageing, we observe a rapidly growing pattern of increase in transnationalism among older adults (Treas, 2008; Walsh and Näre, 2016). For example, in the United States, one in eight foreign-born older adults is a new immigrant over the age of 60 (Treas, 2008). We note with surprise that discussions of the intersectionality of age and migrant status have been notably absent from research focused on urban environment and age-friendliness, leading to a lack of knowledge regarding the particularities of the lived experiences of older adult immigrants (Becker, 2003; Treas and Torres-Gil, 2008). We suggest that this scholarly absence is likely for two reasons, both of which we explicate further below: first, research, policy and social service agencies tend to consider migration and settlement issues to be 'ageless' without consideration of the special needs or assets of older adult immigrants; and second, state-sponsored social welfare benefit structures effectively erase older immigrants from income and medical supports designed to help older adults. We discuss each of these in turn.

First, cultural and media narratives of older immigrants tend to focus on destination moves for immigrants to be reunited with their successful children in a new country (Carr and Tienda, 2013) and/or settlements into high-resource 'ethnoburbs' with culturally appropriate resources (see Jones, 2008, for a review; for a discussion of Chinese ethnoburbs in San Gabriel Valley, see Li, 1998; Zhou et al, 2008). Yet the stark reality is that the living conditions of older immigrants are more frequently characterised by living in inner cities where they face conditions of poverty, crime, poor-quality housing and inadequacies in the basics of comfort and safety (Becker, 2003; Phillipson, 2007, 2011; DeSena and Shortell, 2012).

The intersection of older age and new immigrant status provides both challenges and opportunities for social service providers and policymakers. On the one hand, some characteristics of older immigrants may interact with neighbourhood and community characteristics to render them especially vulnerable. For example, immigrants generally have lower levels of educational attainment and incomes below established levels of poverty relative to native-born residents (Buffel et al, 2012). Many of these older immigrants settle in poorer neighbourhoods with few resources, which also have poor-quality housing, close proximity to environmental toxins (including poor air and water quality) and higher crime rates. For this population, the personal resources available to respond to adverse neighborhood conditions are inevitably limited, increasing the risk of adverse outcomes (Iceland, 2009). Even in resource-rich neighbourhoods and economically established households, new older immigrants could be at high risk of social isolation and loneliness, particularly in car-dependent suburbs located away from ethnic activities and resources (Treas and Mazumdar, 2002; Ajrouch, 2008).

On the other hand, special strengths deriving from some circumstances may be overlooked by policymakers and professionals if their focus is limited to the immediate context. Older foreign-born adults who live in ethno-homogenous neighbourhoods may receive socio-cultural benefits that protect against health decline, even if the social spaces are not resource-rich (Markides et al, 2013). A neighbourhood context with high ethnic homogeneity can be rich with supportive and expansive social networks that are linguistically and culturally compatible to facilitate close personal friendships and assistance with instrumental activities of daily living (Almeida et al, 2009). For example, older Mexican immigrants residing in high-density immigrant areas have been seen to have better health profiles and slower health declines over time than older Mexican immigrants who reside in areas with a low concentration of immigrants (Eschbach et al, 2004). Thus, a neighbourhood context can be either disabling or enabling, based on opportunities for supportive relationships and exchanges, fostering a sense of social and environmental safety to ensure wellbeing.

A particularly interesting and growing population segment in most developed nations is that of long-term immigrants who migrated as children or young adults and are now ageing in place as long-standing residents. In many ways, these immigrants may share the cultural and economic advantage of being long-term residents in the host nation, and in some respects may be quite similar to their ageing native-born counterparts (Angel et al, 2012; Wilmoth, 2012). Yet in other ways, these long-term immigrants are quite distinctive from each other and from native older adults. For example, fluency in the host country's language can vary widely, based on geo-political forces such as colonialism and national policy on accepting refugees. Language barriers are less likely among older Northern African immigrants to France, for example, relative to Mexican immigrants to the United States (Silverstein and Attias-Donfut, 2010). Religious congruity with the host nation is another issue that may serve to exclude older immigrants, particularly those who settle in rural areas of their new nation (Jones, 2008). Despite the differences in countries of origin, destination countries, and even circumstances of migration, older immigrants are substantially more likely to depend on and invest in intergenerational relationships as a strategy for survival and success (Treas, 2008; Silverstein and Attias-Donfut, 2010; Wilmoth, 2012).

A second reason for the limited attention to the intersectionality of age and immigration may be due to the erasure of older immigrants from the welfare state. Examples of this tendency can readily be found: first, employment-based pension structures such as social security in the United States do not apply to older immigrants who have not had any or a sufficient amount of paid labour to qualify for income benefits. Second, based on the 1996 Welfare Reform Law, supplemental security income (SSI), which is designed to provide financial support to very low-income seniors, carries the restriction that the recipient must be a naturalised citizen (Van Hook, 2000). As a result, many – and a growing number – of elderly immigrants may be living with minimal to no financial assistance for extended periods of time. As a third example, in some countries (for example, England and the US), eligibility for health insurance and other benefits carry residency restrictions whereby benefits receipt is conditional on limiting the number and duration of return visits to the recipient's home country (Buffel and Phillipson, 2011).

The assumptions underlying the purpose and execution of benefits in a welfare state are not explicitly designed to exclude older immigrants.

Indeed, this form of erasure from policy is most likely due to the ways in which trends towards globalisation and transnational migration are out-pacing traditional structures of the welfare state. In the era of increasing globalisation, migration is no longer properly conceptualised as a one-time move, but as a process that entails increased inter-linkage of two (or more) contexts and the endurance of social ties that transcend geographic boundaries to create a transnational population (Smith, 2005; Schunck, 2011). Whether recent or long-residing, many immigrants participate in the social, political and economic spheres in both the host country and the country of origin through transnational activities or involvement (for example visits; voting). Even when host communities provide various religious, cultural and social opportunities designed for integration, older immigrants can have enduring, dual attachments to both the county of origin and the receiving country. The neglect of global trends such as transnational caregiving limits our understanding of these older immigrants' lives (Treas, 2008; Walsh and Näre, 2016).

Thus, revisions to the structure of the welfare state to make older immigrants visible to their new home country must necessarily acknowledge trends in globalisation and transnational social ties. Yet, even when older immigrants are explicitly included in benefits structures, policymakers and social service providers must also recognise the unique needs older immigrants may have, such as limited host-country language proficiency or particular types of challenge relating to health and functioning.

For example, in highly regulated markets such as the Netherlands, the transition from a welfare state to more of a 'participation society' where residents are expected to take a more active role, may result in older residents becoming more vulnerable, especially those with multiple intersecting disadvantages such as older immigrants (Van der Greft and Fortuijn, 2017) . For instance, relative to older native Dutch residents, Moroccan and Turkish older immigrants face multiple disadvantages to such 'participation' requirements, including increased risk of lack of support in the face of the deinstitutionalisation of elderly care in the Netherlands and withdrawal of other local community resources to support ageing in place (Van der Greft and Fortuijn, 2017). This may be further complicated by the precariousness of the living conditions of older migrants in disadvantaged areas of the city, especially in terms of a lack of basic comfort and safety, and housing quality (Scharf et al, 2002; Becker, 2003).

However, little is known about the ways in which older migrants manage issues of daily life in disadvantaged communities. Furthermore, there is a need to explore how different resources and assistance programmes may differentially enable or disable older immigrants in their quest to create a sense of 'home' in their locality. It is vital that social gerontology addresses these issues (Buffel et al, 2013; Buffel, 2015).

Conclusion

Population ageing is a demographic reality, not only in postindustrial societies but in virtually all societies. Although this trend is certain to continue through the 21st century, the social and physical worlds of individuals continue to be premised on ageist assumptions that privilege youth and discount the needs and interests of older adults. Both environmental gerontology and the age-friendly cities movement are dedicated to changing and ameliorating these circumstances by identifying problems and needs and creating fresh and innovative approaches to recognise the special potentials as well as the special needs of older people. Herein, we have argued that despite the resultant successes of both of these enterprises, the predisposition to focus on the micro-level without interrogating some fundamental assumptions of our ageist society and culture continues to limit their effectiveness in realising their objectives. We suggest that the value and effectiveness of both of these enterprises will increase through a systematic interrogation of the tendency to accept social and cultural narratives and circumstances that define older people as irrelevant, residual and useless, as a population to be segregated or otherwise marginalised without recognising their interests, capabilities and potential for active engagement and growth, along with possibly significant limitations.

We have focused on the limiting effects of microfication and erasure on two issues – processes of gentrification occurring in urban neighbourhoods, and immigration trends and policies and the struggles of older immigrants – as representing domains within which greater awareness of broader and macro-level realities could benefit both environmental gerontology and the age-friendly movement. We have shown how, too often, developments in these domains have had their potential for advancing the needs of older people thwarted by a conceptual scope that too readily accepts conventional and dominant narratives of individualism and ageism. These examples suggest that much can be gained by clear and deliberate attention to macro- as well as micro-level factors, as they shape the daily experience of 21st-century elders. Thus, we suggest that a critical, sociologically informed approach is essential to enhance awareness of these tendencies and to provide a conceptual framework within which elders' needs will not remain invisible, nor their voices inaudible.

References

Abramson, C.M. (2015) *The end game*, Cambridge, MA: Harvard University Press.

Ajrouch, K.J. (2008) 'Social isolation and loneliness among Arab American elders: cultural, social, and personal factors', *Research in Human Development*, 5(1): 44-59.

Almeida, J., Molnar, B.E., Kawachi, I. and Subramanian, S.V. (2009) 'Ethnicity and nativity status as determinants of perceived social support: testing the concept of familism', *Social Science & Medicine*, 68(10): 1852-8.

Angel, J.L., Torres-Gil, F. and Markides, K. (eds) (2012) *Aging, health, and longevity in the Mexican-origin population*, New York, NY: Springer Science & Business Media.

Andrews, G.J. and Phillips, D.R. (2005) *Ageing and place: Perspectives, policy, practice*, London: Routledge.

Becker, G. (2003) 'Meanings of place and displacement in three groups of older immigrants', *Journal of Aging Studies*, 17: 129-49.

Browning, C.R., Cagney, K.A., and Boettner, B. (2016) 'Neighborhood, place, and the life course,' in M.J. Shanahan, J.T. Mortimer and M.K. Johnson (eds), *Handbook of the life course, volume II*, Cham: Springer Publishing, pp 597–622.

Buffel, T. (2015) 'Aging migrants and the creation of home: mobility and the maintenance of transnational ties'. Article first published online: 27 October 2015, DOI: 10.1002/psp.1994

Buffel, T. and Phillipson, C. (2011) 'Experiences of place among older migrants living in inner-city neighbourhoods in Belgium and England', *Diversité Urbaine*, 11(1): 13-37.

Buffel, T., Phillipson, C. and Scharf, T. (2012) 'Ageing in urban environments: developing "age-friendly" cities', *Critical Social Policy*, 32(4): 597-617.

Buffel, T., Phillipson, C. and Scharf, T. (2013) 'Experiences of neighbourhood exclusion and inclusion among older people living in deprived inner-city areas in Belgium and England', *Ageing & Society*, 33(1): 89-109.

Burns, V.F., Lavoie, J.P. and Rose, D. (2011) 'Revisiting the role of neighbourhood change in social exclusion and inclusion of older people', *Journal of Aging Research*, *2012*, Article ID 148287.

Campbell, F.A.K. (2008) 'Exploring internalized ableism using critical race theory', *Disability & Society*, 23(2): 151-62.

Campbell, K.E. and Lee, B.A. (1992) 'Sources of personal neighbor networks: social integration, need, or time?', *Social Forces*, 70: 1077-100.

Carr, S. and Tienda, M. (2013) 'Family sponsorship and late-age immigration in aging America: revised and expanded estimates of chained migration', *Population Research and Policy Review*, 32(6): 825-49.

Chaskin, R.J. and Joseph, M.L. (2013) '"Positive" gentrification, social control and the "Right to the City" in mixed-income communities: uses and expectations of space and place', *International Journal of Urban and Regional Research*, 37(2): 480-502.

Chaskin, R.J., Sichling, F. and Joseph, M.L. (2013) 'Youth in mixed-income communities replacing public housing complexes: context, dynamics and response', *Cities*, 35: 423-31.

Coleman, J.S. (1988) 'Social capital in the creation of human capital', *American Journal of Sociology*, 94: S95-S120.

Crystal, S. and Beck, P. (1992) 'A room of one's own: the SRO and the single elderly', *The Gerontologist*, 32(5): 684-92.

Dannefer, D. and Kelley-Moore, J.A. (2009) 'Theorizing the life course: new twists in the paths', in V.L. Bengtson, D. Gans, N.M. Putney and M. Silverstein (eds) *Handbook of theories of aging* (2nd edn), New York, NY: Springer, 389-411.

Davidson, M. and Lees, L. (2010) 'Newbuild gentrification: its histories, trajectories, and critical geographies', *Population, Space and Place*, 16(5): 395-411.

DeSena, J. (2012) 'Gentrification in everyday life in Brooklyn', in J. DeSena and T. Shortell (eds) *The world in Brooklyn: Gentrification, immigration and ethnic politics in a global city*, Lanham, MD: Lexington Books.

DeSena, J.N. and Shortell, T. (eds) (2012) *The world in Brooklyn: Gentrification, immigration, and ethnic politics in a global city*, Lanham, MD: Lexington Publishing.

Eschbach, K., Ostir, G.V., Patel, K.V., Markides, K.S. and Goodwin, J.S. (2004) 'Neighborhood context and mortality among older Mexican Americans: is there a barrio advantage?', *American Journal of Public Health*, 94(10): 1807-12.

Fitzgerald, K.G. and Caro, F.G. (2014) 'An overview of age-friendly cities and communities around the world', *Journal of Aging & Social Policy*, 26(1-2): 1-18.

Estes, C.L. and Phillipson, C. (2002) 'The globalization of capital, the welfare state, and old age policy', *International Journal of Health Services*, 32(2): 279–97.

Gennetian, L.A., Sanbonmatsu, L. and Ludwig, J. (2011) 'An overview of moving to opportunity: a random assignment housing mobility study in five US cities', in J.B. Newburger, E.L. Birth and S.M. Wachter (eds) *Neighborhood and life chances: How place matters in modern America*, Philadelphia: University of Pennsylvania Press.

Gillborn, D. (2005) 'Education policy as an act of white supremacy: whiteness, critical race theory and education reform', *Journal of Education Policy*, 20(4): 485-505.

Gooberman-Hill, R. and Ebrahim, S. (2007) 'Making decisions about simple interventions: older people's use of walking aids', *Age and Ageing*, 36(5): 569-73.

Goodsell, T.L. (2013) 'Familification: family, neighborhood change, and housing policy', *Housing Studies*, 28(6): 845-68.

Greason, W.D. (2013) *Suburban erasure: How the suburbs ended the civil rights movement in New Jersey*, Madison, WI: Fairleigh Dickinson University Press.

Hagestad, G. and Dannefer, D. (2001) 'Concepts and theories in aging: beyond microfication in social science approaches', in R.H. Binstock and L. George (eds) *Handbook of aging and the social sciences*, San Diego, CA: Academic Press.

Hagestad, G. O., and Uhlenberg, P. (2007) 'The impact of demographic changes on relations between age groups and generations: A comparative perspective,' in K.W. Schaie and P. Uhlenberg (eds), *Social structures: Demographic changes and the well-being of older persons*, New York: Springer Publishing, pp 239–61.

Haney-López, I. F. (1998) 'The evolution of legal construction of race and "Whiteness"', in *Major problems in American immigration and ethnic history*, Boston, MA: Houghton Miflin, pp 299-304.

Hankins, K.B. (2007) 'The final frontier: charter schools as new community institutions of gentrification', *Urban Geography*, 28(2): 113-28.

Holstein, J.A. and Gubrium, J.F. (2000) *Constructing the life course*. Dix Hills, NY: General Hall, Inc.

Iceland, J. (2009) *Where we live now: Immigration and race in the United States*, Oakland, CA: University of California Press.

Iezzoni, L.I. (2003) *When walking fails: Mobility problems of adults with chronic conditions*, Berkeley, CA: University of California Press.

Jones, R.C. (2008) *Immigrants outside megalopolis: Ethnic transformation in the heartland*, Lanham, MD: Lexington Books.

Kelley-Moore, J.A. and Thorpe, Jr., R.J. (2012) 'Age in place and place in age: advancing the inquiry on neighborhoods and minority older adults', in K. Whitfield and T. Baker (eds) *Handbook of minority aging*, New York, NY: Springer.

Klinenberg, E. (2002) *Heat wave: A social autopsy of disaster in Chicago*, Chicago, IL: University of Chicago Press.

Lawton, M.P. and Nahemow, L. (1973) 'Ecology and the aging process', in C. Eisdorfer and M.P. Lawton (eds) *The psychology of adult development and aging*, Washington, DC: American Psychological Association,

Lewin, K. (1951) *Field theory in social science*, New York, NY: Harper & Row.

Li, W. (1998) 'Anatomy of a new ethnic settlement: The Chinese ethnoburb in Los Angeles', *Urban Studies*, 35(3): 479-501.

Mahmood, A. and Keating, N. (2012) 'Towards inclusive built environments for older adults', in T. Scharf and N.C. Keating (eds) *From exclusion to inclusion in old age: A global challenge*, Bristol: Policy Press, pp 145-62.

Markides, K.S., Peek, M.K. and Angel, R. (2013) 'Aging, health, and families in the Hispanic population: evolution of a paradigm' in M. Silverstein and R. Giarrusso (eds), *Kinship and cohort in an aging society: From Generation to Generation*, Baltimore, MD: Johns Hopkins University Press, pp 314-31.

Marshall, N.L., Noonan, A.E., McCartney, K., Marx, F. and Keefe, N. (2001) 'It takes an urban village parenting networks of urban families', *Journal of Family Issues*, 22(2): 163-82.

McKee, K. (2012) 'Young people, homeownership and future welfare', *Housing Studies*, 27(6): 853-62.

Nagourney, A. (2016) 'Old and on the street: the graying of America's homeless', *The New York Times*, 31 May, available at www.nytimes. com/2016/05/31/us/americas-aging-homeless-old-and-on-the-street.html.

Newman, O. (1972) *Defensible space: Crime prevention through urban design*, New York, NY: Macmillan.

Normoyle, J. B. and Foley, J.M. (1988) 'The defensible space model of fear and elderly public housing residents', *Environment and Behavior*, 20(1): 50-74.

Peterson, P.G. (2004) *Running on empty: How the Democratic and Republican parties are bankrupting our future and what Americans can do about it*, New York, NY: Farrar, Straus, Giroux.

Phillipson, C. (2007) 'The "elected" and the "excluded": sociological perspectives on the experience of place and community in old age', *Ageing & Society*, 27(3): 321-42.

Phillipson, C. (2011) 'Developing age-friendly communities: new approaches to growing old in urban environments', in J.R.A. Settersten and J.L. Angel (eds) *Handbook of sociology of aging*, New York, NY: Springer.

Resnik, L., Allen, S., Isenstadt, D., Wasserman, M. and Iezzoni, L. (2009) 'Perspectives on use of mobility aids in a diverse population of seniors: implications for intervention', *Disability and Health Journal*, 2(2): 77-85.

Sampson, R.J., Morenoff, J.D. and Earls, F. (1999) 'Beyond social capital: spatial dynamics of collective efficacy for children', *American Sociological Review*, 64(5): 633-60.

Scharf, T. and Keating, N.C. (2012) *From exclusion to inclusion in old age: A global challenge*, Bristol: Policy Press.

Scharf, T., Phillipson, C., Smith, A., and Kington, P. (2002) *Growing older in socially deprived areas: social exclusion in later life*, Help the Aged, London. Available at: www.ageuk.org.uk/documents/en-gb/for-professionals/communities-and-inclusion/id2255_a_growing_older_in_socially_deprived_areas_social_exclusion_in_later_life_2002_pro.pdf?dtrk=true

Scharlach, A.E. (2016) 'Age-friendly cities. For whom? By whom? For what purpose?', in T. Moulart and S. Garon (eds), *Age-friendly cities and communities in international comparison*, New York, NY: Springer, pp 305-29.

Schunck, R. (2011) 'Immigrant integration, transnational activities and the life course', in M. Wingens, M. Windzio, H. deValk and C. Aybeck (eds), *A life-course perspective on migration and integration*, New York, NY: Springer, pp 259-82.

Silverstein, M. and Attias-Donfut, C. (2010) 'Intergenerational relationships of international migrants in developed nations: The United States and France' in D. Dannefer and C. Phillipson (eds), *The Sage handbook of social gerontology*, London: Sage Publications, pp 177-89.

Smith, D. (2008) 'The politics of studentification and (un)balanced urban populations: lessons for gentrification and sustainable communities?', *Urban Studies*, 45(12): 2541-64.

Smith, R. (2005) *Mexican New York: Transnational lives of new immigrants*, Oakland, CA: University of California Press.

Stuckelberger, A., Abrams, D. and Chastonay, P. (2012) 'Age discrimination as a source of exclusion in Europe: The need for a human rights plan for older persons', in T. Scharf and N.C. Keating (eds) *From exclusion to inclusion in old age: A global challenge*, Bristol: Policy Press, p 125.

Treas, J. and Mazumdar, S. (2002) 'Older people in America's immigrant families: dilemmas of dependence, integration, and isolation', *Journal of Aging Studies*, 16(3): 243-58.

Treas, J. (2008) 'Transnational older adults and their families', *Family Relations*, 57(4): 468-78.

Treas, J. and Torres-Gil, F. (2008) 'Immigration and aging: The nexus of complexity and promise', *Generations*, 32(4): 6-10.

Van der Greft, S. and Fortuijn, J.D. (2017) 'Multiple disadvantage of older migrants and native Dutch older adults in deprived neighbourhoods in Amsterdam, the Netherlands: a life course perspective', *GeoJournal*, 82(3): 415-32.

Von Hoffman, A. (1996) 'High ambitions: the past and future of American low income housing policy', *Housing Policy Debate*, 7(3): 423-46.

Van Hook, J. (2000) 'SSI eligibility and participation among elderly naturalized citizens and noncitizens', *Social Science Research*, 29(1): 51-69.

Wahl, H.-W., Scheidt, R. and Windley, P.G. (eds) (2004) *Annual review of gerontology and geriatrics. Aging in context: Socio-physical environments*, New York, NY: Springer.

Walsh, K. and Näre, L. (eds) (2016) *Transnational migration and home in older age*, New York, NY/Abingdon: Routledge.

WHO (World Health Organization) (2007) *Global age-friendly cities: A guide*, Geneva: WHO. Williamson, J.B., Watts-Roy, D.M. and Kingson, E.R. (eds) (1999) *The generational equity debate*, New York, NY: Columbia University Press.

Williamson, J.B. and Watts-Roy, D.M. (2009) 'Aging boomers, generational equity, and framing the debate over social security', in R. Hudson (ed), *Boomer bust? Economic and political issues of a fraying society*, Westport, CT: Praeger, pp 153-69.

Wilmoth, J.M. (2012) 'A demographic profile of older immigrants in the United States', *Public Policy & Aging Report*, 22(2): 8-11.

Woldoff, R. (2011) *White flight/black flight: The dynamics of racial change in an American neighborhood*, Ithaca: Cornell University Press

Young, R.M. and Meyer, I.H. (2005) 'The trouble with "MSM" and "WSW": erasure of the sexual-minority person in public health discourse', *American Journal of Public Health*, 95(7): 1144-9.

Zhou, M., Tseng, Y.F. and Kim, R. (2008) 'Rethinking residential assimilation: the case of a Chinese ethnoburb in the San Gabriel Valley, California', *Amerasia Journal*, 34(3): 53–83.

Part 2
Case studies from Europe, Asia and Australia

Age and gentrification in Berlin: urban ageing policy and the experiences of disadvantaged older people

Meredith Dale, Josefine Heusinger, Birgit Wolter

Introduction

Berlin is a young city in the German context. It attracts people from all over the world, and is a magnet for German, European and international migration. Population growth and investor-friendly legislation are creating growing pressure in the housing market: rents have risen sharply and the signs of displacement processes forcing less affluent groups to the city's outskirts and large housing estates are unmistakable. These processes also affect older people, especially those whose income fails to keep pace with rising rents, or who need to move to more suitable accommodation due to illness and frailty.

This chapter begins by sketching gentrification processes in Berlin since the fall of the Wall and examining their relationship to the distribution of older populations across the city. The second section investigates how the city responds politically and administratively to the demands of age-friendly urban development. After examining city policies directed at older people, the focus shifts to the central borough of Mitte. Finally, in the third section, attention turns to one part of Mitte, the traditional working-class district of Moabit, which is today increasingly affected by gentrification. Two studies conducted in this community explore the everyday experience of older, in the main socially disadvantaged people, many of them in need of assistance and long-term care. The conclusion provides an overview of developments in the context of political processes, where urban transformation driven by economic interests generates growing conflict and contradiction with the needs of an ageing and increasingly less affluent population.

Age and gentrification in Berlin

Gentrification arrived comparatively late in Berlin. Holm (2010) dates the beginnings in West Berlin to the late 1980s, while the process did not affect East Berlin until the 1990s, following reunification and the relocation of Germany's seat of government. Since then, however, the city has rapidly 'caught up' with international developments, such that the process can be observed here in a compressed form. One or other stage of gentrification, in the sense of 'the transformation of inner-city working class and other neighbourhoods to middle- and upper-middle-class residential, recreational, and other uses' (Smith, 1987, p 99), can now be said to affect virtually all of Berlin's pre-1914 housing stock. This comprises largely five-storey tenement buildings and encompasses large parts of all the innermost boroughs. In the early 1990s this included many of the city's most disadvantaged districts, having been regarded as generally the city's worst and least desirable housing. Those with the means to do so tended to move to the suburbs and outskirts. As elsewhere, the populations of the gentrified quarters are disproportionately young.[1] In the super-gentrified areas of Prenzlauer Berg, the population aged 65 and over had fallen to just 4,360 by 2012 (5.2%); if the proportion had been the same as for the city as a whole (19%), it would have been nearly 16,000.[2] This occurred as part of a process that 'in Prenzlauer Berg and other East Berlin areas of renewal ... caused the displacement of up to 80 per cent of their original (mainly East German) residents' (Bernt et al, 2013, p 15).

In the early 1990s, older cohorts were already underrepresented in large parts of the central boroughs. In fact, the central areas of underrepresentation largely match the areas of pre-1914 tenement housing where gentrification has since been most intense. Only in the south-western sector (Charlottenburg-Wilmersdorf), where the housing was of better quality (often with lifts) and more expensive, were older people significantly overrepresented; this is also the area where gentrification has to date been least intense.

Examining the central areas more closely 20 years later, it turns out that the small areas with above-average older populations now correspond largely to areas of post-war social housing. The inner boroughs of former West Berlin, with the exception of most of Charlottenburg-Wilmersdorf, are also where the city's highest concentrations of old-age poverty are found (Senatsverwaltung für Gesundheit, Umwelt und Verbraucherschutz, 2011).

The question thus arises, whether the further loss of older residents over this 20-year period has been caused by relocation, or by an initial underrepresentation of the relevant ageing cohorts. Examination of population register data shows that between 1992 and 2012 the 1933-52 cohort reduced in size in the central, gentrifying areas much more strongly than in the city overall. In other words, significant numbers of those who would have otherwise formed the older population of the inner boroughs instead moved elsewhere at some intervening point.[3] The trend is quite different for older cohorts during the same period, with the 1918-27 cohort, for example, showing a much smaller volume of change in location.

It would be of considerable interest to learn where those displaced, in whatever form, end up. Unfortunately, as others have already noted (for example, Holm, 2013), such information is notoriously difficult to acquire (not to mention the topic itself being marginalised in gentrification research as a whole). What can be said is that affordable housing has become scarce in the central boroughs and the lowest-income households tend to find themselves – in the stratified process of housing market allocation described by David Harvey (1973) – moving to the outskirts of Berlin. This has become the location of the least desirable housing, with a small number of very large high-rise housing estates. While countermeasures have recently been introduced in response to public pressure (mild rent restrictions, a ban on conversion to holiday flats), these may slow but will not reverse this trend.

In terms of the geography of residential status, the city could be said to be in the process of turning itself inside out. Thinking through the implications for age and social exclusion, the mechanisms described would suggest that in decades to come, Berlin's concentrations of disadvantaged older people will be more likely to be found on the periphery rather than (as at present) in the centre of the city.

But to return to the present and recent past: in eastern Berlin, where the gentrification process began early and was particularly intense, there is evidence (from Population Register figures and reports by involved professionals) suggesting a movement of older tenants from gentrifying pre-1914 tenements to nearby modern public housing. Holm (2006) demonstrates how public spending and state regulation in the 1990s blunted displacement in eastern Berlin. These instruments lost much of their bite in the early 2000s through severe municipal budget cuts and court rulings. As we shall see, these elements of intervention are largely lacking today.

Gentrification in Moabit

While the Moabit quarter in which our research was conducted is not one of the areas of most intense gentrification in Berlin, the impact is felt nonetheless. Moabit is in the western part of the inner city, close to the seat of government. The main railway station is at its eastern end, and it is bounded to the south by a large city park, the Tiergarten. It is a densely populated district characterised by great architectural and socio-structural heterogeneity, and has become a site of massive processes of urban change. Until reunification Moabit was closed off to the east by the Berlin Wall, and was thus a peripheral location in West Berlin. Some parts of the district are affected by multiple social problems, and are therefore home to long-established advice centres (for example, for homeless people). The district contains two neighbourhood management areas established to address social problems.

The removal of the Berlin Wall and the closure of local factories over the past two decades have greatly improved the attractiveness of a district that has now become – with a large stock of pre-1914 tenements in a central location – a desirable place to live. The district has also come to the attention of the national and international property markets, with clear signs of gentrification and displacement. The principal manifestation here is tenement blocks being bought up (often by large international investment funds), modernised heavily and sold off as individual flats, in many cases as buy-to-let properties. While Berlin's rent controls generally offer greater security than in many other contexts (for example, the UK and US), legal (rent increases, modernisation surcharges) as well as extra-legal pressures are applied to create vacant properties.

In the early 2000s, most of Moabit's municipal housing stock was sold off, and by 2015 only a small proportion of rented housing was publicly owned. This development affects many older people in lower-income groups who have already been living in the district for years and have to date been able to cope with everyday life despite limited financial resources.

The housing market in Moabit, like the whole of central Berlin, has been characterised by significant rent increases over recent years. In Moabit-Südost, the average rent for new leases rose by 59% between 2009 and 2015, to reach a level of 10 euros per square metre (*Berliner Morgenpost*, 2016). By comparison, the system of legal constraints on redevelopment measures overturned by the Federal Administrative Court in 2006 capped the rents on newly modernised properties at 4.54 euros per square metre. For benefits recipients and low-income groups new leases are largely unaffordable in this area – and throughout the central boroughs.

The housing situation for lower-income groups has been further exacerbated by the privatisation of social housing. Between 1990 and 2005, the city sold nearly half of its stock of social housing, reducing the number of units from 500,000 to 270,000 (Holm, n.d.). This included the sale of 65,700 social housing units to Cerberus/Goldman Sachs and Contest in 2004, representing Germany's largest single municipal housing privatisation (Held, 2011). A recent decision to reverse the policy has halted the decline but achieved little rebuilding of stocks. As well as increasing the pressure on affordable rents across the city's housing market, the privatisation of social housing has also robbed the boroughs of one of their principal options for local rehousing of tenants affected by modernisation and redevelopment.

Earlier phases of gentrification occurred within an official redevelopment framework, until 2001 involving public subsidies tied to a requirement to rehouse tenants (ended after a municipal budget crisis led to deep spending cuts). In eastern Berlin, that arrangement frequently led to relocation to nearby social housing. Today, in areas like Moabit, not only is the statutory framework much looser, but the nearest social housing complexes, Hansaviertel and Zille-Siedlung, were privatised in the early 2000s. Borough housing officials thus no longer have access to the stock, and for many tenants seeking housing on their own initiative rents there too have now become unaffordable.

So what does all this mean for the older residents of the city and in particular the most affected districts? What political responses has the city developed for its older citizens?

Ageing policy in Berlin

Responsibility for ageing policy in Berlin lies with the city's Department of Health and Social Affairs. It prepared the Guidelines for ageing policy in Berlin (*Leitlinien Berliner Seniorenpolitik*) (Senatsverwaltung für Gesundheit und Soziales Berlin, 2013), which were adopted in 2013 (updating and replacing the original guidelines of 2006). The guidelines aim to stimulate and coordinate activities in all departments of the city government, in order to promote age-friendliness. As such, they represent the local policy programme with which the WHO's age-friendly cities criteria can be compared, even if Berlin is not a member of the WHO Global Network for Age-Friendly Cities and Communities (GNAFCC) . The GNAFCC currently plays no major role in German gerontological or urban development discourses, and no German city or region has joined. We can only speculate as to the reasons: one might be the strongly fragmented governmental and administrative responsibilities for urban development, infrastructure, accessibility, care and participation at all levels from local to national. In the following we therefore examine selected aspects of the guidelines that are closely connected with questions of residential quality of life and participation in Berlin.

The policy document: Guidelines for ageing policy in Berlin

The Guidelines for ageing policy in Berlin document (Senatsverwaltung für Gesundheit und Soziales Berlin, 2013) comprises 17 chapters, including those on housing, mobility and old-age poverty. Under housing, the guidelines name 'adapting housing stocks to the requirements of age-appropriate housing in social neighbourhoods' (p 28) as the 'key task' for Berlin's future housing policy. However, the formulations used to describe measures to create new, age-adapted housing, accessible quarters and adapt existing housing stock reveal the lack of determination with which the task is being pursued. The city government 'wishes to exert influence' so that older people can live 'as self-determinedly as possible' in 'increasingly accessible' housing. To that end, the quality and infrastructure of residential environments 'should be examined'. The guidelines suggest better publicity for existing home adaptation loan programmes and refer to an information brochure on technical home adaptations published by the City's Department of Urban Development in 2011. But the city does not propose providing funds of its own. In municipal housing projects, the legally prescribed number of barrier-free units 'should if possible' be exceeded, but no commitment is made. Private landlords are requested to exempt tenants who make adaptations at their own expense from the obligation to have the original state of the property restored after they move out or die. Altogether under the heading of housing, problems are identified but only isolated solutions floated. Recommendations for action are addressed largely to others, not least to older people themselves, who are expected to adapt their own (rented) homes, if need be using borrowed funds. A very brief chapter on old-age poverty announces the city's intention to enable older people with low incomes to participate in social and cultural life, but identifies no concrete measures.

With respect to mobility, the guidelines list more projects and describe them in greater detail. Berlin has a long track record of working to make public space and public transport barrier-free. This has already been achieved for many streets and squares, railways stations, and bus and tram lines; the next steps are timetabled and budgeted for. In 2013, Berlin received the European Commission's Access City Award. The city has a comparatively good public transport system, although in the outer districts there are calls for more frequent services and less distance between stops, especially in relation to the mobility needs of older people. The cost of mobility is not mentioned in the guidelines, even though more than 11% of 50- to 64-year-olds and 5.2% of over-65-year-olds in Berlin live on less than the city's risk-of-poverty income of €743 per month (Senatsverwaltung für Gesundheit und Soziales Berlin, 2011, p 36). The large difference in risk between the two age groups indicates rising poverty among the city's older residents in the coming years, as very few of today's poverty-endangered 50- to 65-year-olds will be expecting an improvement in their incomes when they reach pension age.

Implementation of the guidelines is overseen by a working group comprising representatives of the departments of the city government, the 12 boroughs and the City Senior Citizens' Advisory Board *(Landesseniorenbeirat)*. The advisory board is composed of delegates from the borough committees and representatives appointed by the city parliament. Members of the City Senior Citizens' Advisory Board were also involved in developing the guidelines and have pressed for funding to support their enactment of the guidelines. While the advisory board represents older people's interests at the level of the city, the elected borough senior citizens' committees do the same in the 12 boroughs. All residents of the city aged 60 and over are eligible to vote, regardless of nationality. Although the elections to the local senior citizens' committees secure a level of participation in municipal politics, their role is largely consultative and they possess no real power.

A city-wide advice agency on housing projects for older people, *Netzwerkagentur Generationenwohnen*, advises individuals and groups interested in collective housing projects whether as flat-sharing, co-housing or multi-generational projects.[4] Targeted advice for persons requiring long-term home care, including on home adaptations and co-housing, is offered by 33 care coordination centres distributed throughout the city.[5] Some care coordination centres participate actively in developing age-friendliness in their local area, for example by linking up services for people in need of care. There is no provision for participation by older people in defining the tasks and work of the care coordination centres. In certain boroughs there are also specialist centres that advise older people on housing adaptations.

Borough action concept in Mitte

Alongside the guidelines for ageing policy and the work of the city-wide agencies, most of the boroughs have drawn up their own guidelines and concepts. The borough of Mitte introduced its first policy on ageing in 2006. In 2014, the borough council adopted a new policy document *Gemeinsam Älterwerdenin Mitte (Growing old together in Mitte)*, which includes the area of housing (BA Mitte, 2014). While parts of the borough, which has a population of 30,000, are relatively prosperous, particularly the city centre around Alexanderplatz, Moabit itself is not. Almost one-third of its roughly 76,000 residents depend on state welfare benefits. All of these are classed as poor (BA Mitte, 2013, p 2f, p 35 onwards). About 10,000 residents of Moabit are aged 65 and over, of whom almost one quarter have a 'migration background'.[6] Eleven percent of all those aged 65 and over in Moabit receive the means-tested minimum pension (around €400 per month plus rent).

The action concept for Mitte laid out in the aforementioned policy document opens by pointing out the limits on the borough's potential to provide support, created by shrinking financial resources for coping with the cross-cutting task of 'demographic change' and the council's restricted statutory powers. Increasingly, funds for necessities must be sourced from project grants. These circumstances are built into the formulation of recommended actions in the action concept. Local actors are included in the process, including the senior citizens' committees and professional staff from neighbourhood centres, charities, voluntary sector organisations and other service providers. A chapter is devoted to 'cooperation with the target group'. As well as a survey of older residents commissioned by the borough, neighbourhood walks are mentioned where older people identify issues for potential action. These are conducted in collaboration with local committees such as the Round Table on Ageing in Moabit. The borough commits itself to supporting the work of the borough senior citizens' committee, in particular in involving older people with a migration background, but the mechanism for achieving this is left open (BA Mitte, 2014, p 21).

With respect to social participation, the action concept emphasises the relevance of the heterogeneity of the borough's older population in terms of inter-culturality, and the need to tackle isolation and poverty. It recommends ensuring affordable access to libraries, art and culture. It notes, citing various surveys of older citizens, a great demand for social centres where activities can be pursued and contacts made and maintained. In reality, almost all the municipal social centres in Mitte borough have been closed in recent years, in some cases in the face of vigorous protests by their users. In another borough, plans to close a day centre and sell the property were overturned through direct action by the elderly users. A few days before it was due to close for good, users occupied the building and lived there for 112 days with considerable local support, conducting imaginative actions and generating enormous media coverage. Ultimately, they achieved their goal (http://stillestrasse.de, accessed 30 May 2016). In 2013, users of the old people's social centre in Schulstrasse (Mitte borough), organised a demonstration against its closure – unfortunately without success. The social centre in Moabit also closed its doors.

In the section on accessibility and mobility, the contributions from various departments demonstrate growing awareness of the issue. The borough is aware of many material barriers, the inadequacy of mobility assistance services and the inadequate levels of knowledge of existing support and advice services, especially among those who need them most. The listed recommendations suggest relevant improvements, but are not backed up by concrete planning, still less resources. The borough does support the networking of local service providers in various committees.

Affordable housing that meets the needs of older people, including those with functional impairments, is a stated goal, as is establishing and maintaining local services and infrastructure and a suitable residential environment. However, referring to the previously mentioned city-wide guidelines for ageing policy, the document emphasises that the required financial resources are not available. The consequences of rapid rent rises in the borough are viewed critically, because they contradict the borough's aim to 'retain a generationally mixed, socially and ethnically heterogeneous population structure' (BA Mitte, 2014, p 41).

These policy statements generally turn out to be a blunt sword. In 2008, the city sold a block of 62 adapted flats for low-income retirees in Moabit to an international property fund that plans to renovate the building and massively increase the rents. Determined and creative protests by tenants (aged between 70 and over 90) who fear they will no longer be able to afford to live in the modernised building attracted considerable media attention, and Justice Minister Heiko Maas even participated in a discussion with the residents. But the problem itself remains unresolved.

In essence, the action concept for Mitte represents a solid description of the problems and needs of older people in the borough, and reflects a strong awareness and in parts clear ideas about what an age-friendly city could look like. But concrete action is restricted almost entirely to networking and coordination, which are supported with political goodwill but no funding. The participation of older people is regarded as desirable but apart from the institutionalised senior citizens' committee, involvement tends to be left to chance and again depends on project funding. The comparatively large proportion of older people with a migration background and/or in poverty are therefore largely excluded, as are older people with functional and mobility restrictions.

The next section examines the everyday lives of older people in two neighbourhoods, and how they feel when they see their neighbourhoods changing as they themselves grow frailer and their financial resources fail to keep pace with rising costs.

Coping with care needs and low income in Moabit

This section reports on neighbourhood studies exploring the interaction between the spatial and social infrastructure and the social, economic and cultural resources of older people. This is assessed in terms of support provided for those in need of care and the potential for and barriers to self-determined living.[7] Qualitative case studies were conducted in Moabit, in the GDR-era housing estate of Marzahn on the city's eastern outskirts, and in a small rural town in Brandenburg.

In Moabit, the research team conducted structured interviews with 24 older people in need of care, including seven with a migration background. Fourteen were highly dependent on care, while the remainder needed assistance at least five times weekly.[8] The central question was how the interaction of socio-spatial and individual resources influences whether and how socially disadvantaged older people are able to access help and exercise self-determination. The team interviewed professional and volunteer actors in the borough administration, such as care services, senior citizens' committees, churches and mosques to discover how they assess older people's situations, the content and spatial reach of their services and the extent of local cooperation and networking initiatives.

The study found that people used different, milieu-specific strategies and resources to maintain their self-determination despite needing care. The three central factors here are maintaining mobility (despite progressing functional restrictions), access to information and support, and maintaining social participation.

Mobility

The study found that many older people needing care wish to retain as much mobility as possible, for example to do their own shopping and maintain social contacts. Mobility restrictions were viewed as creating threats to self-determination and health, resulting in isolation and loneliness. The possibility to move about independently and unhindered is itself determined by the conditions of the spatial/ technical environment, especially where financial resources for overcoming restrictions – such as regular use of taxis – are unavailable. The principal problems in Moabit are the absence of lifts in the pre-1914 tenement buildings, uneven pavements and barriers in public space, and difficulty boarding public transport. Very few respondents were aware of the mobility services that will accompany older people occasionally for a small monthly fee. These examples underline yet again the observation that mobility restrictions are not a question of individual impairment, but only become (or do not become) a disability in interaction with the spatial and social environment (Oliver, 1996; Putnam, 2002).

Social participation

Social participation was very important to the majority of those interviewed in need of care. Only those who were so ill that they were largely confined to bed were less interested in social events outside their immediate surroundings. As already described, there are now few low-threshold opportunities to socialise in Moabit without the need to purchase food or drink. Moabit's community centre only identified older people as a local target group in 2009. The few existing social and cultural services and opportunities rely heavily on volunteers, job-creation measures and staff paid for just a few hours for specific activities. Such a framework cannot supply the continuity that is especially important for disadvantaged, isolated older people. Two examples may be used to illustrate the point.

First, for many years the minister of a centrally located church in Moabit offered various free afternoon activities for older people, such as a book club and discussions. In the interview for the study, he related how these group activities had become impossible to maintain, because the lack of other services in the area led to increasing numbers of older people coming with worries and problems that he and his church were unable to address, including illnesses such as dementia. While such services are often more attractive to older women, the older men in the study missed the pubs that used to be found on almost every street corner in this formerly working-class area. As well as rent rises and displacement, the cultural change wrought by gentrification is highly disruptive to personal lifestyles. The only remaining place to drink a beer together, one man told us, was the bench outside the supermarket. The interviews for the research found that not only were there too few services and opportunities, but those that did exist were insufficiently adapted to the needs of the various target groups of disadvantaged older people (for example, those on low-incomes, living alone, or with a Turkish or Arab migration background). At the same time, they also paid little heed to older people with mobility problems and in need of care: only those who have the means and ability to attend can participate.

Second, cooperation between those involved in care provision and those involved in advice work and social and cultural participation is poorly developed in Moabit, and relies overwhelmingly on bilateral professional contacts. This exacerbates the neglect of possible synergies and opportunities. Care providers were aware of the huge problems of isolation and loneliness of many older people in need of care, just as some organisers of advice and social contact expressed regrets that older people were no longer able to attend because of impairments. But in most cases neither side had any idea of the need for action, nor did they possess the power or resources to act. Disadvantaged older people, lacking knowledge and money, find it especially difficult to overcome the inadequacies of these structures.

Networking and exchange: the capital of neighbourhoods

The research team also investigated the district of Marzahn, a very large area of GDR-era high-rise housing in eastern Berlin. Here, the borough (Marzahn-Hellersdorf) has handled certain issues differently from Mitte. For example, it has avoided closing its social centres, which has contributed to the survival of a very active local senior citizens' committee – drawing on traditions dating from the GDR era – that unequivocally asserts the rights of senior citizens and publicises their needs. Another factor was the large housing associations, which until about 2010 were still experiencing problems with excessive vacancies and the area's declining image following reunification. In response, they supported neighbourhood activities, providing rooms and occasionally also staff. The borough participated actively in improving and networking services through the very committed care coordination centre. The large number – in comparison to Moabit – of well-networked opportunities for participation and advice means that disadvantaged older people in particular are better informed and have easier access to support and participation. Actors who know what others offer can easily supply information about these opportunities and encourage their use. Older people who converse with others tend often to receive useful information. The comparison of the two districts shows that the local authorities do in fact possess leeway within the restricted statutory framework. Better use should therefore be made of the given political and institutional circumstances – and they should be further improved.

Access to assistance and care

People with restricted economic resources who require assistance and care have very limited opportunities to purchase support. Beyond their rights to care insurance services and state benefits, they are dependent on social networks and neighbours. It became apparent in the research that those with limited cultural capital and/or significant language barriers tend to receive information about possibilities to access care insurance services through *informal networks* such as relatives and neighbours, rather than through official care advice services. In fact many of the older people interviewed in Moabit possessed few resources of any kind and only learned about services to which they were entitled after an emergency such as hospital admission. Those who received assistance from a care provider at least received support in asserting rights associated with their care. In Moabit, there are few low-threshold institutions in the immediate area. The example of an advice centre for Turkish women shows how the existence of such a long-established service can facilitate access to information at least for the target group. But that functioned only because the staff there responded to growing demand by gradually acquiring basic information on questions relating to care and therefore put themselves in a position to refer clients on appropriately. In order to do so, however, as described earlier, they have to know about the other services in the area and be well networked with them – which nobody was organising in 2009 at the time of the study in Moabit. Presentation of the research findings at a local meeting and to the interviewed actors did, however, lead to informal cooperation between certain institutions and activists, who founded the Round Table on Ageing in Moabit. This group remains active today, and was an important partner in the research project to which we now turn.

Self-Determined Living and Participation in the Quarter

The research project Self-Determined Living and Participation in the Quarter (SWuTiQ) was conducted in Moabit in 2015 and 2016 by the *Institut für Gerontologische Forschung.*[9] The goal of the project was to develop a local concept to promote independent living and social participation among socially disadvantaged older people (60 and older) needing support or care. The project cooperated with three partners in the quarter: the borough department of social affairs, the neighbourhood centre and a self-help advice centre for people needing care and their families. These organisations are in turn members of the Round Table on Ageing in Moabit and as such were in a good position to facilitate access to the target group. Together with the cooperation partners, other actors, local networks, and older people in the study area, local problems and potential were identified and starting points for strengthening self-determined living and social participation explored.

The study was designed as an exploratory, qualitative investigation in three phases. The first phase comprised a comprehensive social and geographical analysis, numerous preparatory discussions, and structured interviews and workshops with experts. In the second phase, group discussions and interviews were conducted with German and Turkish older people.[10] In the third phase, the findings of the first two phases were brought together and discussed with the actors and local older people in the framework of a workshop.

Remaining in the local area

Once central problem in Moabit is that of rising rents in combination with high demand. In some cases, this leads older people to remain in homes that have become too large, too expensive or unsuitable because moving to a smaller, cheaper, accessible flat locally would be impossible or too expensive. It has been shown that older people only slowly rebuild neighbourhood relationships and networks after moving (Oswald, 2012). The fear of being forced to leave the area and thus losing useful informal networks is especially great among socially disadvantaged older people, who partially compensate low incomes, mobility restrictions and support needs through neighbourhood assistance (Wolter, 2013). For older Turkish migrants, who frequently speak little German, living close to people who share the same background and language often represents a fundamental precondition for coping with everyday life. Especially for dealings with authorities, such as applying for benefits and services, many depend on Turkish neighbours who speak better German.

In this connection, we discussed the borough's possibilities to create age-friendly living conditions with representatives of urban development agencies. It became clear that the borough administration finds it difficult to even communicate with the housing sector. International property funds, which have purchased growing stocks of housing here, as well as private landlords, demonstrate little interest in the collective process of developing positive local conditions. As one professional put it:

> "We can think up great concepts and planning proposals. We have the ideas. But who will carry it through, is it viable in the long term, are the property owners' expected returns maybe exaggerated? It simply does not work. I believe that the system needs to be tweaked at a higher level if there is to be any effect in our area." (Interview with Herr Linden, local government, Berlin-Mitte, IV1, 38)

Developments in the property market, along with privatisation of public services, also have repercussions on the diversity of local provision for older people in need of support. Here, as elsewhere in Berlin in recent years, municipal facilities such as sheltered housing and social centres have been closed or privatised: *"... the borough has pulled out of provision for senior citizens. There are no more council facilities, they have been privatised. Provision for the old is no longer a local authority responsibility"* (interview with Herr Linden, local government, Berlin-Mitte, IV1, 15). The care agency based in the area, which offers targeted services for older people with migration backgrounds, is planning to move its offices to the outskirts of the city on account of rising commercial rents in the centre.

Frequently it is help from neighbours that plays a central role in permitting socially disadvantaged older people to continue to cope with everyday life in their own home, despite health-related restrictions. Without the financial resources to have shopping or meals delivered, the people we interviewed depend on their neighbours: *"I can't use my hands any more. My neighbours help me. They cook for me."* (WIt1-61; female, Turkish). Sometimes the support is reciprocal, with the recipient for example looking after the children in return.

But we also heard the ambivalence with which support from neighbours is sometimes perceived, and the dissatisfaction created by dependency:

> "... my neighbour. He lives downstairs and he comes up now and then and sees how I am. Or he goes with me ... to the bank or goes shopping with me.... Well sometimes I get sick of that.... You can't say anything if he's helping

you, can you? You do have to … I have to pipe down."
(OLd1-90; female, German)

Possibilities and limits of involvement

Moabit still has a lively culture of participation and diverse self-help structures. Civic initiatives work to develop and improve their neighbourhoods and resist gentrification and displacement. Self-help initiatives offer assistance and services for people aged over 50 and for relatives of people needing care. Two parts of Moabit are neighbourhood management areas, established to strengthen local neighbourhood and social structures. The neighbourhood management initiates and manages projects, in particular to support socially disadvantaged residents and moderate conflicts between groups. The neighbourhood management system includes a development committee and a grant committee. Locally elected residents participate in both, to influence local project development and the spending of certain public funds.

In the context of our project, we were especially interested in whether and to what extent older and very old people, those needing care and older people of Turkish origin participate in the development of their quarter and whether and how they assert their interests in the existing structures. In the discussions and interviews with civic initiatives and neighbourhood management it became clear that older people with and without a migration background certainly make use of the opportunities for participation. In particular, the so-called 'young old' between 55 and 70 organise neighbourhood activities and self-help, including a notable proportion of Turkish people in that age group.

In our survey, however, we found no example of participation by very old people or older people in need of care. One expert confirmed that mobility is a crucial precondition for participation: *"I would say, as long as they are mobile they can actually participate quite well"* (IV3, 82). But as soon as mobility becomes restricted, participation in the development of the quarter becomes difficult or impossible. Restricted mobility influences more than just chances to participate in decision-making; it limits the scope of social participation altogether. Even beyond this problem, in the view of local actors, the possibilities and opportunities for social participation for older people with restrictions are insufficient, above all because of the preconditions for taking part: *"Because of their small pensions many of them simply cannot afford many activities and excursions. And there are language barriers too"* (WS1, 8Y; social worker).

The privatisation of sheltered housing and the transfer of municipal social centres to voluntary sector organisations leave the borough lacking the premises, staff and concrete points of contact it would require to actively promote the social participation of older people in need of support. To an extent, churches and mosques now offer services for older people – which generates friction among older Turkish people on account of the conservative orientation of the Islamic organisations. Informal structures and meeting places have emerged, possibly in response to the lack of social centres. In one example, Turkish women 'took possession' of a public bench in their street, where they meet regularly to drink coffee. Because the bench can only be used in good weather, they have now applied to the neighbourhood management for a roof.

At the end of the project, the findings from the research were discussed at a workshop with socially disadvantaged Turkish and German older people, experts and stakeholders. At the same time, the use of participatory, problem-solving workshop techniques was explored in collaboration with local actors. At the workshop, ideas for the quarter were developed jointly with local older people and actors. In mixed groups, German and Turkish older people with and without care needs and experts discussed collective living arrangements, social participation and access to information. For the older people themselves, the overarching objective was to remain in their own home. Participants also wished for self-managed social centres where they could eat together and advisers to supply information about possibilities for local support and opportunities. The discussion was to continue in working groups to develop the project ideas. Autonomy and independence are uppermost, and remain of central importance to those needing care. Being able to remain in one's own home in the area one knows is an important goal, and forms a constant in everyday life. This is presently massively endangered by the developments.

Conclusion

For several decades, Berlin's inner boroughs, to which Moabit belongs, have seen processes of gentrification and displacement of less affluent groups, among which older residents, and even more so those who are socially disadvantaged, are also affected. The processes of displacement and in particular the consequences of this development for older people have yet to be adequately researched. In particular, with respect to the effects of gentrification on the autonomy, health, social participation and everyday coping of older people, there is a need for further research. Nor is it known where older people move to when they leave their quarter, or how displacement processes affect other parts of the city, particularly the outskirts.

Although the city-wide and borough policy documents name many of the problems affecting older people with limited resources, and to that extent demonstrate a certain awareness of the consequences of urban change for older people, there is little in the way of verifiable planning for rigorous measures and solutions. The WHO's age-friendly cities initiative is not explicitly mentioned in the programmes and has not made any discernible impact in Berlin. Engagement and awareness of the problems exist among local actors and the willingness to act is often great. Their networking supports occasional improvements, above all in relation to sharing knowledge about services. Interdisciplinary cooperation and close coordination between actors involved in developing local responses creates synergies and places neighbourhood development on a broader footing. Successful networking requires resources, including time, premises, and a willingness to cooperate – even in cases of competing commercial interests.

However, financial constraints on borough budgets and limited political powers at the local level mean that only isolated measures are taken to strengthen the position of socially disadvantaged older people. The powerful and well-funded interests of the global capital and property markets, whose effects permeate down to the local level, have to date gone largely unopposed – indeed long encouraged – by the city government. Meaningful opposition has been left to citizens' groups. Now pressure has resulted in modest restrictions at national (limits on rent increases) and city level (restrictions on holiday lets and sale of individual flats). This is far from enough, however, because rent increases may still far exceed income growth. Instead, speculation treating housing as a commodity needs to be prevented. Stricter regulations could ensure that new-build and redevelopment projects produce significantly more age-friendly housing, which is scarce and therefore generally expensive.

What older people want in their local area, and believe would make it age-friendly, are secure, affordable and accessible homes, shops and doctors nearby, social centres and opportunities to participate, and accessible and safe public spaces. Quarters that meet these requirements are not only age-friendly, but also make it easier for all people who have limited resources and/or restrictions to cope with everyday life. The goal should be therefore not age-friendly but integrative quarters that exclude nobody and offer secure living conditions for all, including socially disadvantaged people. Enabling people needing care, especially those with low incomes, to lead a self-determined life and participate in society represents a further challenge within that context. That means promoting social participation and the involvement of older people, including those in need of support and care, in shaping their residential environment. Important preconditions for this include accessible public spaces, availability of local meeting places and structures for low-threshold participation. The willingness of actors, politics and administration to involve older, frail and socially disadvantaged citizens actively in societal processes – as opposed to simply supplying services – is of fundamental importance for strengthening inclusive neighbourhoods.

Strategic measures that promote integrative local development include inter-sectoral cooperation, especially between urban development and social affairs, the provision of budget funds for local development, and residents' participation. Special encouragement to participate should be given to those residents whose voices are easily overheard: those who are socially disadvantaged, very old people and people needing care, as well as children and young people. Ultimately, however, integrative local development can only be a lasting success if it is supported politically and financially at the city-wide level. As well as guidelines, that would require above all concrete planning outlining specific measures and deadlines, complete with funding and assigned responsibility. Simply describing problems and making statements of intent does not itself produce change.

Notes

[1] The question of age, and specifically the place and role of older residents in gentrification processes has to date been largely neglected. Compare for instance the handful of entries for 'elderly residents' in the index of *The gentrification reader* (Lees et al, 2010) with its copious lists relating to class, gender, ethnicity and sexual orientation. While the subjective experiences of older residents in the course of gentrification processes have been addressed by a number of researchers (for example, Petrovic, 2007), their structural role in those processes has been largely neglected (leaving aside passing mention as one of the groups subject to displacement).

[2] Unless otherwise indicated, population data are sourced from the Berlin population register, small-area (LOR) data by age for 1992 and 2012 (*Amt für Statistik Berlin-Brandenburg, Einwohnerregisterstatistik*, 1992, 2012).

[3] The model as such does not account for moves out of or into the city, nor for geographical differentiation in life expectancy. The relocation it identifies is a net cumulation.

[4] For more information, see Stattbau and Senatsverwaltung für Stadtentwicklung Berlin (2015).

[5] The role of the care coordination centres is to advise people requiring long-term care and their relatives about how home-based care can be arranged. They are also supposed to contribute to developing the services offered, including by

improving cooperation. The extent to which this actually occurs varies widely. These organisations are funded by the Berlin city government and the statutory health and care insurers.

⁶ The concept of 'migration background' widely used in Germany is a broad definition including anyone with at least one parent born outside Germany.

⁷ The neighbourhood project was funded from 2008 to 2011 by the Federal Ministry of Education and Research, as part of the Berlin-based research group on Autonomy Despite Multimorbidity in Old Age. It was conducted by the *Institut für Gerontologische Forschung e. V.* and *Wissenschaftszentrum für Sozialforschung* Berlin.

⁸ For a detailed description of the study in Moabit see Falk et al (2011); the project as a whole is described in Kümpers and Heusinger (2012).

⁹ SWuTiQ was funded by the National Association of Statutory Health Insurance Funds *(GKV-Spitzenverband)* as part of a pilot project on developing new living models (§ 45f SGB XI).

¹⁰ Some of the interviews were conducted as walking interviews (Carpiano, 2009; Evans and Jones, 2011).

References

Bernt, M., Grell, B. and Holm, A. (2013) 'Introduction', in M. Bernt, B. Grell and A. Holm (eds) *The Berlin reader: A compendium on urban change and activism*, Bielefeld: Transcript, pp 11-25, available at www.transcript-verlag.de/978-3-8376-2478-6/the-berlin-reader?c=87 (accessed 30 May 2016).

Berliner Morgenpost (2016) 'Berliner Mieten seit 2009 – Wo sich die Preise verdoppelt haben', available at www.morgenpost.de/interaktiv/mieten/article136875377/So-stark-steigen-die-Mieten-in-Berlins-Kiezen.html?config=interactive (accessed 27 February 2016).

BA Mitte (Bezirksamt Mitte von Berlin) (2013) *Basisdaten zur Bevölkerung und sozialen Lage im Bezirk Berlin Mitte, bearbeitet von Jeffrey Butler*, Berlin: BA Mitte.

BA Mitte (2014) *Gemeinsam Älterwerden in Mitte: Handlungskonzept zu den zukünftigen Anforderungen des demografischen Wandels bezogen auf die älter werdende Bevölkerung im Bezirk Mitte: Definition von aktuellen Handlungsfeldern, Darstellung der aktuellen Maßnahmen und Planungen, Formulierung von Handlungsempfehlungen*, Berlin: BA Mitte.

Carpiano, R.M. (2009) 'Come take a walk with me: the "go-along" interview as a novel method for studying the implications of place for health and well-being', *Health & Place*, 15: 263-72.

Evans, J. and Jones, P. (2011) 'The walking interview: methodology, mobility and place', *Applied Geography*, 31: 849-58.

Falk, K., Heusinger, J., Khan-Zvornicanin, M., Kammerer, K., Kümpers, S. and Zander, M. (2011) *Arm, alt, pflegebedürftig: Selbstbestimmungs- und Teilhabechancen im benachteiligten Quartier*, Berlin: Edition Sigma.

Harvey, D. (1973 [rev. ed. 2009]) *Social justice and the city*, Athens, GA: University of Georgia Press.

Held, T. (2011) 'Verkäufe kommunaler Wohnungsbestände – Ausmaß und aktuelle Entwicklungen', *Informationen zur Raumentwicklung*, 12: 675-82.

Holm, A. (n.d.) 'Wohnungsprivatisierung', Berliner Mietergemeinschaft website, available at www.bmgev.de/fileadmin/redaktion/downloads/privatsierung/konferenz-dokumentation/praesentationen/praesentation-andrej-holm.pdf (accessed 27 February 2016).

Holm, A. (2006) *Die Restrukturierung des Raumes: Stadterneuerung der 90er Jahre in Ostberlin: Interessen und Machtverhältnisse*, Bielefeld: Transcript.

Holm, A. (2010) 'Die Karawane zieht weiter – Stationen der Aufwertung in der Berliner Innenstadt', in C. Bacik, C. Ilk and M. Pschera (eds) *Intercity Istanbul Berlin*, Berlin: Dagyeli, pp 89-101.

Holm, A. (2013) *Wir bleiben Alle! Gentrifizierung – Städtische Konflikte um Aufwertung und Verdrängung*, Münster: Unrast.

Kümpers, S. and Heusinger, J. (eds) (2012) *Autonomie trotz Armut und Pflegebedarf? Altern unter Bedingungen von Marginalisierung*, Bern: Huber.

Lees, L., Slater, T. and Wyly, E. (eds) (2010) *The gentrification reader*, Abingdon: Routledge.

Oliver, M. (1996) *Understanding disability*, Basingstoke: Palgrave Macmillan.

Oswald, F. (2012) 'Umzug im Alter', in H.-W. Wahl, C. Tesch-Römer and J. Ziegelmann (eds) *Angewandte Gerontologie: Interventionen für ein gutes Altern in 100 Schlüsselbegriffen*, Stuttgart: Kohlhammer, pp 569-75.

Petrovic, A. (2007) 'The elderly facing gentrification: neglect, invisibility, entrapment, and loss', *Elder Law Journal*, 15: 533-79.

Putnam, M. (2002) 'Linking aging theory and disability models: increasing the potential to explore aging with physical impairment', *The Gerontologist*, 42(6): 799-806.

Senatsverwaltung für Gesundheit, Umwelt und Verbraucherschutz (ed) (2011) *Sozialstatistisches Berichtswesen Berlin Spezialbericht: Zur sozialen Lage älterer Menschen in Berlin: Armutsrisiken und Sozialleistungsbezug*, Berlin: Senatsverwaltung für Gesundheit, Umwelt und Verbraucherschutz.

Senatsverwaltung für Gesundheit und Soziales Berlin (2013) *Leitlinien der Berliner Seniorenpolitik*, Berlin: Senatsverwaltung für Gesundheit und Soziales Berlin, available at www.berlin.de/sen/soziales/themen/seniorinnen-und-senioren/leitlinien-seniorenpolitik (accessed 14 March 2016).

Smith, N. (1987) 'Commentary: gentrification and the rent gap', *Annals of the Association of American Geographers*, republished in L. Lees, T. Slater and E. Wyly (eds) (2010) *The gentrification reader*, London and New York, NY: Routledge.

Stattbau and Senatsverwaltung für Stadtentwicklung Berlin (2015) *Wohnen in Gemeinschaft: Von der Idee zum gemeinsamen Haus (Living in a community: From the idea to the joint home)*, Berlin: Stattbau and Senatsverwaltung für Stadtentwicklung Berlin, available at http://www.stadtentwicklung.berlin.de/wohnen/alter/de/download.shtml (accessed 15 March 2016).

Wolter, B. (2013) 'Nachbarschaft: förderliche und hinderliche Effekte auf die Gesundheit älterer Menschen', *Jahrbuch für Kritische Medizin und Gesundheitswissenschaften*, 48: 71-87.

SIX

Towards an 'active caring community' in Brussels

An-Sofie Smetcoren, Liesbeth De Donder, Daan Duppen, Nico De Witte, Olivia Vanmechelen, Dominique Verté

Introduction

Theoretical insights from environmental gerontology suggest that improving the environment where older people live has a positive impact on reducing disability and minimising the loss of autonomy as people age (Wahl and Oswald, 2010). Frail[1] older people living in urban environments, however, often experience neighbourhood exclusion – or what Kelley-Moore and colleagues have termed 'erasure' (see Chapter Four), an extreme form of social exclusion whereby frail older people remain 'unseen' in cities. Hence, the need to develop urban communities able to increase opportunities for maintaining and enhancing the quality of life of vulnerable and excluded groups of older people is assuming greater urgency within social policy.

Against this background, this chapter addresses the following question: how can an age-friendly urban environment support frail older people to 'age in place'? To answer this research question, the chapter describes the Active Caring Community project, a 'care living lab' that aims to support frail older adults to age in place in two disadvantaged neighbourhoods in Brussels, Belgium. A 'living lab' comprises an experimental environment in which new innovative technologies, services and products can be tested. Such labs benefit from the fact that end users and stakeholders are involved in the development, testing and evaluation of innovative developments in a real-life environment. The value of this approach, however, has yet to be assessed in the context of the complexities that beset disadvantaged urban neighbourhoods, especially those that arise from accelerated social and economic change.

The chapter, first, presents the demographic and social context of the Brussels-Capital region; second, it describes the 'living lab' concept as it was applied in two disadvantaged urban neighbourhoods; and third, it presents qualitative research findings highlighting how age-friendly social environments can support active ageing and ageing in place. Finally, the chapter concludes with critical reflections and a discussion about those local social environmental opportunities that are key to counterbalance the frailty of older people living in disadvantaged urban neighbourhoods.

Facts and figures about Brussels

Brussels, the capital of Belgium and Europe: a complex political system

Belgium is a federal state subdivided into three regions: the Flemish region, the Walloon region and the Brussels-Capital region. The Flemish region – Dutch-speaking Flanders – represents the most populated (6,410,700 inhabitants) and oldest region, with 19.1% of its population aged 65 and older. In the Walloon region, the southern French-speaking region, the population comprises 3,576,300 people, with 17.3% aged 65 and older. The third region, the Brussels-Capital region, which is the focus of this chapter, is referred to as the 'youngest' region, with a total population of 1,163,500 people, of whom 13.3% are 65 and older (see Figure 6.1). This region has a relatively young age structure and will retain this over the coming years: in 2000, the mean age in Brussels-Capital region was 39.1 years, which decreased to 37.4 years in 2014 (FPBS, 2015).

The low percentage of older people in this region can be explained by the relatively large share of younger age groups. According to Hermia (2015), this is caused, on the one hand, by the process of suburbanisation resulting in middle-aged groups leaving Brussels, and, on the other hand, by the impact of international immigration, which mainly represents younger age groups, resulting in an increased birth rate in Brussels. Although relative numbers could suggest that population ageing is not an issue in Brussels, absolute numbers clearly indicate a growth in the ageing population: from 207,259 older adults in 2015 to 276,529 in 2030, an increase of 25% older adults in 15 years (FPBS, 2016). Furthermore, the share of people aged 80 and older comprises one third of the ageing population in Brussels, which is the largest number in Belgium.

Belgium is well known to have a somewhat complicated and unstable political structure. It has governments for each of its three regions, each of its three communities (represented by the three official

Figure 6.1: Demographic projections: older populations in the three Belgian regions

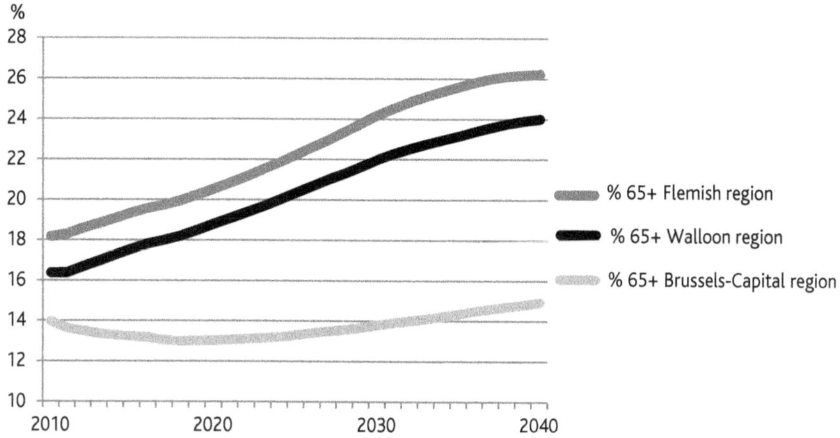

Source: FPBS (2016).

languages of Belgium: French, Flemish and German) and one federal government (Deschouwer, 2012). Each of the three **regions** have authority over various policy fields within **their territory** relating to, for example, employment, housing, transport and urban planning. The three **communities** have authority relating to fields concerning **the person**, such as education, culture, language and welfare. The **federal government** retains limited but important powers relating to the **public interest**, such as justice, defence and social security (Deschouwer, 2012). Some domains, such as healthcare, are organised by both federal government and regional communities, leading to a high degree of fragmented authority (Eeckloo et al, 2011). The complex political structure is especially true for Brussels, which is an **official bilingual region** where both Flemish as well as the French communities have jurisdiction. Furthermore, the Brussels-Capital region is divided into 19 autonomous local municipalities, each with their own governments for local-level responsibilities (Deschouwer, 2012). In summary, political power in Brussels is subdivided among institutions that relate to a number of governments on different levels, that is, the federal state; the regional institution (the Brussels parliament); the community or linguistically determined, cultural and political institutions; and the local institutions (Delwit and Deschouwer, 2009).

In addition to the complex political structure of the Brussels-Capital region, there is the additional presence of the European Union (EU) within the city, marking Brussels out as the political capital of Europe.

It is in Brussels where the European Commission has its headquarters and where all the important political meetings are held (Baeten, 2001; Deschouwer, 2012). The continuous expansion of EU offices and activities puts a certain pressure on the city and its inhabitants. For example, the rapidly expanding internationalisation of the city has led to an increase in real-estate prices and rent in the past decade (Bernard, 2008). The presence of European institutions has spurred on new real-estate developments in better-class districts aiming at well-off EU officials (often expatriates), which in turn has led to the gentrification of more deprived areas. These tendencies are often to the detriment of the more vulnerable residents who are pushed out of their familiar environments (Bernard, 2008). Furthermore, Brussels-Capital region has held a great attraction for immigrants throughout the history. At present, many cities in Europe, including Brussels, are challenged with a growing number of migrant populations reaching retirement age (Buffel, 2015). In 2013, the Housing and Care Expertise Centre Brussels (Vanmechelen et al, 2014) estimated that 27% of people aged 65 and older had a non-Belgian background in comparison with Flanders where the figure was only 4%. By 2020, it is projected that this group will account for almost half of the older population in Brussels.

Socioeconomic characteristics of Brussels

The annual report of the Brussels-Capital Health and Social Observatory (2015) describes the vulnerable socioeconomic and health situation of the inhabitants of the Brussels-Capital region. The report reveals that this region contains a (much) higher proportion of people who experience poverty compared with the two other regions in Belgium. For example, 38.4% of the Brussels population is at risk of poverty or social exclusion. This percentage is significantly lower in the other regions: 26.3% in the Walloon region and 15.3% in Flanders, respectively. The report also indicates a significantly higher unemployment percentage (18.5% compared with an average of 8.6% in Belgium); the highest percentage of people from the lowest income category and an increasing percentage of older people relying on a minimum income in the Brussels region (Brussels-Capital Health and Social Observatory, 2015). Furthermore, the latest census data of 2011 point out that the Brussels-Capital region has a low amount (39%) of owner-occupied dwellings compared with the other Belgian regions (less than 65%) (FPBS, 2014). Moreover, the housing stock in Brussels is rather old (30% of it was built before 1919). Many dwellings in Brussels lack basic facilities and the most frequently mentioned problems are poor electricity, faulty heating systems, high risk of carbon monoxide intoxication and presence of damp (Van Mieghem, 2011).

Despite this, significant internal socio-spatial polarisation of inequalities exists within the Brussel region (Grippa et al, 2015). The Brussels–Capital region includes the municipality with the lowest average income in Belgium per person (Sint-Joost-ten-Node: €8,509) as well as municipalities that rank largely above the Belgian average (Watermaal–Bosvoorde: €19,191) (FPBS, 2013). The socioeconomic situation of those living in the inner city is especially precarious (Grippa et al, 2015).

Necessity of care living labs in the city of Brussels

A living lab is an active structure comprising an experimental environment in which new innovative technologies, services and products can be tested. Such labs benefit from the fact that a population representative of users is involved to test these innovative developments in their real-life environment. The development of such living labs builds on findings from three consecutive studies that underlined the need for innovative projects and initiatives that have the capacity to respond to the care needs of a diverse ageing population in Brussels.

The first piece of research involves the Belgian Ageing Studies (BAS), conducted in 2009 in the city of Brussels. BAS is a **quantitative** research project monitoring local challenges and opportunities as well as issues of quality of life among home-dwelling people aged 60 and older. Findings from this project indicated a more precarious healthcare situation for older adults in the city of Brussels in relation to their Flemish peers. Care-dependent older adults in Brussels were shown to receive less care than those in the Flanders region (2.81 hours per week versus 6.48 hours per week). But while the study showed the many constraints facing older people in Brussels, it also revealed opportunities associated with living in the city: older people's attachment to, and involvement in, their neighbourhoods was significantly higher, for example, compared with the average in Flanders (De Donder et al, 2012).

A second study involved a large **qualitative** research project – Care Needs in Brussels: Different Perspectives (2012) – conducted by *Kenniscentrum Woonzorg Brussel* (the Housing and Care Expertise Centre Brussels), in close collaboration with the BAS research team. In total, 32 focus groups with nearly 300 stakeholders (older people as well as policymakers, informal carers and service providers) were brought together as part of the project. Analysis showed strengths and weaknesses

101

in the organisation of housing and care in Brussels. Neighbourhood services were shown to have an important role in prevention (of falls, for example) and the social activation of older people. On the other hand, informal caregivers felt insufficiently supported by formal caregivers. Care services in Brussels were found to be fragmented and their cost was a burden for many users (Vanmechelen et al, 2012).

The third study in this area was the Programming Study of Brussels. This project was a joint initiative of the three governments in Brussels. The aim was to establish structures that would allow older people to remain in their own homes for as long as possible. An evaluation of the current policy was performed, and based on current gaps and needs, a variety of policy recommendations were proposed. The research drew attention to several problems regarding the provision of care for older adults. For example, there was evidence for growing inequality among the older population regarding access to care. This was attributed to the complex political structure in Brussels whereby the organisation of care involves shared ministerial accountabilities that offer different services accompanied by different charges and rules (care services of the Flemish Community, for example, are generally more expensive in comparison with care services provided by the French and Common Community). Inequalities were reinforced by the uneven geographical distribution of care services. For example, some areas have a shortage, while other areas have an abundance of home-care provision. Another concern was the growing population of older adults from different minority ethnic backgrounds, and the lack of access to care services experienced by many of these groups (De Donder et al, 2012).

The above three studies underlined the potential for developing innovative living labs to address the challenges faced by older people in Brussels (such as financial vulnerability and care shortages). At the same time, the assets of the city (for example, the strong sense of neighbourhood cohesion and the proximity of well-developed local community centres) suggested the potential of reliable, appropriate care services for older people. Drawing on these findings and observations, the idea of the Active Caring Community living lab was born.[2]

Active Caring Community

Living labs in the Flemish community

In September 2013, the Flemish government launched a tender to call for innovative projects named 'care living labs' to tackle future care challenges, such as the rising demand for care, staff shortages and budgetary restrictions. The main objective of these labs was to create new care concepts, services, processes and products and to test them in practice. An imperative was to include both end users and stakeholders in the development, testing and evaluation of care innovations. In order to ensure innovation, a broad partnership was needed, and developed with different types of care and health stakeholders.

Living labs are defined as real-life, everyday environments in which products, services and societal infrastructures can be tested. A living lab represents various users who try out and test products or services while performing daily activities at home or at work. This enables researchers to collect direct feedback from users and to systematically observe, monitor and analyse user behaviour in a natural environment. It provides a method for assessing whether a good idea or concept can be converted into a successful product or service (Bergvall-Kareborn and Stahlbrost, 2009). A central feature of a living lab is the intensive involvement of the end user – in this case older people.

As part of the Flemish government's initiative, a total of six care living labs were funded. Each of these six labs comprised a number of individual projects, including projects around the themes of ageing in place, online communication for older people, quality of life for older adults with complex care requirements, care mobility, and community care. Each of the six living labs was funded for three years. One living lab took place in Brussels: the Active Caring Community project (www.zorgproeftuinen.be/en).

The Active Caring Community living lab in Brussels

For the Active Caring Community project, two disadvantaged neighbourhoods[3] in Brussels were identified. The first district, Jacht, is located in the municipality of Etterbeek, a medium-sized Brussels municipality of 46,228 inhabitants, close to the centre on the south-east side of the city. Situated in the 'first crown' of Brussels (these are the municipalities located around the inner centre), Jacht demonstrates a number of characteristics associated with 'disadvantaged neighbourhoods' (Grippa et al, 2015), including a high number of unemployment and a high proportion of minority ethnic elders. Furthermore, the neighbourhood has a lower proportion of older people (11.3%) compared with the average for the Brussels-Capital region (13.4%).

The second neighbourhood, Brabantwijk, is among the most deprived areas in the Brussels-Capital region and is located in the municipalities of Schaarbeek and Sint-Joost-ten-Node, both of which have the lowest average income per person in Belgium (FPBS, 2013). The neighbourhood represents a concentration of features associated with intense urban deprivation (Grippa et al, 2015), including above-average rates of unemployment (36.7% compared with 22.7% in Brussels-Capital Region as a whole), a high proportion of people receiving benefits and low-income households, high population turnover and high population density (Brussels Institute for Statistics and Analysis, 2015). Furthermore, the area has a significant number of minority ethnic groups, with 40.6% of the population in Brabantwijk having a nationality other than Belgian. Finally, Brabantwijk is characterised by the presence of a major railway station, low-priced shops and (clandestine) prostitution, all of which, indirectly, attract accompanying problems of street litter, vandalism, illegal dumping and nuisance (LOGO Brussel, 2008).

The main goal of the living lab in Brussels was to explore whether it was possible to create or facilitate an 'active caring community', an environment able to support frail older people to 'age in place' (De Donder et al, 2014). The emphasis was to move towards a neighbourhood-organised model of care that reinforced the autonomy of the older adult, supporting and valuing informal care. As part of this, professional home-care helpers or organisations were involved as facilitating, supportive and complementary partners. An active caring community is defined as: a community supporting ageing in place; where residents of the community know and help each other; where meeting opportunities are developed; and where individuals and their informal caregivers receive care and support from motivated professionals. This type of 'socially responsible care' refers to high-quality care that remains affordable for the user as well as for society.

Within this idea of an active caring community, three projects were central: the OPA project (Dutch abbreviation for *Ouderen wonen PAssend*, which can be translated as adapted housing for older adults); the Informal Neighbourhood Care Networks project; and the Case Management project. All three projects involved one or more of the WHO age-friendly domains (see Chapter Two) such as housing, civic participation and employment, communication and information, community and health services, and transportation (WHO, 2007).

OPA project: adapted housing for older adults

The OPA project examined the adequacy of older people's homes through the direct involvement of older volunteers. The growing number of older people is expected to have a significant impact on the housing sector in Brussels, presenting various challenges for current and future housing policies (Pittini and Laino, 2011). Given the low quality of housing stock in Brussels (Van Mieghem, 2011; Winters and Heylen, 2014), and the high number of older people living independently at home, informing older people about their housing options is an urgent priority. Empowering older people in relation to housing may also be achieved by stimulating proactive behaviour. Within this project, older volunteers performed home visits, using a professional checklist, to offer older residents advice about the appropriateness and safety of their house. These volunteers, together with the older resident, searched for possible solutions and provided advice concerning ageing safely at home. This project was primarily aimed at promoting age-friendly housing, but attention was also given to other domains of age-friendliness (see Chapter Two), such as social participation, respect and inclusion, civic participation and employment, and communication and information.

Informal Neighbourhood Care Networks project

Taking a broad vision of care relating to physical, psychological and social support, this project aimed to develop a working model that recognises and values informal care networks, making visible informal care practices. In addition, it aimed to create, facilitate and support informal neighbourhood care networks. Another goal was to ensure that both informal and formal supports were based on the capabilities of older adults and the strengths of the neighbourhood together with local residents. As such, the main age-friendly themes for this project involved civic participation (valuing older people's contributions), community support and health services, and social participation (need for volunteers).

Case Management project

Individual guidance is of great value in helping frail older people connect with appropriate services for their care needs and addressing any questions or concerns they may have. Frail and vulnerable older people often struggle with finding the right kind of care within the fragmented and complex healthcare system of Brussels. A case manager, however, who is well known within neighbourhood social services as well as within community-based organisations, can often support people in their search for help. This case manager can also bring older people into contact with informal caregivers such as local volunteers. The main goal of this project concerned the consolidation, cooperation and alignment of services that supply care and wellbeing at the neighbourhood level. In addition, the case manager guided older adults along their care pathway, supporting their autonomy within that process and enabling them to retain control of the care they received. This project involved a wide range of health services, home-care and community services, with the main age-friendly domain addressed being that of community support and health services (although other themes, such as communication and information, were also covered).

How can an active caring community support age-friendliness?

From the perspective of environmental gerontology, research suggests that improving the physical dimension of neighbourhoods has a positive impact on ageing in place (Wahl and Oswald, 2010). However, the same is equally true of the social dimension, an area that remains underresearched in the age-friendly literature (Buffel et al, 2012; Steels, 2015). The research presented in this chapter addresses this gap in knowledge, emphasising the role of the **social** environment in the process of creating age-friendly communities for frail older people (see also Chapter Three). The social environment is conceptualised as a multidimensional concept, involving a range of aspects relevant to the process of ageing in place, including the perceived neighbourhood social environment (Van Cauwenberg et al, 2014); social participation (Buffel et al, 2014a) and volunteering (Dury et al, 2016); place attachment (Buffel et al, 2014b); and neighbourhood cohesion and safety (De Donder et al, 2013).

Given the above context, the next sections will focus on addressing the following research questions: how can an age-friendly, social environment support **frail** older people to 'age in place'? Which **dimensions** of the social environment are key in that process? What are the main social environmental **opportunities and constraints** that affect older people's frailty?

Findings come from a qualitative study involving 11 focus groups in the two neighbourhoods in Brussels (Brabantwijk and Etterbeek/Jacht) where the Active Caring Community project took place (De Donder et al, 2014). Three focus groups were held with frail older people (n=33); three with informal carers (n=17); three with volunteers who were active in community organisations (for example, social service centres, community centres and social associations) (n=15); one with social and healthcare professionals' active in both communities (n=12);

and one with living lab coordinators and staff (n=10) (see Table 6.1). All participants were recruited by the living lab staff. Of the total 87 participants who took part in the focus groups (56 female; 31 male), 21 participants were from a variety of minority ethnic groups, from countries such as Greece, Turkey, Morocco, Iran.

Towards an age-friendly social environment supporting frail older people

The findings indicate that in order to create age-friendly social environments that support frail older people to age in place, five issues need to be taken into consideration: first, the decreasing availability of kinship support networks; second, the significance of neighbours in support networks; third, the idea of making existing connections and networks 'visible'; fourth, the multidimensional relational aspects of support in the neighbourhood; and fifth, the need to move beyond care and support. These are examined in the following sections.

Table 6.1: Overview of the number of respondents in the focus groups

	Brabantwijk	Etterbeek	Total
Older adults	20	13	33
Informal carers	12	5	17
Volunteers	5	10	15
Neighbourhood professionals	12		12
Living lab staff	10		10

Decreasing availability of kinship support networks

Much of the published work on social support and care networks for older people has focused on the help and support provided by close relatives (Keating et al, 2003). However, the availability of support from kinship networks may contract in later life, with the loss of same-generation kin or with close relatives moving away from the areas in which older people live. The birth of children, relocations, cohabitations, divorces or remarriages have been documented as limiting the availability of social support (Bengtson, 2001). These were all issues that were discussed in one way or another during the focus groups. Some participants talked about the impact of not having children, while others highlighted obstacles to getting help from children, especially those living some distance away. A few interviewees explained that if they wanted help from their children, they were expected to move to closer to their children's homes, which they were unwilling to do. Several interviewees also highlighted how difficult they find it to ask their children for help and support because they do not want to become dependent on their help. A recently retired woman from the Brabantwijk expressed this in the following way: *"My children? No, that's not possible: their life is too busy, they're so overworked, so overly committed; it's difficult to ask them anything. I have always been a very independent person and I wouldn't want to claim them."*

Significance of neighbours in the support networks

Our research findings demonstrate that informal support and care should be seen in a broader social context, taking account of friends and extended family, but also, importantly, neighbours (Barrett et al, 2014; see also Chapter Three). While some older people pointed out that they greeted their neighbours, while not knowing most of them, several participants explicitly highlighted the significance of just a few, but very important, neighbours in the care and support network of frail older people. Such neighbourly support can take on many forms, varying from (intense) practical and emotional support to creating a sense of security by social monitoring (van Dijck et al, 2013). Examples of practical support provided in the neighbourhood were the translation of mail, and help with grocery shopping and cooking. In Brabantwijk, a 62-year-old woman tells the following story: *"Come and have a look at my place, I'll tell you, you'll have a good laugh! Every day, there are about 18 people I feed, and I do it all, 18 people, at my place"*. Neighbourly help and support may be perceived as a small effort by those providing it but its importance to the recipients is often highly significant. One of the participants, a 53-year-old woman, for example, talked about her friend, Marie, who lives in the neighbourhood and who is a full-time carer for her husband. She explains how she supports Marie by occasionally keeping her husband company so that Marie can leave the house:

> "Her husband is at home all the time. There are two nurses who come round to take care of him. But sometimes my friend needs to go out, to buy something, and then she phones me and I go round and stay with her husband until she returns. I live round the corner from them.... Their children live far away."

Making existing networks 'visible' rather than creating new connections

As suggested previously, much of the social support and informal care provided tends to go unrecognised by policy and practice, as it is not visible and largely takes place 'under the radar' (Barrett et al, 2014). Professionals in the focus groups therefore highlighted the need to promote a better understanding of how neighbourhood support networks can play a role in supporting older people to age in place and supporting what neighbours at present already contribute to the care needs of frail older people. According to some participants, when creating an age-friendly social environment, the focus *should not* be on the development of new support networks, but rather on making existing networks visible and supporting and valorising them. A professional expressed this as follows:

> "Actually, there are a lot of good things going on in the neighbourhood that are not visible. And such things are often undertaken by people who are equally invisible, or by people who are often looked at in a negative way. And yet there are so many things that happen here.… I truly hope that this [Active Caring Community] project can reveal those positive things and that we can make them visible."

Acknowledging the multidimensional relational aspects of support

Many of the focus group participants drew attention to the issue of *support givers* (caregivers) who were themselves frail. Thus, neighbours who support frail older people appear to be often frail and vulnerable themselves. Discussions in this regard call for a more diverse conceptualisation of the support giver to understand the complex interrelational nature of support in the neighbourhood instead of the simple dichotomy of 'support giver' versus 'support recipient'. Moreover, frail older people, who are often considered solely as care and support recipients, suggested that they themselves were helping other neighbours, or expressed their desire and the willingness to do so. Equally, in the focus groups with informal carers, several participants underlined their personal needs for additional support and care.

Moving beyond care and support

In reflecting on the concept of active caring communities, several participants mentioned the need for a broader perspective to developing such communities, one that moves beyond a focus on care and support. They stressed that a community that is supportive of frail older people should not only pay attention to help, care, support and reciprocity, but also involve issues linked to dimensions of place attachment, social engagement, community cohesion and safety (De Donder et al, 2013; Buffel et al, 2014a). Some talked about the importance of friendship, fun, small talk and ambience, for example, while others emphasised the importance of intergenerational contact, that is communities that are inclusive of, and promote relationships between, both young and old. 'Combating stereotypes attached to "frail" older people' and 'counteracting anti-care sentiments', which may not only be voiced by community members but also by employers and governmental institutions, were also seen as priority issues to address. An active caring community should thus not focus on 'care' alone, nor should it oblige anyone to provide care, it was argued; however, what is absolutely crucial is that it promotes a **cultural shift** towards **valuing, welcoming and praising care and caregiving**. Yet all too often, governmental organisations fail to recognise the valuable contributions made through informal and community caregiving. A staff member in Brabantwijk expressed this issue with particular vigour:

> "What if an unemployed woman who receives unemployment benefits cares for one of her sick parents? When she goes to the RVA [the governmental organisation that controls unemployed people] and says: 'I'm a part time caregiver', their response is: 'We don't care. You have to work.' ... But if people get penalised when they care for each other, we can promote informal care as much as we like; it just won't work. You can't deprive people from their pride and self-esteem by saying: 'What you are doing is completely irrelevant. You should find a real job'. That's just harsh.... On the one hand, the government asks for more citizen participation in community care, but on the other that same government says 'You have to find a real job, and this informal care? That is your own problem.'"

Discussion

Age-friendly social environments can support frail older people to age in place

The findings from this study demonstrate the various ways in which age-friendly environments can support the most vulnerable groups of older people to age *well* in place in disadvantaged neighbourhoods. While many frail older people who live in urban environments experience exclusion (see, further, Chapter Three), this research has pointed to a range of issues linked to a supportive social environment that help to compensate for, or even counteract, some of the individual pressures or vulnerabilities experienced by older people (see also Chapter Three). Although urban elders often experience a decreasing availability of kinship support networks, the importance of a few significant neighbours in the support networks was a remarkable finding, for example. Rather than creating new support networks and connections, a key challenge here is to make existing networks and connections visible and invest in valuing, promoting and supporting those.

The findings further suggest that the often-used dichotomy of 'carer' versus 'care recipient' is a somewhat artificial distinction. A shift towards a 'relational' conceptualisation of care in the neighbourhood – which recognises that 'carers' may need as much care and support as 'care recipients' with the latter group often also *providing* care – is seen as one way forward to move beyond this dichotomy. At the same time, if the potential of active caring communities to support the ageing in place of frail older people is to be fully realised, other dimensions beyond the caring and supportive aspects also need be taken into account. This study has demonstrated the importance for example of issues linked with community cohesion and place attachment as well as promoting positive images of care and combating stereotypes of ageing and anti-care sentiments.

As this chapter has illustrated, a number of structural pressures and obstacles associated with the urban context have a significant impact on the issue of creating and sustaining an age-friendly active caring community. First, due to Brussels' complex political structure, people in need of care face enormous difficulties in finding and accessing the right kind of care. Indeed, available services are subject to different regulations, under different communities and governments, operating through different channels of communication, via different financing methods, and in different languages. Well-functioning organisations appear to operate next to, rather than collaborate with, each other, thus limiting the development of an integrated care approach. The challenge here is to create an overview of accessible and available care for all residents as well as develop models that enhance cooperation on a *neighbourhood* rather than an organisational level.

Second, the neighbourhoods in which these projects were carried out demonstrate a high annual population turnover, presenting particular challenges to the active caring community model. Brabantwijk, for example, is a typical 'entry neighbourhood' where newly arriving migrants tend to settle because of the affordable housing rents; however, most groups also tend to leave the area as soon as they have the resources to move out. The rapidly changing composition of the neighbourhood often has a detrimental effect on the social networks and relationships of long-term residents who do stay put (Buffel et al, 2013) – an issue that may substantially limit the potential of an active caring community. Gentrification, a feature of the second research neighbourhood (Etterbeek), similarly presents particular challenges to long-term older residents who feel that they have had little impact on how their neighbourhood has changed over the years, with up-market bars and restaurants replacing local and familiar places (see also Chapters Four and Five). An important question that remains unanswered for this particular research neighbourhood is how the mix of EU expatriates and long-term residents can both be integrated into one active caring community.

This research underlines the importance of continuous investment in local care networks, an issue that is especially crucial in disadvantaged urban neighbourhoods characterised by community change. An active caring community cannot simply be 'launched' and then expected to become instantly self-sustaining. Indeed, the model should not be exploited or misused to justify budget cuts and savings in the health and care sector. In contrast, if such models of care indeed save societal costs, these should be reinvested in the organisational support available in the neighbourhood to protect support givers, for instance, from being overburdened as well as supporting existing initiatives and networks that enhance a 'caring' and 'social' age-friendly environment.

Conclusion: critical reflections

This chapter concludes with some critical reflections, both in relation to the definition of a living lab as well as the concept of age-friendliness in this project. First, living labs are defined by the European Network of Living Labs as 'user-centred, open innovation ecosystems based on a systematic user co-creation approach integrating research and innovation processes in real life communities and settings'. Living labs were originally created as an arena to develop digital services and to test new technological devices in home(-like) environments (Bergvall-Kareborn and Stahlbrost, 2009). Although the definition sounds very promising, applying this concept of living labs in real-life (disadvantaged) communities presents several challenges. The ideas of 'co-creation' and 'co-construction', for example, raise several important questions: what do we mean by co-creation? Is co-creation different from the concept of participation, a concept more popular in the 1990s and early 2000s? And how can we enhance co-creation processes with frail older people in disadvantaged neighbourhoods? The experience from the Active Caring Community project indicates that including very frail and vulnerable people is possible, but it takes a lot of time to develop the necessary trust, networks and relationships. This time is not always available within the short timeframe of a project.

Second, a number of critical observations on how the age-friendly cities concept has been implemented within this research can also be made. Through its focus on the *social* aspects rather than the physical aspects of the environment, this study has been able to address a number of issues that have largely remained underresearched in the age-friendly field (Lui et al, 2009: Scharlach et al, 2013). These include the importance of accounting for social attitudes towards frail older people; the need to combat stereotypes around ageing and anti-care sentiments; the significance of a 'relational' conceptualisation of support and care; and the impact of community change and population turnover on social networks in disadvantaged urban neighbourhoods. Such findings lend support to Buffel and Phillipson's (2016) argument that research on age-friendly cities requires stronger integration with analyses of the impact of global forces transforming not just the physical, but also the social context of cities. Furthermore, there is also a need to reconnect the age-friendly debate to broader issues around autonomy, control and power – an issue of particular importance in relation to frail older residents in need of long-term care and assistance. In this respect, it is worth to explore age-friendly issues from a *rights-based perspective*, moving beyond an approach that focuses on identifying older people's *needs* towards one which defends their *rights,* shifting the representation of older people from 'passive beneficiaries' to 'active rights-holders'.

A final critical question relevant to this research has been formulated by Golant (2014, p 11): 'Are age-friendly communities intended to help healthy older people live more meaningful lives or to help the most frail older people age safely in place?' Age-friendliness, broadly understood, could have a significant impact on all age groups living within a given neighbourhood, but it could be particularly beneficial to those who lack the means to improve their situation and to those more reliant on their immediate locality for support, providing new support prospects for 'ageing *well* in place'. In conclusion, the dynamic interplay between the varying and changing needs of frail and non-frail older people on the one hand and the challenging environmental conditions characterising disadvantaged neighbourhoods on the other will be a key issue to address in developing age-friendly cities.

Acknowledgements

The authors wish to acknowledge the support of the community organisations that were involved in the Active Caring Community living lab: Emancipatie Via Arbeid vzw, Buurtwerk Chambéry vzw, Aksent vzw, vzw Maison BILOBA Huis and Kenniscentrum Woonzorg Brussel vzw. We would also like to thank all the other researchers of the Belgian Ageing Study team who contributed to qualitative data collection, including Dorien Brosens, Sarah Dury, Bram Fret, Deborah Lambotte, Sofie Van Regenmortel and Emily Verté. And finally, this project would not have been possible without the financial support of the government agency for Innovation by Science and Technology.

Notes

[1] Frailty is an emerging concept that is often referred to as a (clinical) phenotype (Fried et al, 2001) or an accumulation of health deficits (Rockwood et al, 1994). Yet older people, as well as researchers, perceive frailty as broader than solely a physical problem (Grenier, 2007; De Witte et al, 2013). Therefore, this article approaches frailty from a multidisciplinary perspective (bio-physical, cognitive, psychological, social and environmental).

[2] In Antwerp, Belgium's second largest city, a parallel living lab was tested as this city faces comparable metropolitan challenges. Without ignoring Antwerp's efforts, we only focus on the Brussels living lab in this chapter.

[3] To describe these locations, we handle the definition and indicators as they are drawn by the Brussels Institute for Statistics and Analysis (2013) in light of the district monitoring. We have chosen a neighbourhood definition based on physical and natural boundaries, not necessarily following the municipal boundaries (one of the districts, for example, extends across several municipalities).

References

Baeten, G. (2001) 'The Europeanization of Brussels and the urbanization of "Europe". Hybridizing the city. Empowerment and disempowerment in the EU district', *European Urban and Regional Studies*, 8(2): 117-30.

Barrett, P., Hale, B. and Butler, M. (2014) *Family care and social capital: Transitions in informal care*, Dordrecht: Springer Netherlands.

Bengtson, V.L. (2001) 'Beyond the nuclear family: the increasing importance of multigenerational bonds', *Journal of Marriage and Family*, 63: 1-16.

Bergvall-Kareborn, B. and Stahlbrost, A. (2009) 'Living lab: an open and citizen-centric approach for innovation', *International Journal of Innovation and Regional Development*, 1(4): 356-70.

Bernard, N. (2008) 'De impact van de Europese Unie op vastgoed in Brussel: tussen cliché en onderschatting' ('The impact of the European Union on real estate in Brussels: between stereotypes and underestimations'), *Brussels Studies,* 21, available at www. brusselsstudies.be/medias/publications/NL_63_BruS21NL.pdf (in Dutch).

Brussels-Capital Health and Social Observatory (2015) 'Brussels poverty report', available at http://www.observatbru.be/documents/ publications/publications-pauvrete/rapports-pauvrete.xml?lang=en.

Brussels Institute for Statistics and Analysis (2015) 'Online tool for district monitoring', available at www.statistics.irisnet.be/themes/ population#.VwO6xzaLRR0.

Buffel, T., De Donder, L., Phillipson, C., Dury, S., De Witte, N. and Verté, D. (2014a) 'Social participation among older adults living in medium-sized cities in Belgium: the role of neighbourhood perceptions', *Health Promotion International*, 29(4): 655-68.

Buffel, T., De Donder, L., Phillipson, C., De Witte, N., Dury, S. and Verté, D. (2014b) 'Place attachment among older adults living in four communities in Flanders, Belgium', *Housing Studies*, 29(6): 800-22.

Buffel, T., Verté, D., De Donder, L., De Witte, N., Dury, S., Vanwing, T. and Bolsenbroek, A. (2012) 'Theorising the relationship between older people and their immediate social living environment', *International Journal of Lifelong Education*, 31(1): 13-32.

De Donder, L., Verté, E., Teugels, H., Glorieux, M., Bernard, M., Vanmechelen, O., Smetcoren, A.-S., Persyn, P. and Verté, D. (2012) *Programmatie-studie Brussel. Onderzoek naar het opzetten van de programmatie inzake structuren voor het thuishouden en huisvesten van ouderen (Programmation Study Brussels)*, Zelzate: University Press (in Dutch and French).

De Donder, L., Buffel, T., De Witte, N., Dury, S. and Verté, D. (2013) 'Perceptual quality of neighbourhood design and feelings of unsafety', *Ageing & Society*, 33(6): 917-37.

De Donder, L., Dury, S., Smetcoren, A.-S., Van Regenmortel, S., Verté, E., De Witte, N., Brosens, D. and Lambotte, D. (2014) *Actief zorgzame buurt. Noden en verwachtingen – een stakeholdersbevraging (Active Caring Community. Needs and expectations – stakeholders' perspectives)*, Brussels: Vrije Universiteit Brussel (in Dutch).

Delwit, P. and Deschouwer, K. (2009) 'The institutions of Brussels', *Brussels Studies* (electronic journal), Synopsis no 14, available at www.brusselsstudies.be/medias/publications/NL_85_SGB14.pdf.

Deschouwer, K. (2012) *The politics of Belgium: Governing a divided society*, Basingstoke: Palgrave Macmillan.

De Witte, N., De Donder, L., Dury, S., Buffel, T., Verté, D. and Schols, J. (2013) 'A theoretical perspective on the conceptualisation and usefulness of frailty and vulnerability measurements in community dwelling older adults', *Aporia: The Nursing Journal*, 5(1): 13-31.

Dury, S., Willems, J., De Witte, N., De Donder, D., Buffel, T. and Verté, D. (2016) 'Municipality and neighbourhood influences on volunteering in later life', *Journal of Applied Gerontology*, 35(6): 601-626.

Eeckloo, K., Callens, S., Fornaciari, D. and Vleugels, A. (2011) 'Monitoring quality in a federal state with shared powers in healthcare: the case of Belgium', *European Journal of Health Law*, 18(4): 413-22.

FPBS (Federal Planning Bureau and Statistics) (2013) 'Tax-income overview Belgium in 2013', available at http://statbel.fgov.be/nl/statistieken/cijfers/arbeid_leven/fisc/ (in Dutch).

FPBS (2014) 'Census data 2011', available at http://census2011.fgov.be/index_nl.html (in Dutch).

FPBS (2015) 'Demographic projections 2014-2060', available at www.plan.be/publications/publication.php?lang=en (in Dutch).

FPBS (2016) 'Bevolking op 1 januari en per leeftijd 2016-2061' ('Population for all ages 2016-2061'), available at http://statbel.fgov.be/nl/modules/publications/statistiques/bevolking/downloads/bevolking_op_1_januari_2016-2061.jsp (in Dutch).

Fried, L.P., Tangen, C.M., Walston, J., Newman, A.B., Hirsch, C. and Gottdiener, J. (2001) 'Frailty in older adults: evidence for a phenotype', *The Journals of Gerontology. Series A, Biological Sciences and Medical Sciences*, 56(3): M146-56.

Golant, S. (2014) 'Age-friendly communities, are we expecting too much?', *IRPP Insight*, 5(Feb): 1-20.

Grenier, A. (2007) 'Constructions of frailty in the English language, care practice and the lived experience', *Ageing & Society*, 27(3): 425-44.

Grippa, T., Marissal, P., May, X., Wertz, I. and Loopmans, M. (2015) 'Dynamiek van de buurten in moeilijkheden in de Belgische stadsgewesten' ('Dynamics of deprived neighbourhoods located in Belgian cities'), available at http://forms.mi-is.be/Atlas_NDL.pdf (in Dutch).

Hermia, J.P. (2015) 'Demografische barometer 2014 van het Brussels Hoofdstedelijk Gewest' ('Demographic barometer 2014 of Brussels-Capital Region'), *Focus*, 7, available at www.bisa.irisnet.be/bestanden/publicaties/focus-van-het-bisa/focus_07_februari_2015 (on Dutch).

Keating, N., Otfinowsky, P., Wenger, G.C., Fast, J. and Derksen, L. (2003) 'Understanding the caring capacity of informal networks of frail seniors: a case for care networks', *Ageing & Society*, 23(1): 115-27.

LOGO Brussel (2008) 'Gezondheidsportret: Brabantwijk beweegt!' ('Health survey: the Brabantwijk is moving'), available at http://docplayer.nl/15100058-Gezondheids-portret-brabantwijk-beweegt.html (in Dutch).

Lui, C.-W., Everingham, J.-A., Warburton, J., Cuthill, M. and Bartlett, H. (2009) 'What makes a community age-friendly: a review of international literature', *Australasian Journal on Ageing*, 28(3): 116-21.

Pittini, A. and Laino, E. (2011) *Housing Europe Review 2012. The nuts and bolts of European social housing systems*, Brussels: CECODHAS Housing Europe's Observatory.

Rockwood, K., Fox, R.A., Stolee, P., Robertson, D. and Beattie, B.L. (1994) 'Frailty in elderly people: an evolving concept', *Canadian Medical Association Journal*, 150(4): 489-95.

Scharlach, A.E., Lehning, A.J., Warburton, J., Ng, S.H. and Shardlow, S.M. (2013) 'Ageing-friendly communities and social inclusion in the United States of America' *Ageing & Society*, 33(1): 110-36.

Steels, S. (2015) 'Key characteristics of age-friendly cities and communities: a review', *Cities*, 47: 45-52.

Van Cauwenberg, J., De Donder, L., Clarys, P., De Bourdeaudhui, I., Buffel, T., De Witte, N., Dury, S., Verté, D. and Deforche, B. (2014) 'Relationships between the perceived neighbourhood social environment and walking for transportation among older adults', *Social Science & Medicine*, 104: 23-30.

van Dijk, H.M., Cramm, J.M. and Nieboer, A.P. (2013) 'The experiences of neighbour, volunteer and professional support-givers in supporting community dwelling older people', *Health and Social Care in the Community*, 21(2): 150-58.

Vanmechelen, O., Teugels, H., van Thiel, C., Jeroen, D., Makay I. and Van Osselt, I. (2014) *Masterplan Woonzorg Brussel 2014-2020 (Masterplan housing and care in Brussels 2014-2020)*, Brussels: Kenniscentrum Woonzorg Brussel VZW (in Dutch).

Vanmechelen, O., Verté, D., Teugels, H., Buffel, T., De Donder, L., Glorieux, M., Lamarti, S., Smetcoren, A.-S. and Verté, E. (2012) *Zorgnoden en -behoeften: De kijk van de Brusselaar. Analyse van sterkten, zwaktes, kansen en bedreigingen van de Brusselse Woonzorg (Care needs: The view of Brussels' citizen. Analysis of strengths, weaknesses, opportunities and threaths for residential and homecare in Brussels)*, Brussels: Gillis printing company (in Dutch).

Van Mieghem, W. (2011) 'Zeven jaar ongezonde woningen in Brussel. Conclusies' ('Seven years of unhealthy housing in Brussels. Conclusions'), in Brusselse Bond van Recht op Wonen (BBRoW) (ed) *7 jaar strijd tegen ongezonde woningen in Brussel: De balans*, Brussels: BBRoW.

Wahl, H.-W. and Oswald, F. (2010) 'Environmental perspectives on ageing', in D. Dannefer, and C. Phillipson (eds) *The Sage handbook of social gerontology*, London: Sage Publications, pp 111-24.

WHO (World Health Organization) (2007) *Global age-friendly cities a guide*, Geneva: WHO.

Winters, S. and Heylen, K. (2014) 'How housing outcomes vary between the Belgian regions', *Journal of Housing and the Built Environment*, 29(3): 541-56.

SEVEN

Exploring the age-friendliness of Hong Kong: opportunities, initiatives and challenges in an ageing Asian city

David R. Phillips, Jean Woo, Francis Cheung, Moses Wong, Pui Hing Chau

Introduction

Hong Kong is a small, densely settled Special Administrative Region of China (the HKSAR). Its 2014 mid-year population of some 7.3 million persons had a median age of 42.8 years, with 14.7% aged 65 and, importantly, 4.4% aged over 80 (Census and Statistics Department, 2015a). These percentages of older persons have increased considerably over the past 30 years, as Hong Kong's population has aged demographically, and the HKSAR now also has one of the lowest fertility rates in the world. It faces its most rapid period of population ageing over the next 20 years, with the age 65-plus group set to comprise almost 23% of the 'usually resident' population by 2024 and 30% in 2034, when the median age will be 50. Indeed, United Nations projections indicate that the HKSAR will probably be the sixth oldest territory in the world by 2050, with a median age of almost 53 years (UNDESA, 2015), 10 years older than at present. Clearly, therefore, with a considerable population that is already elderly and the likelihood of very considerable future increase in the proportion of older persons, questions of age-friendliness on all the main domains of the World Health Organization (WHO)'s (2007a, 2007b) age-friendly cities and communities (AFCC) model are of prime consideration as well as certain local additional AFCC characteristics (Wong et al, 2015, 2017). By August 2017, ten HKSAR districts had embarked on the AFCC commitments and received recognition from the WHO by being included in its list of AFCC communities.[1] Hong Kong is also one of 15 countries and territories involved in pilot testing a set of indicators of age-friendliness, under the WHO Kobe Centre for Health Development (WHO, 2015).

Hong Kong is a highly urbanised small territory of only 1,100 square kilometres and, while about 40% of the HKSAR comprises protected country parks, geographical reasons mean that the population is concentrated in only about 25% of the land area. Therefore, overall population density is among the highest in the world, at 6,690 per square kilometer in 2014. In places such as Kwun Tong, the most densely populated district and located in Kowloon, density reaches 57,250 persons per square kilometer (Hong Kong Government, 2015). Therefore, the majority of the territory's population lives in high-rise apartments, in public rental (30.4%), subsidised home ownership (15.5%) and private ownership (53.5%) (Census and Statistics Department, 2015b). Public and subsidised accommodation of various sorts is particularly important for older persons, as noted later in the chapter. Older persons are subject to socioeconomic factors such as high property prices plus dense and crowded urban living, and environmental factors including air pollution, noise and urban design, often affecting their wellbeing and adjustment (Phillips et al, 2009; Chau et al, 2013a) (see also Chapter Two).

This chapter aims to introduce selected age-friendly contexts and concerns that arise from the specific social and demographic context in Hong Kong. Having provided the broad local background, the chapter goes on to consider the possibilities of learning lessons from other large cities in the region. The main sections of the chapter outline, first, the organisations and approaches adopted by AFCC initiatives in Hong Kong. The chapter then focuses on those initiatives concerned principally with the broad domains of social inclusion and participation and, especially important in the dense urban setting, those involving housing and accommodation initiatives. Even though Hong Kong has a mainly Chinese population, there are, nevertheless, smaller groups whose ethnic backgrounds place them at a socioeconomic disadvantage and the chapter provides some innovative insights into initial research into this growing local issue amongst the older population. It then introduces some local initiatives to alert or raise awareness of risks to older persons in weather and emergency situations. In conclusion, the chapter considers some of the positive achievements and some of the negative factors that might hinder future achievement of age-friendliness locally, including the pressing issue of elderly poverty in a rich city.

The AFCC experience in the context of other Asian countries

Given its demographic and urban settings, what can Hong Kong learn from and demonstrate to similar large Asia-Pacific cities in terms of future improvements of age-friendliness, and what opportunities and challenges are likely to be encountered in the next decade or so? Chau and colleagues (2013b) have placed Hong Kong's experience in the context of other world cities such as New York and London, which face similar challenges of ageing in large urban settings. Hong Kong does particularly well on, for example, life expectancy, one of the longest in the world and ahead of the other two cities except for male life expectancy at 65 years, in which London is slightly ahead. Where it seems Hong Kong scores well is also in the proportion of older persons who are married and in terms of health indicators such as obesity and cholesterol levels. However, Hong Kong's older persons often fare worse in terms of financial security and have a much higher poverty rate than their counterparts in London and New York. The older population also, on average, have considerably lower educational levels than comparable groups in these two other world cities, a generational effect that will change over time. The *Hong Kong poverty situation report 2013* (Hong Kong Government, 2014) notes that the post-intervention poverty rate of persons aged 65 years and above was three times higher than that of those aged below 65. In 2013, 30.5% of older persons were identified as being in poverty, even after policy interventions, an unenviably high proportion for a rich world city and a source of considerable local concern. This suggests that public sector policies must become more generous. For example, there is not yet a universal pension in Hong Kong and, in 2017, this remained under vigorous debate. There is pressure for a basic pension to be provided for everyone, but the government is resisting this for philosophical reasons and on the grounds of sustainability and long-term costs.

Resources are important, as evidence from other countries indicates. For example, recent reports note that Thailand may have a serious challenge in becoming age-friendly (Silver Group, 2016). Its population is one of the region's fastest ageing and Thailand is experiencing demographic ageing as rapid as that in Korea and Singapore, but their economic development and national incomes are higher. While efforts are being devoted to local community healthcare for vulnerable older people, without economic growth and a concerted effort towards age-friendliness, the coming decades look problematic for Thailand (Silver Group, 2016; *Straits Times*, 2016). Hong Kong is aware of the importance of devoting resources to older persons, but the issue of elderly poverty remains.

Several other countries in Southeast and East Asia have started to address AFCC domains related to social inclusion and participation, perhaps one of the main areas of concern in many Asian cities. Family changes and their socioeconomic impacts are considerable, and China in particular now acknowledges the reduction of family support and, by extension, social inclusion problems that may result from very small family size (Phillips and Feng, 2015; Phillips, 2018, in press). This issue is likely to be highly relevant for cities elsewhere in the region, including those in Japan, Korea, Taiwan and Singapore, as well as Hong Kong, given their low fertility levels. One policy in China is the development of older people's associations (OPAs), which provide a platform for older people's civic engagement and participation in community affairs as well as being sources of mutual help. They have the potential to be valuable in practical terms, for example in response to natural disasters, floods, extreme weather events and earthquakes. Indeed, older persons in the region have often been disproportionately affected by disasters and emergencies, as the WHO and others recognise. Well-known examples include the tsunamis affecting large areas of Southeast and South Asia in 2004 and Japan in 2011; the Sichuan earthquake in China in 2008; and the super typhoon in the Philippines in November 2013 (McCracken and Phillips, 2012, 2016). Risk reduction activities have been organised, such as disaster preparedness, early warning systems and resilience programmes, in which older people share their knowledge of local community resources. Older people also have knowledge of traditional coping mechanisms and have experiences of previous disaster events. Examples of OPA initiatives were seen in Indonesia after the tsunami in 2004 and in India after a severe flood in Rajasthan (HelpAge International, 2009).

Japan, with its even more elderly population, though broadly comparable demographic structure to Hong Kong's, has identified three priority issues for an ageing society: first, to extend independent living; second, to create environments for ageing in place; and third, to maintain and strengthen human bonds (Akiyama, 2015). Recognition of the importance of an age-friendly community for physical and mental wellbeing is central to these priorities. To try to achieve more age-friendly communities, projects address productive ageing, strengthening social bonds, establishing age-friendly housing, transportation modes, and, a particular Japanese feature, the inclusion of innovative sciences and technologies to designing communities. Two communities (Kashiwa and Fukui) have been selected as pilot future communities for older people, with neighbourhoods designed to include all daily necessities and services close by. This involves collaboration among municipal governments, universities, industries and citizens, and socioeconomic initiatives such as flexible work opportunities for older people that are centrally managed, and housing and transport designed to allow active ageing and ageing in place. Healthcare and assisted living are provided in recognition of different mobility levels. Significant improvements were reported when individual outcomes such as physical and mental health, social relations, levels of happiness, and community indicators such as tax revenues, healthcare costs and social capital were measured (Akiyima, 2015). Such specially planned age communities remain the exception rather than the rule in the region. Their space requirements mean such models are unlikely to be feasible in cities such as Hong Kong. Japan's experience and initiatives do nevertheless illustrate that older people are not necessarily merely clients of welfare-type programmes, but can also influence and change the urban environments in which they live. Moreover, such social innovations help older individuals to remain socially connected and physically mobile, with benefits for the whole community (Sander et al, 2015).

The Hong Kong perspective on age-friendly cities

Given Hong Kong's ageing population and high-rise, its high-density characteristics and its self-proclaimed role as "Asia's world city", there has been considerable local interest in the AFCC concept and the aspects of age-friendliness that could be enhanced. Indeed, Wong and colleagues (2015) and Woo (2013) note that Hong Kong was relatively early in both adopting and promoting the AFCC concept. In 2008, soon after the formal WHO promulgation, the concept received local interest and support from non-governmental organisations (NGOs), governmental bodies, district councils, academic and professional associations, and even from businesses that may have detected elements of the 'silver market' as possible foci. Predating the WHO initiative, an Elderly Commission had been established in 1997 to help formulate policy, coordinate planning and development and monitor and evaluate policies and programmes for 'the elderly' (Elderly Commission, 2016).

The development of an age-friendly environment in Hong Kong is made even more important as government policy is to promote 'ageing in place'. Chui and colleagues (2009) note that this is pursued with a range of measures such as cash support and subsidies in kind. Indeed, ageing in place has been the preferred option for many years and has been promoted since at least the early 1990s (Leung, 1999; Phillips and Yeh, 1999). The policy has been run in conjunction with the earlier approach of 'care in the community', this dating from a 1973 Hong Kong Government working party report. However, critics claim only lip service has been paid over the succeeding decades to the provision of sufficient resources to provide care effectively in the community (Chow, 1999). This makes the development of properly resourced age-friendly environments ever more important and a significant goal for social policy.

In spite of many apparently age-friendly policies in Hong Kong, there is also a fairly high rate of institutionalisation among older persons compared with several other countries, both in the region and internationally. For example, Chui and colleagues (2009) note that Hong Kong's institutionalisation rate for persons aged 65 and over in 2009 was 6.8% compared with 1% in China, 2% in Taiwan, 3% in Japan, 2.3% in Singapore and 4.2% in the United Kingdom, at similar dates. Most institutionalised older persons in Hong Kong live in relatively small residential care units, under either the management of private, public or charitable organisations. Moreover, there has not been the pressure for de-institutionalisation of major residential care units that has been seen in other countries over the years.

In policy terms, 'building an age-friendly community' featured as a specific focus in the Hong Kong Chief Executive's 2016 Policy Address (Hong Kong Government, 2016). This indicates at least some degree of political will and support, although whether this will be developed seriously does seem to be questioned. With respect to the development of many AFCC-relevant services and planning mechanisms, Hong Kong is interesting in that there are many levels of administration and types of provider and participants. For example, the Hong Kong Government and its bureaus and departments have centralised responsibility for the planning of many social, welfare, health and environmental services. Regional and district offices of civil service departments and 18 district councils operate at the more local level throughout the territory. Departments include many directly involved with health, social welfare, planning, housing, and environmental protection, all liaising and working together to varying extents. Healthcare services for older persons are delivered mainly through the public sector and especially via the Hospital Authority (a statutory body) and the Department of Health. A recent study comparing the promotion of an age-friendly city in Hong Kong and Chiayi city (Taiwan) reveals that local contexts, knowledge and mode of governance largely determine the form and making of AFCC policy. The role of government is important, and involvement of different stakeholders such as NGOs, universities and civil society also helps create concerted efforts to achieve integrated outcomes (Sun et al, 2017).

Hong Kong service provision and local AFCC initiatives

Over the years, many elements of welfare provision and services in Hong Kong have been organised and run by charitable organisations, NGOs and other non-profit organisations. Many tend to be services of key importance to older persons and their families, including day care, accommodation, welfare services and home care. A slightly unusual feature is that their infrastructure and some operating costs are financially subvented and monitored by the government, although many recurrent costs are met by the organisations themselves. There is also a wide variety of private services on offer. Many of the official and NGO institutions also collaborate with Hong Kong's universities in terms of research, service delivery and training, including the two medical schools, several departments that provide nursing and social work training, and others involved in many areas of research and teaching in social policy and related areas.

Initial AFCC interests were evident in the formation of an Age-Friendly Hong Kong Steering Committee in 2008, followed by, in 2010, surveys (based on focus groups) of levels of age-friendliness in Hong Kong according to the WHO's eight domains. Subsequently, in 2013, the committee proposed a set of 24 indicators (with three indicators in each domain) based on routine or official statistics to provide an objective and scientific evaluation of the level of age-friendliness in Hong Kong. The numerous 'age-friendly relevant' organisations in Hong Kong often have direct associations with, or even responsibilities for, specific areas under the WHO's AFCC domains. There are numerous age-friendly initiatives being introduced, many of which are in the areas of education and social inclusion, although in an Asian city context, many also focus on housing, infrastructure and health services.

Examples encouraging social participation and inclusion

The Elder Academy scheme, an example of an education and social inclusion and participation initiative, was launched in early 2007 by the Labour and Welfare Bureau and the Elderly Commission. The scheme provides access to learning opportunities in schools and university campuses and is aimed primarily at older people who have had little or no education. This scheme allies with international ideas of the 'university of the third age' approach while optimising the use of existing educational facilities, and has been successful in promoting both lifelong and even initial learning for older persons, encouraging participation and helping to maintain physical and mental wellbeing. The scheme also promotes civic education and intergenerational harmony by engaging school and university students. Currently, some 125 elder academies in various districts and seven tertiary institutions offer a wide variety of courses. In terms of health infrastructure, selected initiatives have emerged. A specific example is **age-friendly hospital wards**, a response to the large numbers of hospitalised frail older people (up to one third of whom may have dementia) who are often receiving poor care arising from a lack of awareness of their needs. At present, two hospitals have adopted this principle when refurbishing their wards (Chui, 2015; Kwok, 2015).

Housing

Given the very high costs of housing in many Asia–Pacific cities and especially in Hong Kong, there has been a strong focus locally on housing-related initiatives and low-cost or subsidised accommodation for older people. Indeed, in 2015, approximately 37% of Hong Kong's over-60s population lived in public rental housing (Hong Kong Government, 2015). Table 7.1 summarises public rental housing schemes (the public sector is Hong Kong's major rental landlord) that focus on older persons. Notably, there has been an attempt to promote multi-generational living to encourage younger generations to live with or close to their older parents. Co-residence has been a declining trend globally and especially in the Asia–Pacific region, where it has raised concerns about the future viability of family care for older people. This decline follows social trends towards nuclear families, which has been exacerbated by the lack of suitably sized affordable multi-generation accommodation, especially in expensive urban areas (Phillips, 2018, in press). These public sector initiatives may be one way to help make multi-generational living somewhat easier, even if the uptake of this policy has to date been somewhat limited.

Hong Kong Housing Society

One particularly interesting local agency, the Hong Kong Housing Society (HKHS), can be highlighted for its contribution to elderly-friendly accommodation design and development (Box 7.1). It is a non-

Table 7.1: Housing schemes and special housing units for older persons

Available schemes (organisations)	Features
Priority public rental housing schemes (Hong Kong Housing Authority)	
Single elderly persons priority scheme	For older persons who wish to live alone
Elderly persons priority scheme	For two or more elderly persons who are willing to live together
Harmonious families priority scheme	For those families who opt to live with or close to their elderly parents/relatives
Special housing for the elderly (Hong Kong Housing Authority)	
Housing for senior citizens units	Come with communal and recreational facilities under the care of a warden
Self-contained small flats	Equipped with facilities such as non-slippery floor tiles and single-lever taps to cater for the needs of older persons
Special housing for the elderly (Hong Kong Housing Society)	
Elderly persons' flats	Approximately 900 units in 9 estates for eligible elderly people at discounted rent

Sources: Hong Kong Housing Authority (www.housingauthority.gov.hk/en/public-housing/meeting-special-needs/senior); Hong Kong Housing Society (www.hkhs.com/eng/business).

profit making body with roots dating from 1948 that provides housing according to the principles of ageing in place, emphasising home safety, care and support, health and wellness. The HKHS specifically promotes age-friendly housing with universal design features and builds on examples from other countries (HKHS, 2016a). While it provides only a relatively small part (just over 4%) of Hong Kong's extensive public housing system, it looks at providing affordable housing in a 'niche position' between the expensive private sector and government public rental housing. The HKHS also has an educational and developmental role, with 'senior housing' highlighted as one of its main activities. It also launched an ageing in place scheme in 2013.

Box 7.1: Hong Kong Housing Society: age-friendly housing example

The Elderly Resource Centre 'Age-friendly housing caring campaign' 2005; a focus on ageing in place, age-friendly design and the 'age-friendly home'. Demonstrates home safety designs and modifications as a showcase and for public education. Provides selected assessment tools and an active volunteer programme on home environment and care for older persons. Provides practical and conceptual foci for Hong Kong's AFCC development. The ERC emphasises interaction between older persons' environmental needs, the ageing process and lifestyles (behaviour, habits and preferences). The ERC conducts experimental design in age-friendly housing, targeted at three income groups, supported by mobile multidisciplinary teams. **Low-income groups:** accommodation with wardens who liaise with existing local services, as necessary. **Middle-income groups:** 500 residential units made up of 250-400 square foot studio/one-bedroom units; with club, clinic, day-care and residential care facilities. Incorporate age-friendly features such as seats in elevators, wireless transmitters in rooms, bedside nurse call buttons and emergency call buttons and monthly medical check-ups. Popular schemes with waiting lists. **High-income groups:** Older persons are 'clients' for developments; applicants are not means-tested; these are not subsidised housing schemes like other HKHS lower-income projects. The only eligibility criterion is that applicants are Hong Kong permanent residents aged 60 and above.

The Tanner Hill, a novel 'quality elderly housing' project on Hong Kong Island, was launched in 2015. It has 580 flats of seven types on mortgageable, lifelong leases or two-yearly short leases. Facilities include a residents' club and a multi-service 'joyous hub' to promote wellness, with Western and Chinese medical clinics and a wide range of older-friendly facilities and a restaurant. Service fees cover a handy-worker service, 24-hour emergency system and nurse support, and various entry security services (HKHS, 2016c). Uptake for earlier schemes was enthusiastic but response by early 2016 was slower for economic reasons (*South China Morning Post*, 2016a). A 16% discount plus waivers on management fees, service charges and rates in mid-September stirred interest. Two-hundred-and forty-eight units were leased within a month, compared with only 75 units before discounts. Only units on long leases remained available (HKHS, 2016c; *South China Morning Post*, 2016b). Future plans include an 'elderly safe-living scheme'. In Tsuen Wan, Kowloon, a housing estate was equipped with remote monitoring to check movements of elderly residents with cognitive impairment as part of that district's application to become a WHO-designated age-friendly district.

Source: HKHS (2016b, 2016c).

Community projects

In recent years, there have been major philanthropic efforts towards making Hong Kong more 'age-friendly', often involving charities and NGOs. An emphasis has been on social improvements and education, including raising health literacy, changing people's attitudes and improving care practices, initiatives that are hopefully sustainable. One project is the Hong Kong Jockey Club (HKJC) CADENZA project, which has a range of aims, including nurturing academic leadership in gerontology and changing the mindset and attitudes of the general public through a range of training and public education programmes. Cross-sectional collaboration between organisations and the implementation of innovative elderly services and programmes are also encouraged in order to bring about a new mode of elderly care services to prepare for a rapidly ageing society, including planning for the needs of the 'soon to be old' (www.cadenza.hk).

The HKJC initiated an age-friendly city (AFC) movement in 2015, in partnership with ageing research centres in four universities, the Chinese University of Hong Kong, Hong Kong Polytechnic University, the University of Hong Kong and Lingnan University, to promote the concept, initially in eight out of 18 districts in 2015, then covering the remaining 10 districts in 2017. The first task will be to conduct an environmental scan, using questionnaires based on the WHO checklist as an audit together with focus groups, to identify areas perceived to require improvement. Meetings at the district level will include older people, district councillors and local government officials, who will review findings and propose improvement projects. The types of projects will be guided by Hong Kong's calculated ranking in the Global AgeWatch Index 2015, a HelpAge International indicator of the wellbeing of older people that enables comparison of these indicators across 90 countries. The index has four domains (income security, health status, capability, and enabling environment) with 13 variables. Calculations made locally for Hong Kong showed low rankings in the areas of participation, income security and psychological wellbeing.

Another example of an NGO leading an AFCC initiative is the Age-link project of the Aberdeen Kai Fong Welfare Association. This focuses on community education, intergenerational learning, intergenerational volunteer development, and promoting continuity of cultural heritage. Older people interacted with students of all ages in activities such as creating stories and plays with primary school children, and mentoring secondary school children and helping with their homework, while secondary school children organised trips with older people to explore sites in Hong Kong. A further example is the Elder Friendly Employment Practice project, developed by the Hong Kong Society for the Aged, another NGO. This looked at the wishes of older people to continue flexible employment post-retirement, to continue social participation and to supplement their incomes. Initiatives included job fairs where prospective employing organisations can advertise and recruit on site and an online job-matching scheme.

In terms of improving access and affordability of private health services, residents aged 65 years and over can enrol in an elderly healthcare voucher scheme.[2] Since 2015, HK $2,000 (US $260) is deposited annually into a recipient's eHealth account to settle healthcare service fees. Healthcare providers involved in the scheme enroll with the Department of Health and their information is made available on the eHealth system. A further means-tested voucher scheme is available for day-care services three times a week, with various levels of co-payment. A second phase covering six days a week and/or home care is being initiated.

Local research and perspectives on age-friendliness

Despite Hong Kong's small size, there is considerable variation in the history, geography, social circumstances and urban design of its 18 districts. Comparative studies in two districts, Sha Tin and Tuen Mun new towns, illustrated this and found significant differences in residents' perceptions of age-friendly characteristics, most likely based on socioeconomic differences between the two populations (Wong et al, 2015). This suggests the need for detailed research including consideration of psychosocial factors that may influence residents' attitudes to and perceptions of local environments. Such comparisons have been extended so far to eight districts and show that there are common areas of concern in the domains of housing, healthcare, civic participation, employment and communication. As noted earlier, a Hong Kong-wide indicator of age-friendliness is being developed based on the Global AgeWatch Index and incorporating the WHO age-friendly indicators (WHO, 2015).

Ethnic variations in perceptions of age-friendliness in a Hong Kong new town

It is generally agreed that older populations are heterogeneous socially and often in other characteristics that may have significant influences on attitudes and wellbeing. As Buffel and colleagues (2012) note, the diversity within older populations will inevitably involve reconciling conflicting interests and concerns in the process of developing age-friendly communities (for example, Becker, 2003; Biggs and Tinker, 2007; Hanson et al, 2012; Buffel et al, 2014; see also Chapter Two). One such factor could include variety in the ethnic backgrounds of an elderly population. In Hong Kong, the older population is rather homogeneous in terms of ethnicity: 99% of Hong Kong's 65-plus population are Chinese. However, there is growing interest in issues related to segregation and disadvantage within the small 'ethnic minority' population, as it is termed in Hong Kong. The majority are of Asian backgrounds other than Chinese (including people of Indian, Pakistani and Nepalese backgrounds). Even though the absolute number of such older individuals in Hong Kong is relatively small, census data from 2001 to 2011 show consistent increases among those aged 60 and above. In view of their linguistic, cultural and religious backgrounds, together with disadvantaged socio-economic status (CCPL, 2015; Cheung, 2015) compared with Hong Kong Chinese counterparts, many encounter difficulties in employment and education, with concomitant increased risk of poverty, poorer accommodation and reduced social integration (CORE, 2001; *South China Morning Post*, 2013; CCPL, 2015).

It is possible that many may also have different needs and expectations both of infrastructure and services provided. The research team extended the Sha Tin and Tuen Mun study (Wong et al, 2015) by comparing two ethnic groups, namely Hong Kong Chinese and Southeast (SE) Asians living in Tuen Mun. One hundred SE Asian respondents aged 50 years and above were interviewed and their responses were compared with those of a local sample from the same district. Compared with SE Asian residents, local Chinese residents reported higher AFCC ratings on outdoor spaces and buildings, transport, social participation, information, and food and shopping. SE Asian respondents reported significantly higher satisfaction on community and health (Figure 7.1).

This comparison provides interesting indications of the importance of studying the ethnic background of older individuals and how ethnicity may relate to different perception of AFCC characteristics. Of the nine AFCC ratings used (which included an additional Hong Kong domain, namely food and shopping), six pairs of comparison were significant. With the exception of community support and health services, SE Asian participants reported lower ratings on five others (outdoor spaces and buildings, transportation, social participation, communication and information, and food and shopping). The findings shed some light on ethnicity as an important factor that may affect perceptions of AFCC domains.

Figure 7.1: Mean domain score of different age-friendly domains in Tuen Mun by ethnic group

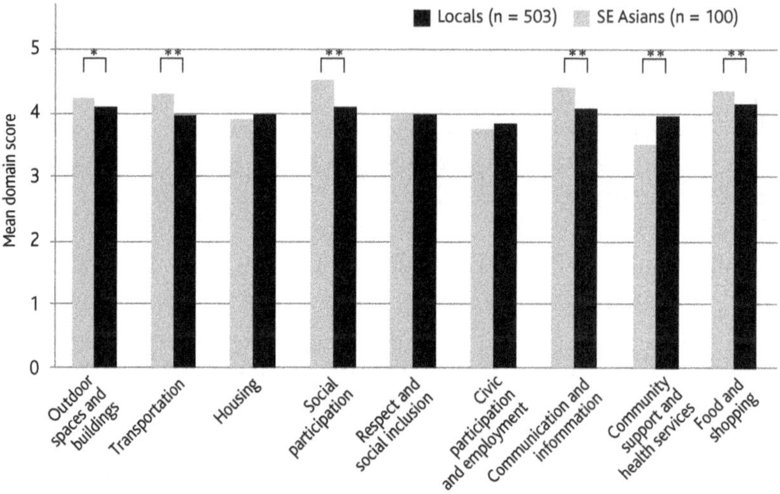

Note: * p<0.05; ** p<0.01

Although the study did not provide detailed empirical analysis of any underlying mechanisms that might contribute to these differences, it can be suggested that cultural, linguistic and social characteristics play an important role. For example, in the social participation and communication and information domains, SE Asian respondents reported significantly lower ratings. The research team reflected on whether this could relate to the fact that most social programmes conducted in the Tuen Mun neighborhood (or, indeed, in Hong Kong at large) are predominately publicised and conducted in Chinese or, more rarely, in English and Mandarin, while languages such as Urdu or Hindi are rarely used. The language barrier may then limit the choice and awareness of services or programmes in which older SE Asians can participate, which could explain lower ratings of these domains among the group. Some NGOs in Hong Kong, for instance the Senior Home Safety Association, do try to provide healthcare services and assistance to older ethnic minority members, but levels of provision are dependent on practice and available resources (CCPL, 2015).

Our findings may reflect the fundamental structural disadvantages of the SE Asian residents in Hong Kong as well. As noted earlier, older individuals may face aspects of social exclusion in Hong Kong society. Older individuals from ethnic minority backgrounds may suffer an extra ethnic exclusion effect, as Chinese culture largely ignores the position of non-Chinese groups by attempting to maintain an ethnically homogeneous culture (Ku, 2006). In a household survey conducted by the Equal Opportunities Commission (2009), Chinese respondents demonstrated the lowest levels of acceptance towards SE Asians compared with other ethnic groups. Although the Race Discrimination Ordinance came into effect in 2009, negative stereotypes and discrimination are not uncommon in modern Hong Kong. As suggested by Crabtree and Wong (2012), SE Asian residents often face problems in accessing public services and resources in Hong Kong, meaning resources and information available to local older Chinese residents may not be readily accessible to older individuals from ethnic minority groups. This is clearly of concern if the desire is to create a comprehensive age-friendly city programme. It is equally important to give a balanced view and consider the attitudes and aspirations of ethnic minority residents. Unfortunately, research on the perceptions of AFCCs among older individuals from ethnic minority backgrounds is very limited, and further studies are planned, including in-depth interviews and focus groups. Such information will be useful to assist the development of more age-friendly environments and programmes in ethnically diverse cities in the region.

Initiatives on social vulnerability

As noted earlier, older persons are often especially at risk in emergencies and vulnerable as well to the effects of climate change (WHO, 2008). Locally in Hong Kong, as an AFCC measure, emergency preparedness for older people is only at an early stage. Based on work by Gusmano and colleagues (2006), the first Social Vulnerability Index in Hong Kong has been developed with the objective of documenting the vulnerability of older people to emergencies and disasters using indicators such as rates of institutionalisation, poverty, the proportion of older population living alone, and access to primary care (Chau et al, 2014a). Plotting the index on the map (Figure 7.2) is useful to identify areas where there is a high concentration of older people who are physically, socially or financially vulnerable. This can inform efficient interventions and the development of social policy to support vulnerable areas and a population in need. The spatial dimension of these environmental challenges has been well documented, demonstrating the effects of extreme temperatures and the risk of adverse health outcomes on both community and institutionalised populations, as well as revealing inequalities of health services provision across the territory (Wong et al, 2009; Chau et al, 2011, 2012, 2014b).

Figure 7.2: Social Vulnerability Index across constituency areas of Hong Kong

Notes: Classification of Social Vulnerability Index values was based on the natural groupings of values in the data, using Jenks Natural Breaks algorithm. This scheme groups similar values into classes while maximising the differences between classes.

Source: Original data from Chau et al, (2014a). Map was produced by the authors, using ArcGIS

Given the extra risks older persons can face in extreme weather, local initiatives include a very hot weather warning issued by the Hong Kong Observatory, which, although not specifically aimed at older persons, has been shown to be of assistance in periods of very hot weather (Chau et al, 2009). Likewise, cold weather warnings are issued, these reflecting temperature extremes experienced in Hong Kong. International experience of morbidity and mortality of older persons in extreme weather conditions indicates that similar initiatives, particularly focusing on the older population, would be helpful to assist these groups in an era of increasingly challenging conditions (McCracken and Phillips, 2016).

Conclusion

Older persons in Hong Kong are as heterogeneous as elsewhere, so stereotyping uniformity will mean AFCC policies are unlikely to be well accepted. However, one important factor that makes older persons more vulnerable is the issue of elderly poverty, noted earlier. This problem was identified in Chau and colleagues' (2013b) comparison of Hong Kong with other world cities and was highlighted in the Hong Kong Commission on Poverty Summit October 2015 (Commission on Poverty Hong Kong, 2015). In particular, 'extremely fast' population ageing was noted as a key issue, but resources devoted to older people's incomes in this wealthy society are trailing. Older persons are relatively worse off in the population, while overall poverty in Hong Kong fell slightly from 1.336 million (2013) to 1.325 million (2014). By contrast, elderly poverty increased by 19% from 366,500 persons in 2009 to 436,400 in 2014. As the majority of older people do not have incomes from work, and income from any savings and investments is limited, they are likely to be classified as poor under the currently limited local definition of a poverty line.

To progress towards being an age-friendly city, Hong Kong does need to tackle several other problems. One is the need to change stereotypes of older persons and even older persons' often negative self-perceptions, as well as to offer equitable opportunities. Ageism exists in society and is practised, involuntarily perhaps, in healthcare at various levels, from primary care, to hospital and end-of-life care. The growing limitations on healthcare resources are often associated with prioritisation of healthcare options. Recent research indicates that the Hong Kong public prioritises technological advances in health services above services such as the care of the elderly and end-of-life care, in contrast to a similar British survey in which end-of-life care was ranked the second highest priority (Mak et al, 2011). In areas ranging from healthcare options to general attitudes towards older persons, local opinions are often still not in favour of supporting a rapidly ageing society. This implies the need to educate and change public ageist attitudes if an age-friendly city is to be achieved.

Moreover, attention should also be given to the social exclusion of older people (Phillips and Cheng, 2012). Many of today's older Hong Kong residents spent their lives in hard work that inevitably restricted their community and social lives. Lacking strong personal networks, many become less 'socially visible' on retirement. Some do participate in social activities organised at local and district levels, but these generally only incorporate a small proportion of older people. A sense of loneliness and social exclusion is commonly reported and encouraging active participation in community life is essential to building and maintaining social connectedness between older people and their communities (see also Chapter Three). As noted earlier, one approach is to promote co-residence to encourage families to support elderly parents.

The extent to which an age-friendly city can in practice be realised also depends on a more age-aware policy change. Hong Kong's legal and administrative framework may itself be a deterrent. For example, the Coroners Ordinance currently does not favour the concept of dying in place, as deaths in (for example) residential care homes for the elderly need to be reported to the police, even if care was provided by the Hospital Authority's comprehensive geriatric assessment team. Similarly, the Fire Service Ordinance requires ambulance staff to attempt to resuscitate even if older people and their families indicate via an advance directive that they do not wish for this to happen. Social and health policies are rarely discussed with or acknowledged by older people. Older people also feel less likely than other age groups to be consulted by public, voluntary and commercial service organisations, as suggested by their poor attitudes towards the civic participation domain in the Sha Tin and Tuen Mun study. There is evidently a significant policy reality gap that militates against promoting age-friendliness in Hong Kong.

In positive terms, perhaps the most obvious progress towards age-friendliness is in the improvement of infrastructure. For example, priority seats have been introduced in almost all forms of public transportation and even in some fast-food shops. However, again, it is not easy to achieve improvements in the more qualitative AFCC domains such as respect and social inclusion. While the priority seats exist, it is common for such seats not to be occupied by people in need, even when older people are standing immediately in front of them. Another example is employment of older workers. While the extension of retirement ages and flexible working hours are being introduced to facilitate employment of older people, there are opinions that such a policy hinders the employment or promotion opportunities of the younger generations, particularly during times of economic recession. While the improvement of infrastructure is relatively quick when resources are available, changes of attitude among the wider population have to be nurtured over many years. In future, greater efforts need to be devoted to cultivating respect towards older people and reducing age-based stereotyping. Promotion of intergenerational harmony may well need to start from kindergarten and carry on for life. A successful AFCC needs all the eight domains of the WHO framework to be achieved simultaneously (see Chapter Two).

Hong Kong does demonstrate considerable enthusiasm and some practical outcomes in the AFCC movement at various levels, from central to local. It is probably one of the most advanced territories in terms of age-friendly policies and concepts in the Asia-Pacific region, which includes the most rapidly ageing areas of the world and many of the largest cities and highest urbanisation rates. As yet, however, there is some distance between official optimism and promulgations such as those outlined in the 2016 Policy Address and the reality of age-friendliness at a local level. Nevertheless, the progress in territory-wide engagement with the concept of age-friendliness at official, charity, NGO, community and even family levels bodes well for future progress in the HKSAR.

Notes

1   See www.jcafc.hk/en/afc-concept/who-global-network
2   See www.hcv.gov.hk/eng/pub_background.htm

References

Akiyama, H. (2015) 'Experience in Japan', in *The Chinese University of Hong Kong Creating Age-friendly Communities*. Hong Kong, China, available at: www.ioa.cuhk.edu.hk/zh-TW/community-outreach/launch-conference

Becker, G. (2003) 'Meanings of place and displacement in three groups of older immigrants', *Journal of Aging Studies*, 17(2): 129-49.

Biggs, S. and Tinker, A. (2007) *What makes a city age-friendly? London's contribution to the World Health Organization's age-friendly cities project*, London: Help the Aged.

Buffel, T., McGarry, P., Phillipson, C., De Donder, L., Dury, S., De Witte, N., Smetcoren, A.S. and Verté, D. (2014) 'Developing age-friendly cities: case studies from Brussels and Manchester and implications for policy and practice', *Journal of Aging and Social Policy*, 26(1-2): 52-72.

Buffel, T., Phillipson, C. and Scharf, T. (2012) 'Ageing in urban environments: developing "age-friendly" cities', *Critical Social Policy*, 32(4): 597-617.

CADENZA (2016) *CADENZA: A jockey club initiative for seniors*. Available at: http://www.cadenza.hk/index.php?lang=en.

CCPL (Centre for Comparative and Public Law) (2015) *Status of ethnic minorities in Hong Kong 1997-2014*, Hong Kong: The University of Hong Kong.

Census and Statistics Department (2015a) *Hong Kong population projections 2015-2064*, Hong Kong: Census and Statistics Department.

Census and Statistics Department (2015b) *Hong Kong annual digest of statistics 2015*, Hong Kong: Census and Statistics Department.

Chau, P.H., Chan, K.C. and Woo, J. (2009) 'Hot weather warnings might help to reduce elderly mortality in Hong Kong', *International Journal of Biometeorology*, 53(5): 461-68.

Chau, P.H., Gusmano, M.K., Cheng, J.O.Y., Cheung, S.H. and Woo, J. (2014a) 'Social vulnerability index for the older people: Hong Kong and New York City as examples', *Journal of Urban Health*, 91(6): 1048-64.

Chau, P.H., Wong, M. and Woo, J. (2012) 'Challenge to long-term care for the elderly: cold weather impacts institutional population more than community-dwelling population', *Journal of the American Medical Directors Association*, 13(9): 788-93.

Chau, P.H., Wong, M. and Woo, J. (2013a) 'Living environment', in J. Woo (ed) *Aging in Hong Kong: A comparative perspective*, New York, NY: Springer, pp 31-67.

Chau, P.H., Wong, M. and Woo, J. (2014b) 'Ischemic heart disease hospitalization among older people in a subtropical city – Hong Kong: does winter have a greater impact than summer?', *International Journal of Environmental Research and Public Health*, 11(4): 3845-58.

Chau, P.H., Woo, J., Goggins, W.B., Wong, M., Chan, K.C. and Ho, S.C. (2011) 'Analysis of spatio-temporal variations in stroke incidence and case-fatality in Hong Kong', *Geospatial Health*, 6(1): 13-20.

Chau, P.H., Woo, J., Gusmano, M.K. and Rodwin, V.G. (2013b) 'Hong Kong and other world cities', in J. Woo (ed) *Aging in Hong Kong: A comparative perspective*, New York, NY: Springer, pp 5-30.

Cheung, K.C.K. (2015) 'Poverty of ethnic minority children in Hong Kong', available at www.ied.edu.hk/media/news.php?id=20151210.

Chow, N.W.S. (1999) 'Housing and environmental needs of elderly people in Hong Kong', in D.R. Phillips and A.G.O. Yeh (eds) *Environment and ageing: Environmental policy, planning and design for elderly people in Hong Kong*, Hong Kong: Centre of Urban Planning and Environmental Management, The University of Hong Kong, pp 53-63.

Chui, M. (2015) 'Dementia friendly ward', in *The Chinese University of Hong Kong, Creating age-friendly communities*. Hong Kong, China, available at: www.ioa.cuhk.edu.hk/zh-TW/community-outreach/launch-conference

Chui, E.W.T, Chan, K.S., Chong, M.L.A., Ko, S.F.L., Law, C.K.S., Law, C.K., Leung M.F.E., Leung, Y.M.A., Lou, W.Q.V. and Ng, Y.T.S. (2009) *Elderly Commission's study on residential care services for the elderly: Final report*, Hong Kong: The University of Hong Kong.

Commission on Poverty Hong Kong (2015) *Commission on Poverty Summit: Poverty situation 2014*, Commission on Poverty Chief Secretary for Administration's Office, available at: http://gia.info.gov.hk/general/201510/10/P201510100726_0726_153439.pdf.

CORE (Coalition for Racial Equality) (2001) *Racial discrimination and new immigrants, ethnic minorities & migrant workers in Hong Kong*, Hong Kong: Human Rights Commission.

Crabtree, S.A. and Wong, H. (2012) '"Ah Cha"! The racial discrimination of Pakistani minority communities in Hong Kong: an analysis of multiple intersecting oppressions', *British Journal of Social Work*, 45(5): 945-63.

Elderly Commission (2016) 'Introduction: Elderly Commission', available at: www.elderlycommission.gov.hk/en/About_Us/Introduction.html.

Equal Opportunities Commission (2009) 'Thematic household survey on racial acceptance', available at www.eoc.org.hk/eoc/GraphicsFolder/ShowContent.aspx?ItemID=8215.

Global AgeWatch Index (2015) 'AgeWatch report card', available at: www.helpage.org/global-agewatch/population-ageing-data/global-rankings-table.

Gusmano, M.K., Rodwin, V.G. and Cantor, M. (2006) *Urban ecology of old age in New York City (NYC): Helping vulnerable older persons*, Final Report to the New York Community Trust, New York, NY.

Hanson, D., Person, M., Phillips, G., Rowan, C., Roughton, C. and Wicks, A. (Orca Planning) (2012) 'Toward an age-friendly Portland', available atwww.portlandoregon.gov/bps/article/425455.

HelpAge International (2009) *Older people in community development: The role of older people's associations (OPAs) in enhancing local development*, London: HelpAge International.

Hong Kong Government (2014) *Hong Kong poverty situation report 2013*, Hong Kong: Hong Kong Government.

Hong Kong Government (2015) *Hong Kong: The facts – Population*, Hong Kong: Information Services Department, Hong Kong Government, available at: https://www.gov.hk/en/about/abouthk/factsheets/docs/housing.pdf.

Hong Kong Government (2016) *Policy Address 2016: Building an age-friendly community*, Hong Kong: Hong Kong Government, available at: www.policyaddress.gov.hk/2016/eng/pdf/leaflet_community.pdf.

Hong Kong Housing Authority (2015) 'Housing in figures 2015', available atwww.housingauthority.gov.hk/en/common/pdf/about-us/publications-and-statistics/HIF.pdf.

Hong Kong Housing Authority (2016) *Housing Authority and Housing Department home page*. Available at: https://www.housingauthority.gov.hk/en/

HKHS (Hong Kong Housing Society) (2016a) *Hong Kong Housing Society*. Available at: www.hkhs.com/index.asp

HKHS (2016b) 'Housing Authority and Housing Department: Age-friendly home', available at www.hkhselderly.com/afh/?lang=en.

HKHS (2016c) 'About the Tanner Hill', available at www.thetannerhill.hkhs.com/en/info/index.html.

Institute of Ageing (2016) *CUHK Jockey Club Institute of Ageing*. Available at: www.ioa.cuhk.edu.hk/en-GB/about-us/organization

Kwok, T. (2015) 'Age-friendly hospital', in The Chinese University of Hong Kong, Creating Age-friendly Communities. Hong Kong, China. Available at: www.ioa.cuhk.edu.hk/zh-TW/community-outreach/launch-conference

Ku, H. B. (2006) 'Body, dress, and cultural exclusion: experiences of Pakistani women in "global" Hong Kong', *Asian Ethnicity*, 7(3): 285-303.

Leung, E.M.F. (1999) 'Housing and environmental issues for elderly people – a health and functional perspective', in D.R. Phillips and A.G.O. Yeh (eds) *Environment and ageing: Environmental policy, planning and design for elderly people in Hong Kong*, Hong Kong: Centre of Urban Planning and Environmental Management, The University of Hong Kong, pp 37-51.

McCracken, K. and Phillips, D.R. (2016) 'Climate change and the health of older people in South-East Asia', in R. Ahktar (ed) *Climate change and human health scenario in South and East Asia*, New York, NY: Springer, pp 29-52.

McCracken, K. and Phillips, D.R. (2012) *Global health*, London: Routledge.

Mak, B., Woo, J., Bowling, A., Wong, F. and Chau, P.H. (2011) 'Health care prioritization in ageing societies: influence of age, education, health literacy and culture', *Health Policy*, 100(2-3): 219-33.

Phillips, D.R. (2018, in press) 'Asia-Pacific and global population aging', in T.R. Klassen, M. Higo, N. Dhirathiti and T. Devasahayam (eds) *Ageing in the Asia Pacific: Interdisciplinary and comparative perspectives*, New York, NY: Routledge, pp 121–44.

Phillips, D.R. and Cheng, K. (2012) 'The impact of changing value systems on social inclusion: an Asia-Pacific perspective', in T. Scharf and N. Keating (eds) *From exclusion to inclusion in old age: a global challenge*, Bristol: Policy Press, pp 109–24.

Phillips, D.R. and Feng, Z.X. (2015) 'Challenges for the aging family in the People's Republic of China', *Canadian Journal on Aging*, 34(3): 290-304.

Phillips, D.R., Cheng, K., Yeh, A.G.O. and Siu, O.L. (2009) 'Person-Environment (P-E) fit models and psychological well-being among older persons in Hong Kong', *Environment and Behavior*, 17: 127-41.

Phillips, D.R. and Yeh, A.G.O. (eds) (1999) *Environment and ageing: Environmental policy, planning and design for elderly people in Hong Kong*, Hong Kong: Centre of Urban Planning and Environmental Management, The University of Hong Kong.

Sander, M., Oxlund, B., Jespersen, A., Krasnik, A., Lykke, E., Gerardus, R., Westendorp, J. and Rasmussen, L.J. (2015) 'The challenges of human population ageing', *Age and Ageing*, 44(2): 185-7.

Silver Group (2016) 'Thailand needs to become age-friendly, and fast!', available at www.silvergroup.asia/2016/04/18/6743/?utm_source=Newsletter+%2350&utm_campaign=Newsletter+50&utm_medium=email.

South China Morning Post (2013) 'Racist Hong Kong is still a fact', 25 May, available atwww.scmp.com/comment/insight-opinion/article/1245226/racist-hong-kong-still-fact.

South China Morning Post (2016a) 'Flats for elderly rich people sweeten the deal after lukewarm response', 8 March, available at www.scmp.com/news/hong-kong/article/1922554/flats-elderly-rich-people-sweeten-deal-after-lukewarm-response.

South China Morning Post (2016b) 'Sales for Hong Kong luxury flats for elderly soar 330 per cent after developer offered discounts', 12 October, available atwww.scmp.com/news/hong-kong/education-community/article/2027173/sales-hong-kong-luxury-flats-elderly-soar-330.

Straits Times (2016) 'Girding Thailand for a greying future', 16 April, available atwww.straitstimes.com/asia/se-asia/girding-thailand-for-a-greying-future.

Sun, Y., Chao, T.Y., Woo, J. and Au, D.W.H. (2017) 'An institutional perspective of "glocalization" in two Asian tigers: the "structure-agent-strategy" of building an age-friendly city', *Habitat International*, 59:101-9.

UNDESA (United Nations Department of Economic and Social Affairs) (2015) *World population prospects: The 2015 revision. Key findings and advance tables*, New York, NY: United Nations.

WHO (World Health Organization) (2007a) *Global age-friendly cities: A guide*, Geneva: WHO.

WHO (2007b) *Checklist of essential features of age-friendly cities*, Geneva: WHO.

WHO (2008) *Older people in emergencies: An active ageing perspective*, Geneva: WHO.

WHO (2015) *Measuring the age-friendliness of cities: A guide to using core indicators*, Geneva: WHO.

Wong, M., Chau, P.H., Cheung, F., Phillips, D.R. and Woo, J. (2015) 'Comparing the age-friendliness of different neighbourhoods using district surveys: an example from Hong Kong', *PLoS ONE*, 10(7): e0131526, http://dx.doi.org/10.1371/journal.pone.0131526.

Wong, M., Chau, P.H., Goggins, W.B. and Woo, J. (2009) 'A geographical study of health services utilization among the elderly in Hong Kong: from spatial variations to health care implications', *Health Services Insights*, 2: 1-13.

Wong, M., Yu, R. and Woo, J. (2017) 'Effects of perceived neighbourhood environments on self-rated health among community-dwelling older Chinese', *International Journal of Environmental Research and Public Health*, 14(6): 614.

Woo, J. (ed) (2013) *Aging in Hong Kong: A comparative perspective*, New York, NY: Springer.

EIGHT

Creating an age-friendly county in Ireland: stakeholders' perspectives on implementation

Bernard McDonald, Thomas Scharf, Kieran Walsh

Introduction

Ireland's Age Friendly Cities and Counties (AFCC) programme, established in 2010, is one of 12 country- or state-level programmes affiliated to the World Health Organization's (WHO) burgeoning Global Network of Age-Friendly Cities and Communities (Age-Friendly World, 2016). As such, it is currently being implemented in all 31 local authority areas across the country. Aside from the scale of the Irish programme, the context in which it was developed has several distinctive characteristics. The programme was initiated at a time of global economic crisis. Because of exacerbating local economic circumstances, this was experienced more severely in Ireland than in many countries, leading to the country becoming one of the 'bailout nations' co-funded by the so-called Troika (European Union, European Central Bank and International Monetary Fund). As a consequence, a severe austerity programme, which saw major cutbacks to public health and social services, including services provided for older people, was introduced contemporaneously with the development of the AFCC programme.

The programme's governance structures are also notable. Unlike in other countries, where research centres, non-governmental organisations (NGOs) or local authorities assume a leadership role, the development of Ireland's national programme was supported and resourced primarily by an independent think-tank, the Ageing Well Network, which was in turn financed by an international philanthropic limited life foundation, The Atlantic Philanthropies (hereafter Atlantic). Ireland's demography is also distinctive. Although its population is ageing, it remains relatively young in comparison with other high-income countries. This combination of circumstances – the scale and coverage of the Irish programme, the particular set of international and local economic forces at play during its implementation, and the organisational and demographic factors that influenced its development – provides a unique context in which to examine the development and implementation of an age-friendly initiative.

Key features of the WHO Age-Friendly Cities and Communities initiative have increasingly been the focus of scientific debate (see Chapter Two). Researchers have examined the various approaches adopted, the conceptual understandings that underpin these approaches, the challenges facing age-friendly initiatives, and the outcomes achieved (Scharlach, 2009; Fitzgerald and Caro, 2014; Moulaert and Garon, 2016). However, as noted by Scharlach (2016), comparatively little attention has been paid to 'community change processes and their implementation' (p 317), that is, to the 'nuts and bolts' of the process of bringing about age-friendly improvements in particular cities or communities. While there has been much debate about older people's role in age-friendly programmes, there has been little research on the role and influence of the political, organisational and administrative systems in which many of these initiatives are situated, other than broad descriptive accounts of a contextual nature. In particular, few studies have explored these influences from the perspective of the major stakeholders involved. This chapter seeks to redress the balance by examining, from the perspective of the major actors involved, the dynamics of the implementation of an age-friendly county programme in one of the participating counties in Ireland, County Fingal. It integrates the views of local, national and international stakeholders to explore the complex interplay of forces at these various levels that have influenced the development and impact of Fingal's local programme.

The chapter first outlines the social and economic context that framed the development of the AFCC programme. It then reviews the programme's origins and development and describes the local development and implementation of Fingal's Age Friendly County (AFC) initiative. Following that, findings arising from ongoing research are used to explore two critical aspects of the implementation process: the understandings, motivations and actions of the key stakeholders that were influential in developing and implementing the programme; and, the attitudes, understandings and actions of these same stakeholders that underpin, and are reflected in, the processes established to involve older people in the programme. The chapter concludes by highlighting key issues that need to be addressed to enhance the potential impact of age-friendly community programmes on the lives of older adults.

Background: overview of demographic, economic and policy context in Ireland

Demography

Two demographic characteristics are particularly relevant to the development of Ireland's AFCC programme. First, Ireland is a relatively 'young' country. Second, only relatively recently has the urban population surpassed that living in rural areas, with almost half of urban dwellers living in smaller towns rather than large urban centres. Of the total population of 4,588,252 people in 2011, over half a million were aged 65 and over (Central Statistics Office, 2012). Projections suggest that the proportion of people in this age group will rise from 12% in 2011 to 17% in 2026 and to 26% by 2050 (Central Statistics Office, 2013).

In 2011, 2.84 million people, representing 62% of the total population, lived in urban areas of Ireland. One-and-a-half million of these urban dwellers lived in the five main cities, Dublin, Cork, Limerick, Galway and Waterford, with the remaining 1.3 million living in towns with populations of between 1,500 and 39,000 people. This in effect means that almost 46% of urban dwellers, and 31% of the total population, live in towns rather than in larger urban settings. This has obvious implications for an AFCC programme that is designed to be implemented not only in large urban settings, such as Dublin city, but also in places like County Leitrim, where almost 90% of the population live in rural settings.

The impact of austerity measures on older people

The AFCC programme was introduced in Ireland at a time of economic turmoil following the collapse of the so-called Celtic Tiger in 2008 and the period of austerity that followed. In the face of what amounted almost to a national existential crisis, this was not the most auspicious time to introduce a new national programme. Although there was a significant improvement overall in the financial position of older people during the Celtic Tiger years 1995-2008, when policy measures reduced the 'at-risk-of-poverty' rate of older people from 27.1% in 2004 to 9.7% in 2011, their situation has been affected by the economic crisis (Connolly, 2015). Despite what seems like a dramatic improvement overall, there is evidence of significant poverty and deprivation among a substantial minority of older people. This is sometimes masked by official statistics and the complexity of indirect impacts. Subgroups of older people affected include those living alone, those with poor health, and those who are deemed 'hard to reach', such as older travellers (Boyle and Larragy, 2010; Walsh and Harvey, 2012; Scharf, 2015a).

The economic crisis has had direct and indirect adverse effects on older people. This can be explained by examining the detail of the austerity programme. While the state pension rate has been maintained, there has been a multiplicity of cuts to ancillary benefits for older people, including, for example, those related to fuel consumption and telephone usage. Austerity measures in the health system have included the reintroduction of means testing for medical cards (which provide entitlement to free medical care), and the introduction of prescription charges for those on medical cards. Since 2009, over two billion euros have been cut from the public health budget, and waiting times for public hospital health services have increased. Community care has also suffered severe budgetary cutbacks, with reductions in home support packages and home-help allocations, both of which are considered crucial to supporting older people in their own homes and communities. The effects of these measures have been compounded by the introduction of new taxes and property and water charges, all of which have had a negative impact on older people, and in particular on those deemed most vulnerable (Age Action, 2014).

The recession has also had indirect adverse effects on older people. High emigration rates among young people can adversely affect the older generation left behind. In rural areas, depopulation can lead to curtailment of public and social services, which has a significant impact on older adults (Walsh et al, 2012). In both urban and rural areas, the recession has led to a reduction in basic infrastructure such as the closure of local grocery outlets, post offices and police stations, and the curtailment of community transport schemes (Walsh, 2015). Older parents are also providing increased financial and other forms of assistance and support to their adult children and their families who have been affected by the high levels of unemployment and the housing crisis brought about by the recession (Timonen et al, 2013).

Policy context

It is somewhat ironic that the period of severe cutbacks in public services and welfare benefits coincided with a more productive phase of development of national social and health policy related to older people. The National Positive Ageing Strategy (Department of Health, 2013a) was published in 2013. This was complemented by a national policing policy for older people (An Garda Síochána, 2010), a first national policy on dementia (Department of Health, 2014) and *Healthy Ireland: A framework for improved health and wellbeing 2013-2025* (Department of Health, 2013b). The latter, although not specific to older people, has identified the AFCC programme as a platform for the implementation of many of its recommendations for older people. Another critical policy development for the AFCC programme during this period was the introduction of Putting People First (Department of the Environment, 2012), a national action programme that radically reformed local government structures. However, due to the economic crisis, and despite the 'recovery' since 2015, these policies, or the age-related components of these policies, were largely introduced without the allocation of sufficient resources for their implementation.

Development of AFCC and Fingal AFC programme

Ireland's Age Friendly Cities and Counties programme

The AFCC programme had its roots in the strategic approach taken by Atlantic to its work in Ireland. Atlantic's influence can easily be overlooked because it operates in a low-key way, mainly through its grant-funding programme. However, its impact on the ageing sector in Ireland, strategically and at more fundamental levels, including its support for the national AFCC programme, has been considerable. The Ageing Well Network (2007-13) and, since 2014, Age Friendly Ireland (AFI), both organisations funded by Atlantic, played a critical role in the development of the national AFCC programme. Atlantic established its Ageing Programme in Ireland in 2008. Before closing in 2016, the programme focused on building capacity across voluntary and research organisations (Cochrane et al, 2013). The broad objectives set by Atlantic in its funding programme reflected perceived weaknesses in the ageing sector in Ireland, including fragmented and uncoordinated public advocacy for older people, a lack of recognition of ageing as a core area in government policy, and a paucity of solid research to inform planning and service provision (O'Shea and Conboy, 2005; O'Neill et al, 2009; Walsh et al, 2015).

The Ageing Well Network was established in 2007 by Atlantic as a leadership networking forum and a think-tank to fill what was identified as a specific gap at that time. Leaders and key decision makers from 75 organisations, including central government, local government, state agencies, academia, the voluntary sector and the corporate sector, comprised the network's membership. The network adopted a strategic focus, developed issue-specific position papers, and included senior civil servants as members to influence policy development and long-term planning (Parker, 2015).

As it developed, the Ageing Well Network began to operationalise some innovation by way of a number of practical projects, including the development of the AFCC programme. Dundalk in County Louth, one of the 33 original research study sites for the WHO's age-friendly cities initiative, was used as a pilot site in which to develop a national age-friendly county programme. As the pilot progressed, national structures were established to support its extension to other counties. As the programme was introduced into additional counties and cities, practical support was provided by means of a team of regional development consultants, and as the initiative was introduced into the bigger cities, it was renamed the Age Friendly Cities and Counties programme.

A four-phase implementation model was developed, based on the WHO approach and the learning from the pilot phase. Similar processes and implementation structures were established in each city and county as the programme expanded (Figure 8.1). The model essentially employs a 'top-down' approach that aims to ground its work in participatory mechanisms developed to involve older people. It promotes the engagement of older people through the use of baseline consultations and surveys, by establishing older people's councils (OPCs) or working with existing older people's forums, and by providing representation for these councils on local city or county stakeholder alliances that oversee the programmes. However, the model is heavily reliant on effective top-down leadership. Ideally, each of the statutory agencies on an alliance should be represented by the local senior executive manager. Core agencies involved include the local authority, Ageing Well Network and Age Friendly Ireland, and those responsible for health, social services, education and policing. This is supplemented by a range of organisations, such as academic institutions and NGOs, depending on local circumstances.

While the multiple stakeholder approach, as evidenced in the alliance, may appear cumbersome as a governance structure, it is necessary because of the way in which essential services are delivered in Ireland. Local government has a limited remit and is primarily tasked with the provision and maintenance of infrastructure and the physical environment (Turley and Flannery, 2013); hence the need to involve the broad range of agencies and organisations represented on the alliance. The programme stresses interagency collaboration, aims to embed the programme in sustainable service delivery structures in these agencies, and, perhaps not surprisingly in light of the prevailing economic climate, promotes the reconfiguration of existing resources so that implementation is cost-neutral. The alliance is established and chaired initially by the chief executive officer (CEO) of the relevant local authority, and, following the development of the local five-year age-friendly strategy, by an independent chairperson. The local authority appoints a coordinator, usually on a part-time basis, to oversee implementation of the programme workplan and to act as a secretariat for the alliance.

Figure 8.1: The four stage approach to developing an age-friendly city or county

1 Start
Secure approval of Local Authority
Secure agreement of critical agencies
Secure consent of political representatives
Create an Age Friendly City or County Alliance
Hold a public launch

2 Consult
Consult with older people
Engage other key organisations
Establish Older People's Council

3 Plan
Complete 1st Draft Strategy
Check strategy reflects priorities
Secure Alliance approval
Finalise and launch strategy
Affiliate to WHO Global Network

4 Act
Begin implementing the strategy
Plan forums
Establish Age Friendly Business and Service
Providers forum
Monitor and review implementation

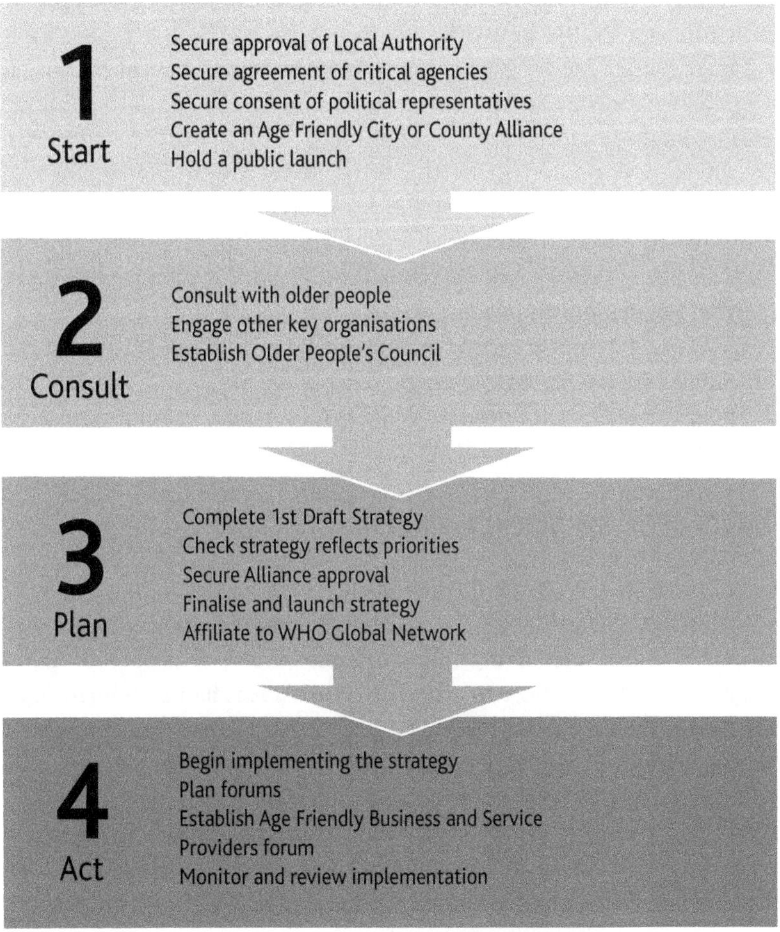

Source: Age-Friendly Ireland (2016)

Ireland's AFCC programme places great emphasis on developing and maintaining international links with the WHO initiative. Before establishing the AFCC programme, international 'experts' on developing age-friendly initiatives made presentations to members of the Ageing Well Network and senior staff in Atlantic. The first international conference on age-friendly cities was held in Dublin in 2011 and co-hosted with WHO and the International Federation on Ageing. In association with the conference, the Dublin Declaration on Age-friendly Cities was developed and signed by municipal representatives of 38 cities worldwide. A further 36 European cities signed the declaration in 2013. As the WHO Global Network for Age-Friendly Cities and Communities grew, Atlantic agreed to provide basic funding for the network's office.

The Ageing Well Network was wound down in December 2013 as originally planned, and AFI was established in January 2014 to continue to coordinate Ireland's AFCC programme. AFI is hosted in Dublin City Council on behalf of the local government network, and is still primarily funded by Atlantic. It coordinates, supports and provides 'technical guidance' to the individual city and county programmes. AFI stresses the pivotal role that local authorities play in creating age-friendly communities, and emphasises the role the AFCC programme plays in supporting the realisation of the objectives of the National Positive Ageing Strategy. It has also continued to highlight the programme's links with the WHO age-friendly cities programme (Age Friendly Ireland, 2015).

Fingal Age Friendly County programme

In 2011, at an early stage in the development of the national AFCC programme, Fingal decided to establish an age-friendly county initiative. Fingal is located on Ireland's east coast, north of Dublin city (Figure 8.2). At the most recent census in 2011, it had a population of 273,000 (Central Statistics Office, 2012), representing an increase of almost 14% on the previous census in 2006. Fingal is the second most populous and 'youngest' county in Ireland, with 7.2% of its population aged 65 or over. Ninety-two per cent of the population live in urban areas. These urban areas vary in size from densely populated suburbs to the north-west of Dublin city to county towns and relatively remote rural villages in the north and west of Fingal.

The Fingal Development Plan 2011–2017 (Fingal County Council, 2011) gives an overview of the council's policies and objectives for the overall development of the county, including measures to improve the development of its economic, environmental, cultural and social resources. The development plan is underpinned by several cross-cutting principles, including the need to ensure social inclusion. Following a county profile of poverty and social exclusion, older people were identified as a target group at risk of social exclusion. Much of the focus of the development plan is on developing economically and socially sustainable communities, improving economic activities, developing employment opportunities, and ensuring sustainable development of the built and natural environments.

Figure 8.2: Fingal County (dark grey) shown within the former County Dublin (lighter grey) and within Ireland

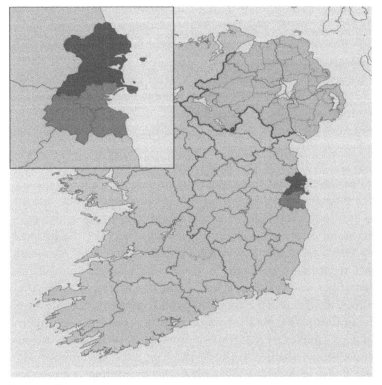

Source: creativecommons.org

This is the local authority policy context in which the Fingal AFC programme was introduced in 2011. The county signed the Dublin declaration in the same year, and shortly afterwards the county manager established the Fingal AFC Alliance. A staff member of Fingal County Council was appointed to coordinate the programme. The alliance, chaired by the county manager for the first year and subsequently by an independent chairperson, meets four times a year. Its membership reflects the national framework, with additional places reserved for several higher education institutions. Following the development of its first five-year strategy, the programme joined the WHO Global Network for Age-Friendly Cities and Communities in 2012.

Not surprisingly, the Fingal Age Friendly County Strategy 2012-2017 (Fingal County Council, 2012) was developed using a modified version of the eight-domain framework outlined in the WHO Guide. The strategy was informed by a range of consultations with older people, an online survey of older adults, and a baseline assessment of current service provision. The strategy identified a range of 'possible actions' across each domain that could be implemented, and the agencies that would be responsible for actioning each of these. Forty of the 58 proposed actions relate to aspects of the social environment, such as social participation, civic engagement, community support, crime prevention and communication. The remaining 18 focus on aspects of the physical environment, including housing, transportation, and outdoor spaces and public buildings.

Between 2012 and 2015, the alliance began to implement the strategy across a wide range of issues (Fingal Age Friendly County Alliance, 2015). It adopted a flexible approach towards the structures needed to develop and implement the programme, and progressed issues by establishing working groups – one on transport, another on information and communications, and a third on housing – rather than creating some of the broader forums recommended by the national model. There was a high turnover of membership – all of the main statutory agencies, including the local authority, changed their alliance representatives during this period – and the impact on the AFC programme of the restructuring happening at local authority level because of Putting People First was of ongoing concern to members. The strategy's implementation was progressed by establishing various projects, seven in total, covering a range of areas identified in the strategy. These included projects on health promotion, support for independent living, transport services, acute hospital services for older people, and a project on the development of an age-friendly town. A formal mid-term review of implementation of the strategy was conducted in 2014 (Fingal Age Friendly County, 2014).

During this period, the alliance also developed its own management and oversight capacity. Capacity-building training was provided to the OPC, and older people were actively involved in developing many of the projects (Box 8.1). Their representation on the alliance was increased from two to three members. In 2015, Fingal's OPC hosted one of the first national meetings of OPCs.

Box 8.1: Collaborative planning in action: Skerries age-friendly town

In 2013, Skerries, County Fingal, was selected to take part in the Age-Friendly Towns initiative, one of Ageing Well Network's national programmes. A town planner was appointed to oversee the development process. Extensive data collection, involving desk research, asset mapping, surveying and consultation, was carried out, and following the initial research period, an existing local community liaison committee agreed to act as a steering committee for the project. This committee has overseen the development of the Age-Friendly Action Plan for Skerries.

The data used to draft the action plan were collected from a number of sources. Twenty-five older residents were recruited to undertake a walkability study that highlighted key areas for improvement in the town's physical environment. The older volunteers were joined by members of the youth council on the nine routes covered by the study and, following the walk, each group completed a walkability audit questionnaire. A public consultation was also conducted with local older people to examine broader social issues affecting them, including local community and recreational resources and local education provision.

Actions outlined in the Age-Friendly Action Plan relate to footpaths, pedestrian crossings, public seating, transport facilities, the local public park, support for independent living, measures to reduce social isolation, support for carers, and the availability of information regarding local services and facilities.

Source: Based on Ageing Well Network (2013).

Implementation: stakeholders' perspectives

The account that follows is based on empirical evidence arising from a study of the implementation of the AFCC in County Fingal. The overall study involves two strands of interviews: one with older people living in Fingal, which explores daily experiences of life in the county; and a second strand that examines the development and implementation of the Fingal AFC programme from the perspective of key stakeholders. The findings reported here arise from interviews conducted between

2013 and 2016 with 16 organisational stakeholders belonging to three different groups: eight members of the Fingal AFC Alliance; five key national policymakers who were involved in developing Ireland's AFCC programme; and three international stakeholders who were heavily involved in developing the WHO programme. Interview data are analysed in relation to two core questions: stakeholder understandings, motivations and actions and how these influenced the development and implementation of the programme; and, how stakeholders perceive and influenced the processes established to involve older people in the programme.

Leadership, planning and working together

Alliance stakeholders

At the time of interview, most alliance members believed that implementation of the AFC programme in Fingal was proceeding 'well' or 'really well'. They accounted for this in terms of how the initiative is managed and the professionalism of the key people involved, the planning approach adopted, and the level of collaboration and commitment evident among the various organisations and interest groups represented on the alliance. Participants recognised the important leadership role of the local authority and the county manager in establishing and chairing the alliance until the strategy was developed, and in 'driving' the initiative in its early stages, and linked this with how the initiative would be perceived and the possibility that significant innovation and change could happen as a result of the initiative. A particularly strong focus was also placed on the role and calibre of the independent chairperson of the alliance, who had a previous long career in national politics, was well networked and knew how statutory organisations worked. Participants felt her appointment sent out a strong message that the initiative 'meant business'. Local stakeholders also stressed the central role played by the programme's coordinator, including her commitment to older people and strong work ethic, and the positive working relationship between the coordinator, alliance chairperson and the regional Ageing Well Network consultant. Overall, there was a strong sense among alliance members that the programme was being well served by the calibre, energy and commitment of the people assigned key leadership responsibilities for its development and implementation.

Many alliance members also commented positively about the planning process used by the alliance. This related to general project planning and management issues, rather than the use of the WHO framework. Stakeholders commended the strategy's action and practical focus, and noted the realistic objectives that were set for the programme, given the resources available, and the 'measured approach' adopted, which demonstrated that the alliance had learned from previous experience of inter-agency planning where objectives had been over-ambitious and little achieved.

Several alliance stakeholders commented on the level of commitment and collaboration displayed by the different agencies represented on the alliance, and in particular by the leadership role different agencies had taken in the various projects that had been initiated. Others, although more qualified in their appraisal of the level of interagency collaboration, remained positive about collaboration even in the context of the severe budgetary restraints that prevailed, highlighting the benefits to all parties involved. Notwithstanding this, some stakeholders stressed the difficulty in ensuring ongoing collaboration, and emphasised the need for follow-up to ensure that commitments were enacted, offering examples of when this had been effective. A number of local stakeholders were concerned about the ongoing local authority reforms and how these might impact on collaboration and implementation of the programme.

National stakeholders

While recognising the significant achievements of the AFCC, national policymakers were more circumspect and critical in their appraisal of the age-friendly initiative. They acknowledged the important leadership contributions of key individuals in developing the national programme, and highlighted the crucial role of the Ageing Well Network and Atlantic. National stakeholders also recognised the considerable achievement involved in developing an initiative from a pilot project in one county in 2009 to its current implementation in all local authority areas.

However, national stakeholders expressed some concerns about the AFCC programme. They expressed concern about interagency collaboration, the outcomes achieved to date, certain aspects of the implementation model, and the level of engagement of politicians at local level. Participants also held divergent views on the impact of WHO involvement on the national initiative. Several national stakeholders were despondent about the levels and quality of interagency collaboration generated by the initiative in some cities and counties. HSE, the health and social service agency, was singled out in particular for negative comment. One stakeholder cited HSE engagement as representing the most significant challenge facing the initiative. Another recognised the need for integrated service delivery and acknowledged the leadership role of local authorities on the initiative, but also highlighted the difficulties in achieving close collaborative working. These included the pressures placed on organisations by austerity-driven cutbacks and organisational downsizing. Some stakeholders, however, were more strident in their comments and doubted if Irish public service in general had developed the capacity at this stage to operate on the collaborative basis envisaged by the AFCC programme.

Some reservations were also expressed by national stakeholders about the implementation approach. One participant felt that the approach was too prescriptive and did not allow for enough flexibility by the alliances. The same participant went further to state that the insistence by the national programme on a common template for implementation had acted as a barrier to extending the initiative to some local authority areas. This participant felt that the NGO national forum had not contributed greatly to the programme's development. National stakeholders also expressed the need for the initiative to be more responsive to the changing priorities of national policy, particularly the new local authority structures being introduced under Putting People First.

National stakeholders held divergent views about the international dimension of the initiative as represented by WHO. One participant felt that the WHO assisted in developing the overall agenda for the initiative at national level, but had only a modest impact on the programme at local level. However, other stakeholders, noting that there was little by way of direct WHO support to the initiative, stressed the importance of the connection with the organisation and the credibility it lent to the initiative, particularly from the viewpoint of local authorities.

International stakeholders

International stakeholders identified what they consider to be the fundamental elements of the implementation process, the rationale for global networking of initiatives, and the contribution that national programmes can make. All were impressed with the rapid growth of the age-friendly 'movement', noting the leadership role of key individuals, and the commitment and enthusiasm these individuals had brought to the task. They agreed on the core elements of what was likely to be a successful age-friendly initiative, including the mobilisation of political support at a senior level to ensure sustainability, and the application of a rigorous assessment process to identify older people's needs. Some stressed the importance of intersectoral or interagency collaboration, with one stakeholder suggesting that this was a fundamental requisite for success as it secured a broad organisational support base for the programme.

Another international stakeholder noted that adopting a collaborative approach was not required for membership of the WHO global network. While admitting that there were some examples of excellent practice in this regard in the network, this stakeholder suggested that in most age-friendly communities the officials with responsibility for older people services were probably 'driving' the initiative.

When discussing the age-friendly movement's progress, some international stakeholders highlighted the importance of the WHO guidelines (WHO, 2007), others the establishment of the WHO global network in 2010. The divergence in opinion was related to whether the primary focus should be on assessment or implementation. Several stakeholders felt that the guidelines, if used flexibly, still had currency, and that the core principles on which they were based continued to be relevant. Another participant expressed regret that there had not been greater emphasis on implementation when the guidelines were originally launched. Yet another was concerned that the guidelines were seen as a prescription for how to proceed rather than as a 'tool' for stimulating ideas. This stakeholder noted that most of the original 33 cities had used the guidelines to determine how age-friendly they were, but had not then proceeded to act on the results. This participant further emphasised the leadership role of municipalities, but was also realistic about the risks involved in having a network, and in particular the way in which some cities used membership to declare that they were already age-friendly, rather than that they were affiliating to a network that committed them to work towards becoming age-friendly.

Some international stakeholders stated that the quality of the plans developed by network members had improved in recent years as individual AFCC programmes matured. However, participants also noted that many network members had yet to develop their plans. International stakeholders were aware of the need for the initiative to cater for geographic and cultural diversity, and emphasised the requirement for flexibility in these different contexts to cater for a full range of diversity. Some questioned whether the needs of these various groupings were being met on current initiatives.

International stakeholders also saw value in developing national programmes, partly because of the lack of resources available to WHO to support initiatives locally. They recognised that the quality of national programmes varied between countries. They were more easily organised in less populous countries and had the advantage of sending a strong message that age-friendliness was a national priority. Where they were working well they could more effectively access resources, and create partnerships to mobilise action. However, national programmes could also have a negative effect if they prevented members from actively engaging in the wider global network, or stymied innovation and creativity by establishing limiting criteria for membership.

The role of older people in developing AFCC: tokenism or real influence?

All stakeholders held strong views on the rationale for involving older people in the initiative. They also felt strongly about the factors that facilitate successful participation, the difficulties associated with utilising a participative approach, and the importance of policy support for participatory approaches.

Participants belonging to all stakeholder groups recognised the value of involving older people in age-friendly initiatives. They referred to the energy, life and colour that older people bring to projects and the increased momentum that often results. Essentially, it was felt important that older people's 'lived experiences' should inform age-friendly initiatives. There was also recognition of a range of ways in which older people could be involved: in consultations to identify priority issues, in planning and framing solutions, in providing implementation advice, and sometimes in being actively involved in implementation itself. Consultation was seen as a basic requirement across all age-friendly developments and viewed as an intrinsic element of promoting and managing effective change.

Some stakeholders contrasted 'expert-led' initiatives with those that involve older people in meaningful ways. While expressing lack of confidence in 'experts' alone identifying the needs of older people and developing effective solutions, some stakeholders were also cautious about having unrealistic expectations about older people's participation. They felt that initiatives led solely by older people would not necessarily do any better than more conventional, 'top-down' programmes. The ideal for many stakeholders would be a combination of a 'top-down' and 'bottom-up' approaches, which they felt would reflect the reality of how decision-making processes operate at municipal level, recognise the multiple constituencies of interest that exist within municipalities and their sometimes conflicting demands, and still ensure that older people's needs were given serious consideration in the planning process.

All stakeholder groups identified age-friendly initiatives where they felt there was successful involvement of older people. National stakeholders were particularly positive about this aspect of Ireland's AFCC programme and felt it represented one of its major achievements, although they also recognised that the quality of engagement varied greatly between counties. In general, alliance members were positive about the engagement of older people at local level. They praised the combination of consultation methods used in Fingal. They instanced Age-Friendly Skerries and the Age-Friendly Dublin Airport project as two exemplars of effective involvement of older people. They referred to the consultation mechanisms that existed prior to the AFC programme in Fingal and felt that these had been enhanced. They noted the comprehensive nature of the initial consultation and praised the focus not only on identifying problems and issues, but also on providing opportunities for older people to generate possible solutions. Some stakeholders felt that older people's relationship with place in Fingal meant that consultations were more local area-focused than in larger urban contexts, and that this added to the results' value. Local stakeholders further commented positively on the working relationship between the OPC and the alliance.

Stakeholders were also keenly aware of the obstacles and challenges involved in engaging older people in age-friendly programmes. International stakeholders referred to cultural barriers that may exist, where participatory democratic mechanisms may not be part of the decision-making landscape in many countries. They felt that this may lead to tokenistic and 'symbolic' involvement of older people where the possibility of influencing decision making in a significant way does not exist. National stakeholders made similar points in discussing organisational resistance to participation because of the changes it can bring about to power structures and how decisions are made. One national stakeholder commented that AFI itself is very cautious in devolving power and influence to OPCs and may be acting as a barrier to more meaningful engagement of older people.

All stakeholders commented on the difficulties in involving effectively more vulnerable or marginalised groups of older people in participatory processes, including people in residential care, older travellers, older members of 'new' Irish communities, and older men. Involving advocates for these groups in the programme was seen as one possible way around this problem. Local stakeholders stressed the need to develop greater awareness among older people about Age Friendly Fingal as one way of promoting their greater involvement in the programme.

Stakeholders at national and local level held various views about the need to develop the capacity of older people to engage fully with age-friendly initiatives. Some felt that older adults were more than capable of expressing their views on their lives and the issues that confront them, particularly through consultation mechanisms. One local stakeholder suggested that capacity building could be used to shape the agenda for older people and 'lead' them in particular directions, rather than be a genuine attempt to develop knowledge and skills to enhance engagement. However, others felt that there was a need to develop further the capacity of older people in order for them to influence decision making effectively and participate fully in Fingal's AFC programme. The training and development programme for OPCs currently being developed was seen as an important step in this process, although it is also a highly resource-intensive activity. As a result, national and local stakeholders were also aware of the need to dedicate specific resources to facilitate and ensure effective participation by older people in age-friendly initiatives.

Further, stakeholders at national level welcomed the policy support for OPCs articulated in the Programme for Government 2011-2016 (Department of the Taoiseach, 2011), and recognition in the National Positive Ageing Strategy of the importance of civic engagement among older people. They felt these provided a policy validation for the development of older people's participation. Finally, some national stakeholders suggested that the national programme now needed to also focus more on involving the political sector at local level in the development of city and county age-friendly initiatives.

Discussion and conclusion

Lui and colleagues (2009) identified the range of governance approaches being used to create age-friendly initiatives, and found that there was limited critical consideration of the effectiveness of the specific approaches, or analysis of the 'drivers' that determine particular approaches. In the intervening years, the WHO approach has been the subject of detailed analysis, which has highlighted both strengths and weaknesses (Buffel et al, 2012; Keating et al, 2013; Liddle et al, 2013; Golant, 2014; Plouffe et al, 2016). Research and discussion papers in Ireland have also explored these implementation issues. The Irish body of work explores the significant influence of austerity measures on Ireland's AFCC programme (Walsh, 2015) and the challenges it has faced from a range of political and systemic factors (Connolly, 2011; Walsh and Harvey, 2012; Fingal Age Friendly County, 2014).

However, despite the adverse economic climate in which Ireland's AFCC was developed, its achievements are still considerable. These include: the development of a national programme that has engaged a diverse range of sectors and stakeholders, one that is now recognised in national policy; the creation of effective structures and processes to support implementation and ensure linkages between local age-friendly initiatives; and emerging evidence of innovative solutions to key issues identified by older people (Scharf, 2015b). So what then are the lessons to be learned from the Irish experience, and in particular, what are the lessons relevant to two critical implementation issues that face all age-friendly initiatives: how to engage political leadership and support, and how to involve older people effectively in such endeavours?

The development of Ireland's AFCC programme demonstrates the importance of political leadership and provides an exemplar of how this has been actively mobilised to support programme development. As demonstrated here, the implementation approach adopted on the AFCC programme has been heavily influenced by the WHO initiative, particularly in the way in which it has used the eight-domain structure of the original guide for local strategy development (see Chapter Two). However, the programme has not slavishly adopted every aspect of the WHO approach, and, following piloting, has tailored the governance framework to fit local service delivery structures and ongoing organisational and policy changes. It has also allowed for some flexibility – some would argue not enough – in establishing these structures at local level. The AFCC programme has been designed to reflect realistically the adverse economic conditions that prevailed at the time, and has developed unique structures at national level to support the establishment of a national programme. The programme's origins in the Ageing Well Network facilitated this, and this opportunity was proactively and effectively exploited to garner government and policy support for the initiative. While the link with Atlantic also helped in this regard, Atlantic's limited funding cycle may have adversely accelerated the programme's extension. The AFCC programme is now formally recognised in national policy (Department of the Taoiseach, 2011), and its sustainability is more secure following its transfer as AFI to the local government support network at national level.

However, in the Irish context, it is not only political leadership that is crucial. The political system has provided a supportive policy context for the development of AFCC, but strong individual and organisational leadership have also been critical. This is evident at county and city level where the quality of commitment and leadership from the local authority CEO, the alliance chair and the programme coordinator is crucial, as it was in Fingal. Individual leadership in the Ageing Well Network and in the Louth AFC pilot programme have also been identified as critical in developing the national programme. One of the challenges now facing the programme is its sustainability, following the departure of some of these individuals from the stage, particularly in light of the pressures on the programme because of shifting priorities stemming from local government reform. This will surely test the programme's collaborative nature and the extent to which it has been successfully embedded in policy and service delivery systems.

While AFCC has successfully mobilised political support, it has found supporting older people's effective engagement in the programme more problematic. This partly reflects a lack of ambition about what older people can contribute, but also an overcautious approach to giving older people more decisive influence on the programme's development. Much has been written about the civic engagement of older people, including its various conceptualisations, its place in public policy and in research, what enables it and what acts as a barrier, and the benefits that accrue to older people (Minkler and Holstein, 2008; Barnes et al, 2012; Ekman and Amna, 2012; Buffel, 2015). Indeed, there is a growing body of research specific to the Irish context (Ní Léime et al, 2012; Ní Léime, 2015; Scharf et al, 2016). What is clear from our growing understanding of civic engagement is that the model developed to date is at the lower end of the scale in terms of older people's influence on the AFCC programme. This partly reflects the low baseline from which the programme began, where there was little if any experience of involving older people in service improvement initiatives. And, to be fair, the AFCC programme has developed processes and mechanisms to facilitate older people's engagement, including, as we have seen, the consultation process that has been utilised in developing local strategies, the establishment of OPCs in many, but not all, local programmes, and providing for the representation of older people on the relevant alliance in each participating city and county. However, despite the positive rhetoric about civic engagement, serious weaknesses continue to mark the model adopted to date. Many of these have been identified by stakeholders, and there are positive signs that they are beginning to be addressed in the capacity-building initiatives currently being developed and rolled out across local programmes. It is important that these initiatives are grounded in a broad understanding of civic engagement, which can promote social and even political activism by OPCs, and which employ effective community education and adult-learning principles to achieve their goals. It may also be time to develop civic engagement capacity-building programmes for service providers to enhance their understanding of civic engagement, and their capacity to involve older people more effectively in age-friendly projects and initiatives.

Representing a rare insight into the local implementation process of an age-friendly programme and its national and international links, this critical review highlights the complex interplay between the many political, economic, policy, organisational and indeed individual influences that have shaped important facets of the governance and implementation approach adopted in County Fingal. These influences have their origins at international, national and local levels, and similar factors are likely to be at play in age-friendly initiatives elsewhere. It is important that we develop a better understanding of these interacting factors so that they are given serious consideration in any attempt to create age-friendly communities. This points to the need for ongoing critical research and evaluation of the implementation of age-friendly programmes, if they are to realise their ambition and potential to have significant impact on the lives of older people.

References

Age Action (2014) *Pre-budget submission 2015,* Dublin: Age Action.

Age-Friendly Ireland (2015) *Age Friendly Ireland's statement of strategy 2015-2017,* Dublin: Age-Friendly Ireland, available at www.agefriendlyireland.ie.

Age-Friendly Ireland (2016) *The 4 stage approach*, Dublin: Age-Friendly Ireland, available at www.agefriendlyireland.ie.

Age-Friendly World (2016) 'What is an age-friendly world?', available at https://extranet.who.int/agefriendlyworld.

Ageing Well Network (2013) *Skerries age-friendly town*, Dublin: Ageing Well Network.

An Garda Síochána (2010) *An Garda Síochána older people strategy*, Dublin: An Garda Síochána.

Barnes, M., Harrison, E. and Murray, L. (2012) 'Ageing activists: who gets involved in older people's forums?', *Ageing & Society*, 32 (2): 261-80.

Boyle, M. and Larragy, J. (2010) *Feeling the pinch: One year on*, Dublin: Older and Bolder.

Buffel, T. (ed) (2015) *Researching age-friendly communities. Stories from older people as co-investigators*, Manchester: The University of Manchester Library.

Buffel, T., Phillipson, C. and Scharf, T. (2012) 'Ageing in urban environments: developing "age-friendly" cities', *Critical Social Policy*, 32(4): 597-617.

Central Statistics Office (2012) *Census 2011 preliminary report*, Dublin: Central Statistics Office.

Central Statistics Office (2013) *Population and labour force projections: 2016-2046*, Dublin: Central Statistics Office.

Cochrane, A., McGilloway, S., Furlong, M. and Donnelly, M. (2013) 'The role and contribution of philanthropy to the lives of older people in Ireland', *The International Journal of Aging and Society*, 2 (2): 14-23.

Connolly, A. (2011) 'Building Ireland's age friendly counties programme', Paper presented at 1st International Conference on Age Friendly Cities, Dublin, 28-30 September.

Connolly, S. (2015) 'Contextualising ageing in Ireland', in K. Walsh, G.M. Carney and Á. Ní Léime (eds) *Ageing through austerity: Critical perspectives from Ireland*, Bristol: Policy Press, pp 17-30.

Department of Health (2013a) *National Positive Ageing Strategy*, Dublin: Department of Health.

Department of Health (2013b) *Healthy Ireland: A framework for improved health and wellbeing 2013-2025*, Dublin: Department of Health.

Department of Health (2014) *The Irish national dementia strategy*, Dublin: Department of Health.

Department of the Environment, Community and Local Government (2012) *Putting People First: Action programme for effective local government*, Dublin: Department of the Environment, Community and Local Government.

Department of the Taoiseach (2011) *Programme for Government 2011-2016*, Dublin: Department of the Taoiseach.

Ekman, J. and Amna, E. (2012) 'Political participation and civic engagement: towards a new typology', *Human Affairs*, 22 (3): 283-300.

Fingal Age Friendly County (2014) *Fingal Age Friendly County Strategy review 2014: Your voice, your say*, Fingal Age Friendly County.

Fingal Age Friendly County Alliance (2015) *Minutes of alliance meetings 2012-2015*, Fingal Age Friendly County.

Fingal County Council (2011) *Fingal Development Plan 2011-2017*, Fingal County Council.

Fingal County Council (2012) *Fingal Age Friendly County Strategy 2012-2017*, Fingal County Council.

Fitzgerald, K.G. and Caro, F.G. (2014) 'An overview of age-friendly cities and communities around the world', *Journal of Aging & Social Policy*, 26(1-2): 1-18.

Golant, S.M. (2014) 'Age-friendly communities: are we expecting too much?', *IRPP Insight*, 5: 1-19.

Keating, N., Eales, J. and Phillips, J.E. (2013) 'Age-friendly rural communities: conceptualizing "best-fit"', *Canadian Journal on Aging/ La Revue Canadienne Du Vieillissement*, 32 (4): 319-32.

Liddle, J., Scharf, T., Bartlam, B., Bernard, M. and Sim, J. (2013) 'Exploring the age-friendliness of purpose-built retirement communities: evidence from England', *Ageing & Society*, 34(9): 1601-29.

Lui, C., Everingham, J., Warburton, J., Cuthill, M. and Bartlett, H. (2009) 'What makes a community age-friendly: a review of international literature', *Australasian Journal on Ageing*, 28(3): 116-21.

Minkler, M. and Holstein, M.B. (2008) 'From civil rights to civic engagement? Concerns of two older critical gerontologists about a "new social movement" and what it portends', *Journal of Aging Studies*, 22 (2): 196-204.

Moulaert, T. and Garon, S. (2016) 'Introduction: toward a better understanding of AFCC', in T. Moulaert and S. Garon (eds) *Age-friendly cities and communities in international comparison. Political lessons, scientific avenues and democratic issues*, New York, NY: Springer, pp 1-16.

Ní Léime, Á. (2015) 'Active ageing: social participation and volunteering in later life', in Walsh, K., Carney, G.M. and Ní Léime, Á. (eds) *Ageing through austerity: Critical perspectives from Ireland*, Bristol: Policy Press, pp 47-62.

Ní Léime, Á., Callan, A., Finn, C. and Healy, R. (2012) *Evaluating the impact of Active Retirement Ireland on the lives of older people*, Dublin: Active Retirement Ireland.

O'Neill, D., Twomey, C. and O'Shea, E. (2009) 'Ireland', in E. Palmore, S. Kunkel and F. Whittington (eds) *The international handbook on aging*, Santa Barbara: Praeger, pp 283-96.

O'Shea, E. and Conboy, P. (2005) *Planning for an ageing population: Strategic considerations*, Dublin: National Council on Ageing and Older People.

Parker, S. (2015) *Ageing Well Network: A case study of an Irish success story in the field of ageing*, Dublin: The Atlantic Philanthropies.

Plouffe, L., Kalache, A. and Voelcker, I. (2016) 'A critical review of the WHO age-friendly cities methodology and its implementation', in T. Moulaert and S. Garon (eds) *Age-friendly cities and communities in international comparison: Political lessons, scientific avenues, and democratic issues*, New York, NY: Springer, pp 19-36.

Scharf, T. (2015a) 'Between inclusion and exclusion in later life', in K. Walsh, G.M. Carney and Á. Ní Léime (eds) *Ageing through austerity: Critical perspectives from Ireland*, Bristol: Policy Press, pp 113-29.

Scharf, T. (2015b) 'Age-friendly cities and communities in Ireland: key challenges for a national programme', Paper presented at Annual Conference of the British Society of Gerontology, Newcastle, 1-3 July.

Scharf, T., McDonald, B. and Atkins, A.M. (2016) *Promoting civic engagement in later life through the Touchstone programme: A resource and research guide*, Galway: Irish Centre for Social Gerontology, National University of Ireland Galway.

Scharlach, A. (2009) 'Creating aging-friendly communities', *Generations*, 33(2): 5-11.

Scharlach, A. (2016) 'Age-friendly cities. For whom? By whom? For what purpose?', in T. Moulaert and S. Garon (eds) *Age-friendly cities and communities in international comparison. Political lessons, scientific avenues and democratic issues*, New York, NY: Springer, pp 305-29.

Timonen, V., Scharf, T., Conlon, C. and Carney, G. (2013) 'Family, state and class: reconceptualising intergenerational solidarity using the grounded theory approach', *European Journal of Ageing*, 10(3): 171-9.

Turley, G. and Flannery, D. (2013) 'The impact of the economic boom and bust on local government budgets in Ireland', *Administration*, 61(2): 33-56.

Walsh, K. and Harvey, B. (2012) *Review of age friendly counties programme*, Dublin: Ageing Well Network.

Walsh, K. (2015) 'Interrogating the "age-friendly community" in austerity', in K. Walsh, G.M. Carney and Á. Ní Léime (eds) *Ageing through austerity: Critical perspectives from Ireland*, Bristol: Policy Press, pp 79-95.

Walsh, K., Scharf, T., Cullinan, J. and Finn, C. (2012) *Deprivation and its measurement in later life: Findings from a mixed-methods study in Ireland*, Galway: Irish Centre for Social Gerontology, National University of Ireland Galway.

Walsh, K., Carney, G., Ní Léime, Á. (2015) 'Introduction – social policy and ageing through austerity', in K. Walsh, G.M. Carney and Á. Ní Léime (eds) *Ageing through austerity: Critical perspectives from Ireland*, Bristol: Policy Press, pp 1-15.

WHO (World Health Organization) (2007) *Global age-friendly cities: A guide*, Geneva: WHO.

NINE

Implementing age-friendly cities in Australia

Hal Kendig, Cathy Gong, Lisa Cannon

Introduction

Australia was among the first countries to contribute in the World Health Organization's (WHO) pioneering age-friendly cities and communities (AFCC) strategy, with ongoing engagement through to the landmark ageing and health report (WHO, 2015). This chapter presents a critical overview of Australian initiatives ensuing from the following seminal WHO statement:

> An age-friendly city encourages active ageing by optimizing opportunities for health, participation and security in order to enhance quality of life as people age. In practical terms, an age-friendly city adapts its structures and services to be accessible to and inclusive of older people with varying needs and capacities. (WHO, 2007, p 1)

The WHO's age-friendly cities (AFC) guide and checklist have provided practical directions for local action on behalf of older Australians in the eight priority areas of urban living: outdoor spaces and buildings, transportation, housing, social participation, respect and social inclusion, civic participation and employment, communication and information, and community support and health services (later amended to include lifelong learning and sustainability) (WHO, 2007). The focus of this chapter is on understanding Australian efforts to apply the AFC approach of bringing 'bottom-up' community perspectives into whole-of-government responses to ageing. This includes efforts to develop learning and action partnerships between government, communities and university researchers.

The chapter begins by briefly reviewing the evolution of Australia's ageing population and spatial structures, including the increasing diversity of the population. We then consider evidence on the liveability of Australian cities, especially for disadvantaged older people, inclusive of the widely used but ambiguous concept of 'ageing in place'. The chapter then provides a critical review of AFC initiatives, comparing Sydney, Melbourne, and Canberra in a state and national context. While there has been valuable AFC work in other cities and non-metropolitan areas, we concentrate on these three capital cities in order to better focus and integrate the discussion.[1] The chapter critically assesses the challenges of implementing age-friendly approaches and concludes with an assessment of achievements and prospects for the future.

An ageing Australia and urban change

Australia is an advanced, industrial society that in contrast to Europe has been advantaged by decades of economic and population growth and rising real incomes. While Australia managed to avoid recession during the global financial crisis of 2007 (Kendig et al, 2013), there are growing uncertainties for the future as the economy transitions away from heavy reliance on the export of resources to China. Contrary to the bucolic image of the 'outback', Australia is in fact one of the most urbanised countries on earth. The capital cities and state governments maintain their economic political hegemony over smaller cities and rural areas that are experiencing variable economic and population decline, notwithstanding some movement by recent retirees to the coast and other ex-urban locations. Sydney and Melbourne, each with populations in the order of five million, had their initial urban development in the mid-19th century. They are increasingly global cities integrated into the international economy: their strong employment and population growth over the past decade has continued to attract large numbers of international migrants, students and tourists to their multicultural society. Canberra, Australia's capital, is an inland city of 400,000 people purpose-designed as the centre of the Australian government and public service in the Australian Capital Territory (ACT) (broadly comparable to the US District of Columbia).

Population diversity and change

Australia is ageing, with the proportion of the population aged 65 years and over having risen from 12% in 1995 to 15% in 2015, and this figure is projected to increase to nearly 20% in 2031 (ABS, 2012, 2015). This is primarily the result of ageing of the large cohort of post-war baby boomers[2] and post-war migrants as well as increasing longevity (Gong and Kendig, 2016). More people are reaching later life after having migrated from Europe in the early years after the Second World War and from Asia over recent decades, including modest numbers of refugees since the Vietnam War and subsequent upheavals in Africa and the Middle East. Diversity is also increasing as younger boomers have a healthy and productive later life while increasing numbers are reaching advanced later life. There also are widening social inequalities between older people advantaged by home ownership and superannuation compared with disadvantaged groups reliant on government pensions, women living alone, tenants in the private rental market, people living with disabilities, and small pockets of intensely disadvantaged Aboriginal people. As in other countries, disadvantage accumulates over the life span and between generations (Dannefer and Kelly-Moore, 2009). Lifelong economic prospects appear to be less favourable for younger people (Kendig, 2017), thus raising social and political concerns for intergenerational equity.[3]

Urban structures, particularly in Melbourne and Sydney, have also been changing. The spatial spread of low-density, single-family housing on the urban periphery has increased to accommodate growing demand, while more recently the supply of serviced land has been expensive for developers and homebuyers. Infill development of medium and high-density housing has intensified in inner-city areas, around radial rail routes, and in growing suburban centres. Increasing land values in accessible locations has led to some redevelopment in established areas, but the main effect has been to increase the cost of housing overall. This has generated substantial wealth increases for the cohort who owned property during the housing boom from the 1980s onwards. Conversely, the cost thresholds of buying for new cohorts have increased, private rents have increased, and the supply of low-cost government housing has slowed over recent years. Overall, older Australians have high rates of outright home ownership; relatively few are public tenants, and there is significant growth of retirement living communities (villages) that provide accommodation, lifestyle and care options (Kendig et al, 2012; Faulkner, 2017).

The Australian Housing and Urban Research Institute (AHURI) '… provides an account of the geography of disadvantage in Australia's three largest cities (Sydney, Melbourne and Brisbane)' (Hulse et al, 2014, p 9). The authors report that the availability of affordable rental properties for low-income Australians has remained a significant issue over the past three decades. Private tenants are increasing in numbers at all ages and they experience significant housing problems in terms of affordability, security and quality (Hulse and Pinnegar, 2015).

Australian cities have relatively few pockets of intense deprivation or very poor-quality housing, with most of these comprising large, older public housing estates or areas of run-down boarding or lodging houses in inner-city areas. There nonetheless is significant social segregation as well as spatial inequalities, with a strong clustering of multiple economic disadvantage and advantage of older Australians, particularly in capital cities (Gong et al, 2014). Economic disadvantage is indicated by high proportions of non-home owners reliant on the universal, means-tested pension only, while advantage is indicated by outright home ownership, higher incomes and occupational superannuation. Those paying rent after retirement are some of the most vulnerable in the country and those in disadvantaged areas are more likely to have poor access to health and social services (Tanton et al, 2016).

Older people's experiences of urban environments

Ageing and the home base

The majority of older Australians, particularly the large numbers of outright home owners, have lived in their homes for decades and have a strong desire to 'age in place' (AIHW, 2013). The home is not only essential for shelter and a key influence on living standards, but its significance also extends to people's emotional attachments and their links to the community and services that surround the home. Qualitative studies attest to the intense meaning of home for the maintenance of identity and autonomy, including ongoing connection to the owner's past and memories (de Jonge et al, 2011; Kendig et al, 2012; Stones and Gullifer, 2016).

For the current cohort of older Australians, buying a home and paying it off has been the fulfilment of a lifelong aspiration that is bound up with family building, social standing and economic security for later life (Faulkner, 2017): "'... this house here has been a silent witness to my own life ..." – Kayley' (Stones and Gullifer, 2016, p 464).

As Australians grow older and experience mobility limitations, 'ageing in place' means they spend increasing amounts of time in their homes and their neighbourhood (Kendig et al, 2012). With increasing age, older people can experience a shrinking 'life sphere', with the home and neighbourhood taking on added importance for their opportunities for social participation, as a base for healthy and productive activities, and as an access point to public transport and community and health services, which vary greatly in their local availability. Along with family support and delivered care and health services, the home is the primary setting of care. It can be adapted to become more supportive through modifications, home maintenance services and technological assistance (such as fall-detection devices), as well as internet access and mobile phones, which increase social connectivity (Faulkner, 2017).

Accommodation and care

New developments in support at home, along with housing innovations such as the resurgence of retirement communities, are increasing the range of options in the community. Australian housing is based primarily in the strong private market and the for-profit sector is gaining an increasing share of provision, and it is leading desirable but costly innovations for older people. User charges are increasing in government-subsidised community and residential care, including substantial capital requirements for accommodation components of care. These trends are accentuating inequalities already apparent in terms of income and also wealth, notably in housing and superannuation assets. While Australian governments have made important advances with community care initiatives as alternatives to residential care, there has been little funding for complementary provision of affordable housing.

Homelessness

Older people can be found among the intensely disadvantaged people in insecure housing. An ethnographic study of homeless older men was conducted in a supportive but run-down part of inner Sydney (Quine et al, 2004). These men had a range of health conditions, many experienced food insecurity, and they were living on or below the poverty line. While many highlighted the importance of social interactions, all informants were living alone without family support. The idea of relocating to a more 'supportive' aged care facility was outweighed by the anticipated loss of independence they associated with such a transition. Access to other resources such as health services becomes more complex and time-consuming, with the lack of transport seen as a barrier.

Older people's views on their suburbs

The 'supportiveness' of homes and neighbourhoods was reported from semi-structured interviews conducted with older people living in economically and geographically diverse suburbs within the greater Sydney region (Mackenzie et al, 2015). Most respondents owned their own home outright, and drove as the main means of transport. Intensifying urban development (including high-rise and medium housing, increased traffic and the lack of parking), in addition to declining health and income, have restricted some individuals' abilities to continue to drive. The development of large shopping centres was reported to have led to the loss of local corner shops and other facilities within walking range. Inadequate pathways, poor lighting at night and the lack of bus shelters were nominated for restricting access by public transport to local facilities and hence capacities to remain socially engaged with their community. Some residents also felt the design of their neighbourhood did not encourage them to walk for pleasure or for exercise. Many felt they had limited control over their changing environments.

Improving local facilities

Several studies have investigated how to improve local environments for older people. A Melbourne study found that walking was enhanced by close proximity of destinations of interest and daily life facilities, such as sporting and recreational facilities (Bentley et al, 2010). Another Melbourne study found that the ability to access basic services and facilities, and social activities by means of public transport is a crucial prerequisite when driving becomes risky or impossible at older ages (Engles and Liu, 2013; see also Berry, 2007). A national review for the AHURI (Judd et al, 2014) reported that modifications of home and site-level environment, such as ramps and hand holders, would increase walkability for pedestrians and reduce risk of falls. The study built a case for universal liveable housing design and the integration of housing, parks, open spaces, community services and facilities that improve safety for older people and better enable them to stay in their own homes as they grow older (Judd et al, 2014; see also ACSA, 2015).

Transportation

Transportation issues are especially important for the majority of older Australians who live in low-density urban locations developed during the post war era (Faulkner, 2017). Approximately 74% of people aged 65 and over have driver licences and still drive their cars regularly (NSW Government, 2012a). The research suggests that older people often adapt to failing health by limiting their driving in terms of distances travelled, day rather than night trips, and avoidance of heavy traffic areas (Berry, 2007). Women as well as men have had a lifelong reliance on private cars, persisting with car driving as long as possible subject to health and financial circumstances. For most, the car is the mainstay of their independence and social participation: '"I use the car all the time; you can't get out here much unless you've got your own transport … if you haven't got a car you're lost" (married woman)' (Mackenzie et al, 2015, p 1700).

Many older people view public transport such as buses as unreliable, time-inefficient, and/or disability unfriendly or non-existent in their local areas. These experiences are reported across a variety of contexts, from various suburbs across Sydney (Mackenzie et al, 2015) to the low-density and relatively uncongested Canberra (CMHR, 2011). The Canberra study found that inadequate public transport as well as damaged or poor-quality footpaths inhibit community engagement especially in socioeconomically disadvantaged neighbourhoods (Pearson et al, 2012).

Implementation and challenges

The small AFC movement in Australia is confronted by the complexity of the federal system of governments, in which each level has its own elected representatives with competing policy directions and fiscal incentives. National government maintains its dominance through income taxes and other revenue as well as grants to state and local government. The states have primary powers over land use and the delivery of education and health services, while local government has limited responsibilities for property services financed by local property taxes. Government departments have primary responsibilities to functions rather than population groups. In this patchwork of political, bureaucratic and economic interests, it is difficult to forge policy directions that take ageing and older people comprehensively into account, notwithstanding the potential benefits that could be achieved for older people and others at all ages.

An overview of AFC developments is provided in Table 9.1 nationally, and in two states (Sydney and Melbourne) and the ACT (Canberra). Their strategic context and key initiatives are shown in columns 1 and 2, while outcomes and challenges are shown in columns 3 and 4.

Table 9.1: Age-friendly developments in Australia: Melbourne, Canberra, and Sydney

	Strategic context	Key initiatives	Implementation outcomes	Challenges and prospects
National (not AFC-specific)	Coalition government elected 2013 Age Discrimination Commissioner ongoingAdvisory Panel on Positive Ageing disbandedIntergenerational reports (IGRs) continuing	Living Longer, Living Better reforms (2012) Ongoing development for home care packages More consumer-directed care Ageing portfolio split between health and social services (2015)	Continuation of Commonwealth and state fiscal restraint More means testing for universal ageing pension and aged care services July 2016 re-election of the coalition government	Infrastructure investment plans (major transport) New Ministry for Cities Can federalism 'gridlock' be better addressed?
Melbourne and Victorian state developments	Strong local government, Council on the Ageing (COTA) Earlier state Positive Ageing Strategy and strong Home and Community Care programme.	AFC pilot initiatives with WHO and councils Boorondara Active Ageing Strategy 2009-2014, then 2019 (an AFC city) Metropolitan Strategic Plan (2002, 2014) Ageing in the Growth Corridor of Melbourne project.	State AFC initiatives lapsed with the 2010 change of government State care and health planning coordination continues Few state or local AFC resources Growth corridor planning basically fails	Can state and COTA leadership be retained? Is it achievable to aim at 'Bringing the views of older people into integrated action by local, state, and even national policy development'?
Canberra and ACT Developments	ACT Strategic Plans for Positive Ageing: 2010-2014, 2012-2014, and 2015 -2019. ACT Older Persons Assemblies 2011 and 2014.	The ACT Age Friendly Cities Survey 2010. Specific initiatives including senior card concessions developing within ACT departments.	Continuing age-friendly 'increments' Community development COTA Minimal engagement with the major rail initiative or bus review Minimal involvement with land use planning	How can ageing be taken into account better in land use planning? How can ageing be taken into account in the major rail initiatives and bus reforms?
Sydney and NSW developments	Election of a reform-focused Coalition government NSW Ageing Plan and Strategy (2012) led by Minister on Ageing Office on Ageing to manage implementation with departmental partners and oversight by the Ministerial Advisory Council on Ageing	Conducting joint initiatives with State government departments, advocacy organisations, and private sector partners State IGR Reports (2012 and 2016) Evaluation of the NSW Ageing Plan (2015)	State Budget has limited funding for the Ageing Plan strategy State replaces some resources lost to Commonwealth cutbacks Ageing projects largely successful. Little influence on Departments e.g. mainstream transport & housing	'Whole-of-government' inter-departmental efforts are difficult. Collaborations with the private sector are promising

National developments

Initiatives complementary to AFC objectives were pursued under a former Labor government (2007-13), notably by its Advisory Panel on Positive Ageing, the Age Discrimination Commissioner, and Living Longer, Living Better reforms of aged care. The coalition (conservative) government elected in 2013 cut a number of what were considered to be 'wasteful' organisations (including the Advisory Panel on Positive Ageing) while turning its emphases to expenditure restraint. For older people, this included tighter means testing for pensions, increased user charges across care services, and the consequences of massive cuts in Commonwealth grants to state governments. In 2005, the Minister on Ageing and Aged Care Division moved to the Department of Health from the Department of Social Services, which retained responsibility for income support, housing, and a new initiative on planning over the life span.

As reviewed from an ageing perspective by Woods and Kendig (2015), Australia's ongoing intergenerational reports have underscored deepening national concern for projected increases in age-related expenditure, growing perceptions of younger people having disadvantaged futures, and (so far unsuccessful) attempts to limit continuing budget deficits.

The *language* of 'ageing in place', had emerged nationally as a cultural and policy construction of ageing in academic reviews (Horner and Boldy, 2008) as well as in the minister's 2012 launch of Living Longer, Living Better policy reforms of aged care. In the reforms of community care, the individual and wider community benefits of ageing in place have been touted as encouraging independence and active ageing and reducing 'burdens' on governments and taxpayers in an ageing society (DoHA, 2012; Productivity Commission, 2011). Underlying these issues is the fact that the community care approach *potentially* can yield savings to government because the costs of accommodation, living expenses and care itself are largely met privately (Jeon and Kendig, 2017).

The challenges faced by AFC initiatives have increased over recent years, with the Commonwealth government continuing major budget cuts, particularly in revenue sharing to state governments. Per Capita (2014), leading a coalition of national advocacy groups, completed the *Blueprint for an ageing Australia* (including a policy priority of 'enabling environments') after the former government's Advisory Panel on Positive Ageing was disbanded by the current government. In the lead-up to the 2017 election, the Australian Prime Minister Malcolm

Turnbull had articulated potentially AFC-relevant investment in transport infrastructure and a new Ministry for Cities. The opposition Australian Labor Party (ALP), which was in a close contest with the sitting government, has a platform calling for restoration of budgets for health and social expenditure. Its major policy document, *Growing together: Labor's agenda for tackling inequality* (ALP, 2016), outlined a range of policies supportive of positive approaches to ageing and communities. Council of the Ageing (COTA) Australia (2016), in its comment on the Budget, noted some reigning in of generous superannuation taxation for those on higher incomes, while also noting limited progress on consumer-led care and housing affordability.

Developments in Melbourne

Victorian Positive Ageing directions through the 1990s set a base for later AFC initiatives working in partnership with local government and pilot WHO efforts (as reviewed in Kendig et al, 2014). The WHO age-friendly cities guide (WHO, 2007), for example, was implemented and reviewed favourably by the Municipal Association of Victoria in 2009. Age-friendly principles were subsequently adopted by increasing numbers of councils, with support from COTA Victoria and the University of Melbourne. Local authorities were required to have municipal public health and wellbeing plans but with government changes and lack of resources a number of the early AFC initiatives lapsed, notwithstanding AFC language serving as a 'banner' during state election campaigns. Over recent years, some AFC activities continued with the Office on Ageing working with COTA Victoria and the City of Melbourne.

The municipality of Boroondara became one of Australia's first age-friendly cities, as reflected in its five-year Active Ageing Strategy (2009-14). The subsequent strategy document *Creating an age-friendly Boroondara: 2014-2019* (City of Boroondara, 2014) focused on key issues identified by national research as well as local community concern. These included social isolation, social connections, health promotion and older people's desires to age well in their homes. The plan aimed to bring the views of older people into integrated action by local, state, and even national policy development. While modest local initiatives were taken, a complementary vision and resources have not been forthcoming from state and national governments.

The Melbourne Strategic Plan 2030, an initiative of the Victoria Government (2002; updated in 2014), had promised to bring the AFC developments already underway into alignment with mainstream urban planning. The plan's ambitious preamble underscored the importance of planning for an ageing population, addressing inequalities of access on the basis of low income and disability, and the vulnerabilities of people with disabilities, the frail, and the aged (p 15). It stated that '... inadequate access affects people's sense of wellbeing, quality of life, and can exclude them from full participation in society' (p 118). The strategic plan included aims to address under-occupancy of the housing stock and improve public transport, but planning initiatives taking ageing into account have not been apparent.

Implementation challenges have been reviewed critically by Brasher and Winterton (2016) from their viewpoints as COTA Victoria director and a university researcher. They focused on the '... lack of AFC uptake in Victoria', attributing responsibility to '... a lack of strategic vision, leadership, and direction across all levels of government' (p 233). They note that the main arena for determining federal relations, the Council of Australian Governments, had not taken up the AFC agenda. They point to the 'lack of vision' in the top-down Commonwealth and state governments, reminding readers of the failure 15 years earlier of the National Strategy for an Ageing Australia. The Australian Local Government Association, in its *Age-friendly built environments: Opportunities for local government* (2006), offered some initial direction, but the association had neither significant authority nor resources.

Difficulties of AFC implementation in metropolitan planning were highlighted in the action research project, Ageing in the Growth Corridor of Melbourne, undertaken as a partnership between the University of Melbourne and the Victorian Department of Health (Ozanne et al, 2014). The department funded six project officers who sought to develop age-friendly actions that could be taken by local and state government in improving infrastructure investment and infill development. The cross-sectorial initiative worked with local governments, regional councils, the state infrastructure department, and the state Department of Human Services. Eighteen months of intense effort were put into considering strategic regional priorities for key infrastructure areas for life-course groups including older people. Yet it was concluded that 'in advocating for an ageing population against other regional priorities ... only a couple [of project officers] felt they were successful in being heard' (Ozanne et al, 2014, p 156).

Significant obstacles were recounted in a section on the lessons learned in relation to project implementation of the corridor development. It was concluded that 'because of the leadership changes and staff adjustments that occurred, this critical regional initiative did not continue in 2013' (Ozanne et al, 2014, p 159). The ambitious, complex, and contested goals proved to be unachievable in an unstable context of continually evolving policy environment at all levels of government, changing management and cutbacks in the state departments, and what was termed a lack of incentive to innovate versus a 'business as usual model'. The project evaluation concluded with a strongly worded recommendation that called for 'directly challenging the institutional ageism evident in project implementation and inherent in the Victorian urban planning policy and practice' (Ozanne et al, 2014, p 160).

ACT strategies and initiatives

The capital city Canberra initiated its AFC strategies a number of years after Melbourne, but activities have since developed rapidly. The ACT effectively serves as a regional government, having state and municipal responsibilities, thus limiting problems of coherency between governments. Canberra was designated an AFC city by WHO in 2012 after having followed the prescribed WHO procedures including community consultations, an AFC survey resourced by the ACT Government and the Australian National University in 2010, and a first Strategic Plan for Positive Ageing.

A first older persons' assembly in 2011 followed by a second in 2014, which had improved representation of community groups, yielded recommendations on infrastructure, transport and 'connecting in an age-friendly city' (ACT Government, 2011, 2014). These developments had some political as well as bureaucratic leadership in explicitly addressing WHO AFC priority areas.

A baseline survey of Canberra as an age-friendly city was conducted in 2009, with funding by the ACT government as part of its participation as a WHO AFC city. The survey, conducted by the Australian National University (ANU) in 2011, reported on older people's views on their city and the relationship between 'ageing well' and their neighbourhoods (CMHR, 2011; Pearson et al, 2012). While most of the older people generally held positive perceptions of their community, such views were most strongly associated with living in the same residence for a longer period. A range of environmental features – including perceived issues with graffiti, vandalism or rubbish in the community, and feeling safe to walk at night – was associated with better general health, while social cohesion was associated with lower levels of loneliness (Pearson et al, 2012).

Older women in Canberra were found to be more likely than men to view their neighbourhoods as unsafe places to walk at night, which arguably limits social opportunity; nearly a quarter did not go out in the evening at all (CMHR, 2011). The report also highlighted socio-demographic and disability factors associated with transportation problems, and found that women, those who rely on the pension as their main source of income, those with mobility issues, and those who lived in public rentals were more likely to report problems with buses and other forms of transport (CMHR, 2011). In partnership with the National Seniors Productive Ageing Centre and the Illawarra Retirement Trust, Pearson and colleagues from ANU (2012) made a case for further research and public health and other initiatives that can improve quality of the neighbourhood and facilitate good health, independence, and 'ageing in place happily'.

A series of AFC plans were developed by an interdepartmental committee of key departments led by the Office on Ageing working with the ACT Ministerial Council on Ageing (MACA) (ACT MACA, 2011). There was the launch of the ACT Strategic Plan for Positive Ageing 2010-2014: Towards an Age Friendly City, aligned with the WHO age-friendly checklist (ACT Government, 2009). The ACT Strategic Plan for Positive Ageing: Action Plan 2012-2014 addressed healthy and meaningful ageing, social isolation and adaptation to retirement (ACT Government, 2012). The ACT Active Ageing Framework 2015-2018 had broad objectives to provide services and programmes that are inclusive and empower older members of society, recognise the needs of older people through urban planning, and provide opportunities for social and economic engagement (ACT Government, 2015a). A Canberra AFC network was established with government agencies and key local seniors organisations (ACT Government, 2011).

The AFC plans and organisation led to a number of specific activities and initiatives in the ACT including an online seniors' information portal, public transport smart cards (MyWay) and a high-profile Grandparents' Day. Further efforts included flexible nightrider bus services, an innovative travel budget scheme, and the promotion of universal design in recent changes to building codes. A major review of the bus system in 2015, while noting a community transport initiative in 2014 and the upgrading of buses towards being disability-friendly by 2020, devoted its attention to rising consumer dissatisfaction and increasing costs (ACTION Expenditure Review, 2015). COTA ACT was provided with modest resources to work with government departments to conduct grassroots community consultations in two ACT suburbs (Tuggeranong Valley and Kaleen) (ACT Government, 2015b). COTA also was resourced by ACT Government to explore older people's transport usage and concerns and produced a guide to getting around in Canberra for older residents and a 'travel buddy' scheme. Modest progress has been made so far on plans to enhance flexible housing options, affordable rental options, address safety and security issues in public housing and provide emergency housing for homeless people.

AFC actions in Canberra have been facilitated by the single level of government in the ACT. A MACA review commented favourably on early initiatives that were modest but of clear value: a seniors' card (to increase access to affordable events and activities), Grandparents' Day (to enhance respect), and an online seniors' information portal (to enable access and participation). Little progress had been made on more significant housing initiatives that would have been costly and difficult. The advantages of individualised and flexible transport were achieved (not as an AFC initiative) by the advent of Uber in the ACT from 30 October 2015, with Canberra becoming the first city in Australia to allow and regulate ride-share services, providing employment for older drivers as well as accessible transport for passengers having special needs. Grassroots neighbourhood consultations provided impetus for specific improvements – such as better lighting on footpaths and seating – that were of value to older people but still affordable within tight departmental budgets.

There has been little engagement from the viewpoint of older people in transport and land-use issues of importance for all people. A light rail system is being developed, at an estimated cost of one billion Australian dollars, notwithstanding the project being rated as a poor investment by the independent Grattan Institute (Terrill et al, 2016). There has been similarly little engagement by AFC efforts with land-use planning, these being dominated by private property interests intensifying commercial centres and redeveloping housing in residential areas. There have been modest efforts (and considerable community opposition) to facilitate small-scale infill development that can increase local housing options for downsizing located near local neighbourhood centres (Kendig et al, 2014). The 'McFluffy' programme – the compulsory acquisition, demolition, and sale of older homes having dangerous asbestos insulation – could also provide better local housing options, but the emphasis here is on maximising cost recovery. The potential for the actions is constrained severely by ongoing budget pressure in large part due to the costs of the light rail initiative, rising health expenditure, and restrictions in Commonwealth revenue sharing.

Sydney and New South Wales developments

New South Wales (NSW) does not have any WHO AFC cities, but it developed an ambitious NSW Ageing Strategy (NSW Government, 2012a) that shares many of the AFC ideals. The strategy amounts to a whole-of-government, whole-of-community initiative for achieving positive ageing, with the aim of empowering people to lead active, healthy and rewarding lives from mid-age onwards. It focuses on participation, liveable communities, age discrimination, security and dignity. At the launch, the Minister on Ageing stated:

> This is a great opportunity to realise the benefits of an ageing population and to harness the contribution of seniors in our communities. Equally important will be empowering people to plan ahead for the future they envisage in their later years. (NSW Government, 2012a)

The NSW Ageing Strategy was actively led by the newly elected State Minister on Ageing, supported by the Premier and Cabinet. The plan aims to make mainstream government services more responsive to and appropriate for older people. The state government required involvement by the main state departments including Family and Community Services (the lead agency), Housing, Health, Planning and Infrastructure, Local Government, Police and Justice, Treasury, Education and Communities. The departments were charged with making their programmes more responsive to older people by identifying priorities for ageing and reallocating resources to achieve them.

Ongoing implementation of the strategy was to be overseen by a high-level interdepartmental committee of senior departmental representatives and a representative from each of the private sector, the non-government sector, local government and MACA. MACA has representation from diverse communities, academia and the ageing sector. The chair, a recognised community leader, plays a pivotal role in supporting the Minister on Ageing and the strategy. The strategy had envisaged that the Treasury would oversee departments' progress in establishing age-friendly priorities and monitoring progress as part of the annual budget process.

To facilitate joint efforts with partner organisations, the Department of Family and Community Services (FACS) committed $A6.4 million to AFC projects (mid-2012 through 2014) and $A2.1 million to peak advocacy bodies (funding matches by departments were small).

Projects targeting 'behaviour change' included Tackling Abuse, Tech Savvy Seniors, and My Life, My Decision (legal documents on end of life). Additional projects included Linking Seniors to Information (to increase use of a seniors' card); Traveling Safely (a review of the Older Drivers' Licensing Scheme and pilot community transport projects); and 'age-friendly communities' small grants to local councils.

The strategy has also worked to increase the responsiveness to older people in the NSW Long Term Transport Masterplan and the Australian Government's Accessible Transport Standards targets. The Office on Ageing also aimed to influence comparable mainstream plans in other portfolios including a rural housing strategy. An external evaluation was conducted on implementation of the strategy (NSW Government, 2015).

A comprehensive strategy evaluation was conducted in mid-2015 (NSW Government, 2015). 'Highlight projects' were identified on the basis of their importance, the opportunities offered, the existence of a willing partner and their 'supporting actions. Factors found to be important for project implementation included 'a concrete commitment', 'funding', a 'willing partner', and 'strong stakeholder engagement' (NSW Government, 2015, pp 52-3). Some major policy announcements, however (such as those on rural health and social housing), were found to '… not directly address the potential concerns of older people' (p 69). Departments' staff effort and direct outlays on AFC projects was found to be modest. Population awareness of the strategy was found to be reasonable, suggesting at least indirect influence on attitudes to ageing.

The NSW Ageing Strategy had envisaged a central role for Treasury in implementing and monitoring age-related reallocations. However, government attention was quickly diverted to opposing and compensating for Commonwealth funding cuts affecting concessions and other outlays important for older people. Two state intergenerational reports (NSW Government, 2012b, 2016) reviewed the long-term implications of demographic change on the state. The *NSW intergenerational report 2016* (NSW Government, 2016), released just before the national election, projected an increasing fiscal gap over the next 40 years and made a case for strengthening the economy, innovating in the area of service delivery, and creating a more sustainable revenue base.

At an April 2016 Roundtable on Renewal of the NSW Ageing Strategy, convened with the private sector by the Minister on Ageing, the MACA chair urged 'that the discourse move [should] away from the consideration of "age" and instead towards a discussion of "life experience"… people "do not come with a use-by date'". Successful private–public partnerships – with Westpac Bank, Bunnings and Telstra, for example – were presented as valuable initiatives facilitating the continuing contributions of ageing workers and provided business opportunities for the partners in targeting growing markets for older people.

Interpretation and directions

Australia has a sound knowledge base on ageing, but few of the population studies have been designed to investigate the community context in which people are living. A small literature has identified the meanings of home and neighbourhood for older people, and urban influences on their independence and wellbeing. Our review has highlighted exemplar Australian studies that illustrate the important, variable community dimensions of ageing, particularly in their impacts on disadvantaged older people. These Australian findings are largely consistent with the international literature applying 'environmental fit and adaptation' models as underpinnings of the global age-friendly movement and its development as led by WHO (see Kendig and Phillipson, 2014; see also Chapter Two).

The WHO aims for bringing a participatory, bottom-up approach into whole-of-government, multi-sectorial action on ageing across levels of government. While having great potential, this approach has proven to be difficult to achieve in Australia. However, the NSW Ageing Strategy evaluation (NSW Government, 2015) drew on an Australian-based review (Lui et al, 2009) to conceptualise the complexity of age-friendly discourse along dimensions from top-down to bottom-up governance, and in terms of the physical and social environments.

The evaluation (NSW Government, 2015, p 17) also added a conceptual interpretation of the 'whole-of-government' strategy. Following Keast (2011), a dynamic process of 'vertical' power and 'horizontal' stakeholder interactions can be posited as a 'normative' policy cycle (Althaus et al, 2012) in the midst of 'messier' real-world negotiations (Colebatch, 2006). The strategy did have vertical authority through an election commitment, but there was a limited mandate, given that there was no legislative requirement and only limited resources. The evaluation noted that: 'The *Influencer* model [indicates that] identifying a target behaviour of the population (e.g. downsizing, using public transport) provides a focus for activity and some clarity about where effort could usefully be directed' (NSW Government,

2015, p 68, emphasis in original). In the 'messy' world of advocacy and interest groups, a measure of empowerment can be enabled by processes of 'co-design' (Stewart-Weeks, 2014) in which knowledge and responsibility are shared by the 'users' in policy and programme design.

Conclusion

In conclusion, AFCC aspirations have to date achieved modest implementation in a context of bureaucratic and property interests at a time of public austerity. Nevertheless, the AFCC approach has facilitated some innovative services for older people, increased recognition of disadvantaged groups, and contributed to more participation and inclusiveness. Older people and their advocates who have been involved with AFCC developments speak positively of measures increasing empowerment, while principles of 'co-design' are facilitating service innovation. Government collaboration with the private sector is providing some 'win-win' partnerships that strengthen corporate marketing and improve products and services tailored for older people. It is important to emphasise that actions towards making communities 'friendly' for older people are also important for other vulnerable people at other points along the life span, for example, parents with young children and no car who are at home during the day.

The AFCC approach in Australia remains at an early stage of development in terms of broader agendas, especially those aiming to bring ageing into multi-sectorial, whole-of government policy development. Notwithstanding the potential value for broader community interests, there has been little achievement demonstrating the benefits of taking age and the life span into account in mainstream policy areas such as transport, housing and land-use planning. For example, actions increasing local housing options for downsizing by older people also can free large homes for younger families and further urban consolidation. The context of financial stringency does limit many actions, but it also strengthens the case for age-appropriate actions that address priority concerns of older people themselves. The value of AFCC approaches could be recognised further as the baby-boomer generation moves through later life, given their expectations and resources for self-determination in their lives and their communities.

Notes
[1] For information on significant AFC developments elsewhere in Australia, see COTA WA (2016).

² 'Baby boomers' are the large cohort of people who were born between 1945 and 1960 (Gong and Kendig 2016).
³ A comprehensive account of the opportunities and challenges of an ageing Australia – across housing, transportation and health, among other areas – can be found in O'Loughlin et al (2017).

References

ABS (Australian Bureau of Statistics) (2012) *Population projections, Australia, 2012 (base) to 2101*, Canberra: Australian Government.

ABS (2015) *Population by age and sex, Australia, states and territories*, Canberra: Australian Government.

ACSA (Aged and Community Services Australia) (2015) *The future of housing for older Australians*, Canberra: ACSA.

ACT (Australian Capital Territory) Government (2009) *ACT Strategic Plan for Positive Ageing 2010-2014: Towards an Age-Friendly City*, Canberra, Australia: ACT Government, Department of Disability, Housing and Community Services.

ACT Government (2011) *2011 ACT older persons assembly*, Canberra: ACT Government, Department of Community Services.

ACT Government (2012) *ACT Strategic Plan for Positive Ageing: Action Plan 2012-2014*, Canberra: ACT Government, Department of Community Services.

ACT Government (2014) *2014 older persons assembly*, Canberra: ACT Government, Department of Community Services.

ACT Government (2015a) *ACT Active Ageing Framework 2015-2018*, Canberra: ACT Government, Department of Community Services.

ACT Government (2015b) *ACT budget 2015-2016. Budget paper 3: Budget outlook*, Canberra: ACT Government, Department of Treasury.

ACTION Expenditure Review (2015) *Action expenditure review: Final public report*, Canberra: ACT Government, Treasury and Economic Development Directorate.

ACT MACA (Ministerial Advisory Council on Ageing) (2011) *Report on implementation of the ACT Strategic Plan for Positive Ageing*, Canberra: ACT Government, Department of Community Services.

AIHW (Australian Institute of Health and Welfare) (2013) *The desire to age in place among older Australians*, Bulletin 114, Canberra: Australian Government.

ALP (Australian Labor Party) (2016) *Growing together: Labor's agenda for tackling inequality*, Victoria: ALP.

Althaus, C., Bridgman, P. and Davis, G. (2012) *The Australian policy handbook* (5th edn), Sydney: Allen & Unwin.

Australian Local Government Association (2006) *Age-friendly built environments: Opportunities for local government*, Canberra: Australian Local Government Association.

Bentley, R., Jolley, D. and Kavangh, M. (2010) 'Local environments as determinants of walking in Melbourne, Australia', *Social Science & Medicine*, 70(11): 1806-15.

Berry, M. (2007) 'Ageing in space: transport, access and urban form', in A. Borowski, S. Encel and E. Ozanne (eds) *Longevity and social change in Australia*, Sydney: UNSW Press, pp 239-64.

Brasher, K. and Winterton, R. (2016) 'Whose responsibility? Challenges to creating an age-friendly Victoria in the wider Australian policy context', in T. Moulaert and S. Garon (eds) *Age-friendly cities and communities in international comparison. Political lessons, scientific avenues and democratic issues*, New York, NY: Springer, pp 229-45.

CMHR (Centre for Mental Health Research) (2011) *A baseline survey of Canberra as an age-friendly city*, Canberra: Australian National University.

Colebatch, H. (ed) (2006) *Beyond the policy cycle: The policy process in Australia*, Sydney: Allen & Unwin.

COTA (Council of the Ageing) ACT (2016) *A guide to getting around in Canberra: Transport information for older ACT residents*, Canberra: COTA ACT.

COTA Australia (2016) *COTA Australia policy alert: Federal budget 2016*, Canberra: COTA Australia.

COTA Western Australia (WA) (2016) 'Age-friendly communities network', available at www.cotawa.org.au/programs-projects/age-friendly-communities-network.

Dannefer, D. and Kelly-Moore, J.A. (2009) 'Theorizing the life course: new twists in the paths', in V. Bengston, D. Gans, N.M. Putney and M. Silverstein (eds) *Handbook of theories of aging*, New York, NY: Springer, pp 389-412.

de Jonge, D.M., Jones, A., Phillips, R. and Chung, M. (2011) 'Understanding the essence of home: older people's experience of home in Australia', *Occupational Therapy International*, 18(1): 39-47.

DoHA (Department of Health and Ageing) (2012) *Living Longer, Living Better*, Canberra: DoHA.

Engels, B. and Liu, G. (2013) 'Ageing in place: the out-of-home travel patterns of seniors in Victoria and its policy implications', *Urban Policy & Research*, 31(2): 168-89.

Faulkner, D. (2017) 'Housing and the environments of ageing', in K. O'Loughlin, C. Browning and H. Kendig (eds) *Ageing in Australia: Challenges and opportunities*, New York, NY Springer, pp 173-91.

Gong, C. and Kendig, H. (2016) 'Ageing and social change in Australia', in H. Kendig, P. McDonald and J. Piggott (eds) *Population ageing and Australia's future*, Canberra: ANU Press for the Academy of Social Sciences in Australia, pp 19-45.

Gong, C., Kendig, H., Harding, A. Miranti, R. and McNamara, J. (2014) 'Economic advantage and disadvantage among older Australians: producing national and small area profiles', *Australasian Journal of Regional Studies*, 20(3): 512-39.

Horner, B.J. and Boldy, D.P. (2008) 'The benefits and burdens of "Ageing in place" in an aged care community', *Australian Health Review*, 32(2): 356-65.

Hulse, K. and Pinnegar, S. (2015) *Housing markets and socio-spatial disadvantage: An Australian perspective*, Melbourne: AHURI.

Hulse, K., Pawson, H., Reynolds, M. and Herath, S. (2014) *Disadvantaged places in urban Australia: Analysing socio-economic diversity and housing market performance*, Melbourne: AHURI.

Jeon, Y.H. and Kendig, H. (2017) 'Care and support for older people', in K. O'Loughlin, C. Browning and H. Kendig (eds) *Ageing in Australia: Challenges and opportunities*, New York, NY: Springer, pp 239–59.

Judd, B., Liu, E., Easthope, H., Davy, L. and Bridge C. (2014) *Downsizing amongst older Australians, Final Report No. 214*, Melbourne: AHURI.

Keast, R. (2011) 'Joined-up governance in Australia: how the past can inform the future', *International Journal of Public Administration*, 34(4): 221-331.

Kendig, H. (2017) 'Directions and choices on ageing for the future', in K. O'Loughlin, C. Browning and H. Kendig (eds) *Ageing in Australia: Challenges and opportunities*, New York, NY: Springer, pp 263-79.

Kendig, H. and Phillipson, C. (2014) 'Building age friendly cities: new approaches and evidence', in N. Denison and L. Newby (eds) *If you could do one thing... Nine local actions to reduce health inequalities*, London: British Academy, pp 102-11.

Kendig, H., Clemson, L. and Mackenzie, L. (2012) 'Older people: well-being, housing and neighbourhoods', in S.J. Smith, M. Elsinga, L. Fox O'Mahony, O.S. Eng, S. Wachter and C. Hamnett (eds) *International encyclopedia of housing & home, vol 5*, Oxford: Elsevier, pp 150-5.

Kendig, H., Elias, A.M., Matwijiw, P. and Anstey, K. (2014) 'Developing age-friendly cities and communities in Australia', *Journal of Aging & Health*, 26(8): 1390-414.

Kendig, H., Wells, Y., O'Loughlin, K. and Heese, K. (2013) 'Australian baby boomers face retirement during the global financial crisis', *Journal of Aging & Social Policy*, 25(3): 264-80.

Lui, C.-W., Everingham, J.-A., Warburton, J., Cuthill, M. and Bartlett, H. (2009) 'What makes a community age-friendly: a review of international literature', *Australasian Journal on Ageing*, 28(3): 116-21.

Mackenzie, L., Curryer, C. and Byles, J. (2015) 'Narratives of home and place: findings from the Housing and Independent Living Study', *Ageing & Society*, 35(8): 1684-712.

New South Wales (NSW) Government (2012a) *NSW Ageing Strategy*, Sydney: NSW Government, Department of Family and Community Services.

NSW Government (2012b) *NSW long-term fiscal pressures report: NSW intergenerational report, 2011-2012. Budget paper no. 6*, Sydney: NSW Government, Department of Treasury.

NSW Government (2015) *Evaluation of the NSW Ageing Strategy*, Sydney: NSW Government, Department of Family and Community Services.

NSW Government (2016) *NSW intergenerational report 2016-2017: Future state NSW in 2056*, Sydney: NSW Government, Department of Treasury.

O'Loughlin, K., Browning C. and Kendig, H. (eds) (2017) *Ageing in Australia: Challenges and opportunities*, New York, NY: Springer.

Ozanne, E., Biggs, S. and Kurowski, W. (2014) 'Competing frameworks in planning for the aged in the growth corridors of Melbourne', *Journal of Aging & Social Policy*, 26(1-2): 147-65.

Pearson, E., Windsor, T., Crisp, D.A., Butterworth, P. and Anstey, K.J. (2012) *Neighbourhood characteristics and ageing well: A survey of older Australian adults*, NSPAC Research Monograph 2, Canberra: National Seniors Productive Ageing Centre.

Per Capita (2014) 'Blueprint for an ageing Australia', available at https://percapita.org.au/wp-content/uploads/2014/11/BlueprintForAnAgeingAustralia.pdf.

Productivity Commission (2011) *Caring for older Australians: Overview*, Report No 53, Canberra: Australia Government, available at www.pc.gov.au/inquiries/completed/aged-care/report/aged-care-overview-booklet.pdf.

Quine, S., Kendig, H., Russell, C. and Touchard, D. (2004) 'Health promotion for socially disadvantaged groups: the case of homeless older men in Australia', *Health Promotion International*, 19(2): 157-65.

Stewart-Weeks, M. (2014) 'Two cheers ... for co-design and co-production', *Public Administration Today*, 38(April): 6-11.

Stones, D. and Gullifer, J. (2016) '"At home it's just so much easier to be yourself": older adults' perceptions of ageing in place', *Ageing & Society*, 36(3): 449-81.

Tanton, R., Vidyattama, Y. and Miranti, R. (2016) *Small area Indicators of Wellbeing for Older Australians (IWOA)*, Canberra: NATSEM University of Canberra.

Terrill, M., Emslie, O. and Coates, B. (2016) *Roads to riches: Better transport investment*, Melbourne: Grattan Institute.

Victoria Government (2002) *Melbourne 2030: Planning for sustainable growth*, Melbourne: Victoria Government, Department of Environment, Land, Water and Planning.

Victoria Government (2014) *Plan Melbourne metropolitan planning strategy*, Melbourne: Victoria Government, Department of Environment, Land, Water and Planning.

WHO (World Health Organization) (2007) *Global age-friendly cities: A guide*, Geneva: WHO.

WHO (2015) *World report on ageing and health*, Geneva: WHO. Woods, M. and Kendig, H. (2015) 'Intergenerational report 2015: A limited and political view of our future', *Australasian Journal on Ageing*, 34(4): 217-19.

Part 3
Age-friendly policies, urban design and a manifesto for change

TEN

From representation to active ageing in a Manchester neighbourhood: designing the age-friendly city

Stefan White and Mark Hammond

Introduction

This chapter explores what it means to use a 'capability' approach to designing an age-friendly city and its potential for developing physical and social environments that respond directly to the lived experiences of older people. Drawing on an interdisciplinary collaborative research/ design project that has informed the development of Manchester's age-friendly cities and communities (AFCC) programme, it describes a community-engaged, urban design research project conducted in the Old Moat area of the city in 2012. The project's aim was to explore the applicability of AFCC design guidance within a specific urban neighbourhood. The chapter focuses on the dynamic relationship between the research and design elements of the project. It examines how the process of discovering and sharing information about the lived experience of older people translates into the development and implementation of age-friendly activities and interventions intended to make a neighbourhood more appropriate to the needs and desires of its older residents.

Capability, design and active ageing

In urban studies, 'capability' models offer new ways of understanding and engaging with the relationship between cities and the individuals and groups within them (Nussbaum, 2011). They focus on the *abilities* of individuals to influence the wider world around them rather than identifying or representing 'users' of the city according to general categories such as disability, race, gender or age. Capability models are at the root of critiques regarding normative, 'universal' or 'inclusive' design approaches to disability and age (Boys, 2016). Such models are central to current conceptions of cities and citizenship in urban studies (Robinson, 2011) and architecture (Rawes, 2013). Moreover, they offer, as this chapter argues, a valuable way of rethinking approaches to age-friendly design. A capability perspective does not consider 'the city' either generally or abstractly 'age-friendly'. Instead, it argues that specific groups of older people in the particular places that they live must not only actually experience a city to be age-friendly but must be **actively instrumental in making this the case**.

In this way, a positive, 'capability' reading of age-friendliness (the distinctive and central feature of the research/design project discussed in this chapter) places the World Health Organization (WHO) concept of 'active ageing' at the centre of the relationship between research and design activity, the local community and its older residents (see Chapter Two). Here, as the WHO concept of active ageing suggests, the potential of age-friendliness becomes defined by the **ability** of older people to **influence** and **control**, individually and collectively, the impact of the eight age-friendly domains on their experience of living in the city (see also Chapters Two and Eleven).

Capability in an age-friendly Manchester: the case of Old Moat

In 2012, Southway Housing Trust (a community-based housing provider and social enterprise that owns and manages half of the stock in the area) commissioned the Age-Friendly Old Moat[1] project in partnership with Manchester City Council's Age-Friendly Manchester (AFM) programme. Led by the PHASE Place-Health Research Group at the Manchester School of Architecture and the Manchester Institute for Collaborative Research on Ageing, the project formed part of a broader programme of work undertaken by groups working together with the local authority to align the AFM Ageing Strategy with 'citizenship' or 'capability' conceptions of ageing (Hammond et al, 2012; see also Chapter Twelve).[2] Following conceptual principles and practical design guidance of the WHO AFCC programme, the basic remit of the project was to work with the local community to make the Old Moat neighbourhood more age-friendly. Its two main objectives were, first – via research – to discover what makes the area age-friendly (or not) and how to make it more age-friendly; and, second – via design – to instigate actions and processes to make it more age-friendly.

By using expertise from architecture, urban design, sociology, gerontology and community development, the Age-Friendly Old

Moat project examined both the social and physical aspects of the neighbourhood, and adopted a capability approach to thinking about the design and development of age-friendly neighbourhoods. Its interdisciplinary research and design team took a multi-faceted approach to community-engaged urban design research in order to explore the dynamic interaction between the social and physical determinants of age-friendliness across the WHO domains (see Chapter Two). Crucially, this approach worked to enable the development of interventions that would increase active ageing, improve individual experiences of age-friendliness and improve resident involvement in decision making in the neighbourhood – in an area previously without an enduring, constituted group of residents or tenants of any age.

A central part of the capability approach involved the co-creation of a neighbourhood 'action plan' together with both residents and institutional stakeholders; increasing resident participation in the project; and improving engagement between residents and city stakeholders (such as transport and service providers). The development of an action plan enabled the project team to not only gather information about older residents' lived experiences of the various WHO domains of age-friendliness, but also stimulated a collective debate about the translation of such findings into practical proposals for interventions. In this way, rather than adopting a conventional process of 'consultation', the co-production of the action plan enabled older residents of Old Moat to be active in designing a programme of improvements that responded to their actual experiences of the neighbourhood. A range of resident activities, instigated during the project, continue at the time of writing, and the capability methodologies are now being tested on a larger scale elsewhere in Greater Manchester. The relationship between the capability model, the WHO age-friendly city principles, and work in the Old Moat neighbourhood is summarised in Table 10.1.

Table 10.1: Relation between three kinds or levels of relationship developed in the Old Moat project

Old Moat project relationships	Manchester City Council Ageing Strategy categories	General models of difference	WHO guidance
Active Older residents determining the positioning of benches through the active cultural appropriation of these territories	**Citizenship** For example: Neighbourhood and city Social capital and participation Age-proofing Reducing exclusion Changing attitudes	**Capability** Relation between city and individual seen as constituting the nature of the city as it is experienced and its capacity as a body	**Active ageing** The WHO Age-Friendly City diagram of the determinants of active ageing lists social, economic, behavioural, personal and physical factors within a wider context of culture and gender (WHO, 2007, Figure 3)
Involved Insights into older residents' lived experience is shared and communicated with a range of stakeholders, affecting understanding and decision making	**Care** For example: Customer Networks Care Vulnerable Prevention of care provision	**Social** Individual is seen as part of a network or community where multiple kinds of relations to others are seen to interact to influence an individual's ability to perform both social and physical functions (not just the relationship between their body and the physical environment)	**Age-friendly city** The WHO Age-Friendly City topic areas that are determinants of how well an individual ages are represented as eight petals making up a flower at the centre of which is the individual experience of an Age-Friendly City (WHO, 2007, Figure 6)
Represented Older residents are more or less consulted through a reductive process that then 'stands in' for any further involvement	**Medical** For example: Patient Individual Clinical 'Frail' Prevention of hospital entry Health	**Environmental** The relationship between the physical dimensions of a body and the physical environment are seen as primary factors for deciding on or locating 'interventions' designed to improve the experience of the general population of people understood to belong in specific, assigned categories	**Disability threshold** The WHO guidance explains how changes to the physical environment can lower the threshold at which it becomes inaccessible, especially as people grow older (WHO, 2007, Figure 4)

Research and design: from representation to involvement to activity

Building on key principles around active ageing and co-production, the project presented here defines 'age-friendliness' as both a **collaborative** and a **spatial** enterprise. This means that the ambition to produce urban conditions, amenable to a diverse ageing population, requires the development of highly collaborative, cross-disciplinary approaches that build on the active participation of different groups of older people. Moreover, to ensure that these various relationships are sufficiently focused to propose effective interventions, a spatial understanding of the locality is also needed. For example, while transport is a city-wide issue that appears to be central to making cities accessible and age-friendly, everyone is affected differently, depending on the journeys they desire and are able to make between their private home, their neighbourhood and the activities available to them.

This chapter revisits the Old Moat project and describes the way in which the programme was able to evolve a **capability approach to age-friendly design** as the project moved, first, from processes of **representation** (drawing on the experiences of local residents) to, second, processes of **involvement** (actively involving older people in the existing structures of decision-making in the area) and, third, **activity** (enabling, in certain instances, older residents to actively determine the emerging character of their own neighbourhood).

Each of the subsequent three sections describes the project via its distinctive research and design perspectives. These two distinct perspectives are made explicit in order to demonstrate how a capability approach to developing age-friendly neighbourhoods implies a parallel, situated development of both knowledge (**research**) and action (**design**).

Beyond representation

From a research perspective, this section argues that architects' and urban designers' reliance on untested representations in the use of urban space (representations developed independently of the actual lived experiences of its residents) can create misleading assumptions that may frustrate neighbourhood-based interventions. To illustrate this, from a design perspective, the chapter takes one intervention (that attempted to transform the use of a particular site in the Old Moat estate – the 'gateway') to show how such interventions may not necessarily respond to older residents' lived experiences.

Representation and research

As observed above, the 'city' is traditionally represented by architects and urbanists through what can be defined as a 'top-down' processes (see Figure 10.1). A typical urban design approach might begin by examining maps of an area in terms of certain components such as 'routes' or 'landmarks', identifying 'key' features of the environment that affect the users of the city. This kind of analysis, however, is usually undertaken independently of any real exploration of the lived experiences of the residents, or those frequently present, in the neighbourhood. While such processes can be highly instructive, this method predominantly understands the relationships between, for example, housing, services and infrastructure based on an *imagined* (by the designer) rather than an actual experience of the area.

In contrast, and following critiques by Boys (2016) and Lawton (Regnier, 1983), the Old Moat project team attempted to develop a more explicit and socially 'involved' approach that focused on how *citizens*, as opposed to professionals, might interpret their relationship with the environment, both in physical as well as in social terms (White, 2017; see also Chapters Eleven and Twelve).

Following Petrescu (2009), de Certeau (1984) and Robinson (2011), a 'neighbourhood', in this project, is not simply defined as an area on a map, but rather as a territory that can only be produced by those who

Figure 10.1: Old Moat 'Movement Hierarchy' map following the format of the 'Image of the city'

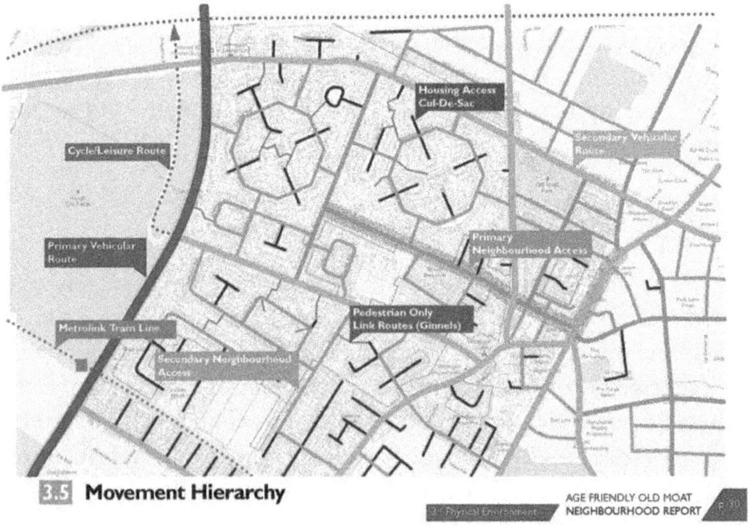

Source: Hammond et al (2012).

live there, relative to the capabilities they have to 'produce' that territory. In this respect, the Old Moat approach examines the 'neighbourhood' as the practical involvement of individual capabilities and desires to access and contribute to the resources of the city, rather than as an abstract representation imagined by designers.

While the Old Moat research project started with a typical, formal, desktop analysis of the physical urban environment, this methodology was only used as a starting point from which to begin engagement with residents. The initial desktop analysis followed a traditional representational 'image of the city' methodology, which understands the legibility of urban environments by identifying a hierarchy of nodes, boundaries, routes, districts and landmarks (Lynch, 1960). There was a specific assumption made, however, while undertaking this work, that older residents living in Old Moat would travel to Manchester city centre for services, rather than using the smaller, less well-resourced local shopping precinct. This appeared to be a sensible assumption to make at the time, given that the city centre was served by frequent bus routes and was only a short distance away. However, through various engagements and interviews, it became clear that the actual city experienced by older residents of Old Moat was at least, partially, created or defined by their own personal relationship with transport services, location and their desire to meet with others. Indeed, local older people tended to travel to district centres in surrounding towns rather than into Manchester city centre. Figure 10.2 shows the

Figure 10.2: Primary transport use for older residents in Old Moat assumed through formal analysis (left) and actual reported transport use

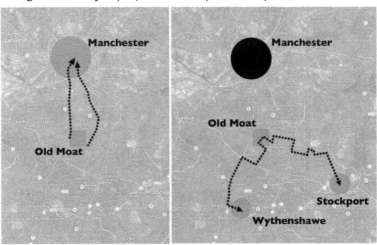

Source: Hammond et al (2012).

difference between the project's initial assumptions and the key features of the actual reported transport use. This changing understanding of the city space in turn changed the project's design responses.

Representation and design

Shortly before the Old Moat project began, Southway Housing Trust had identified a street corner within Old Moat (shown in Figure 10.3) as an important intersection in the neighbourhood. It was described as a 'gateway' to the local estate and had been made subject to a series of environmental improvements. The focus of these landscaping works had been on creating a generally improved perception of the physical environment of the gateway, rather than directly attempting to create a space that would be used by groups of people. This intervention was prompted by reasonable (representational) presumptions about the area, in particular a need for benches and a desire to make it feel less 'run down'. These desires and needs were then allied to a programme of 'consultation'.

Figure 10.3: Photograph of 'gateway' with insert map showing it as a junction of 'access' and 'primary' routes, and inset diagram showing placing of concrete capping

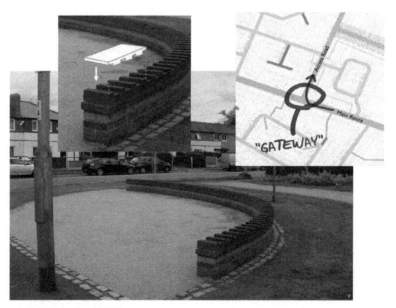

Source: Hammond et al (2012).

Although the WHO AFCC checklist of essential features of Age-Friendly Cities (WHO, 2007a) identifies the provision of benches as a key urban design resource for age-friendly cities, many older people (along with other residents) voted against the provision of benches through the consultation process, fearing that they might attract antisocial behaviour.[3] The response to the consultation was, therefore, to remove benches from the proposal and change the design of the gateway to low walls specifically designed to discourage sitting. In this instance, traditional consultation restricted the involvement of older residents to the limited power and ability to reject proposals made on their behalf, even though those proposals did not necessarily respond to their actual lived experience. To broaden the discussion, it would be worth noting that many local public spaces in Manchester and all around the UK have seen benches removed due to concerns about antisocial behaviour or simply lost through the privatisation of public spaces. While the WHO AFCC guidance recognises the involvement of wider issues such as maintenance and security in the age-friendly nature of a bench, design is not typically assumed to have a role in enabling the creation of situations where actual benches can come to be used in actual neighbourhoods (see further below).

Involving older people in locality research and design

The key argument developed in this section is that a capability approach to understanding the age-friendliness of a neighbourhood requires the development of collaborative working. From the research perspective, it describes how the project moved to a more participatory, involved approach, using a range of spatial and co-production methodologies to explore the different WHO age-friendly domains (see Chapter Two). From the design perspective, this section returns to the gateway site, and describes how older residents came to take ownership of a space that they had previously rejected. Furthermore, it shows how, through the project's involved approach with older residents, the representational understanding of the use of public spaces in the neighbourhood was not just revised; rather, it was reversed.

Involved research

Although the WHO AFCC guidance lists the eight age-friendly domains as interrelated factors affecting the relative age-friendliness of a city, each of these determining factors represented by each of the eight domains are generally assumed to be related to the work of individual disciplines. This was apparent within the Old Moat project, where there was, at least initially, a common assumption among the various stakeholders (from planning, transport to public health executives), that architects and urban designers primarily address the domains of housing, and outdoor space and buildings' (see also Chapter Eleven).

To ensure that the project did not limit the discussion of what enables or prevents age-friendliness and active ageing to purely physical or medical needs, however, the project worked explicitly and simultaneously across several of the WHO AFCC domains. This information from each of the domains was then synthesised geographically. This enabled the project to consider the interaction between all aspects of the research (physical environment, statistical, interpersonal and survey data) in the context of the specific urban environment within which it is located. Figure 10.4, for instance, shows how specific issues arising from interpersonal and spatial data sources were recorded on a map dedicated to the domains of outdoor space and buildings, and social participation, for example. This exercise was also undertaken for the other domains.

Figure 10.4: Drawing showing separate recording of issues related to the domains of outdoor space and buildings, and social participation, which are integrated into the action plan

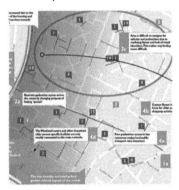 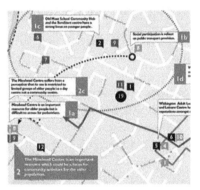

Outdoor Space and Building   Social Participation

Source: Hammond et al (2012).

This process of combining different types of research information was a key feature of the project's research report and its methodological toolkit. It featured in project presentations to stakeholder groups as well as in the project's final executive summary report (Hammond et al, 2012). In this report it is possible to see how the project is broken down into a range of different research approaches that were summarised both in terms of each of the studied domains and in terms of an integrated action plan map addressing all of the domains.

The project used a range of different research techniques from analysing the physical environment using spatial analysis, to conducting interpersonal research. First, analysis of the physical environment involved a survey of the area with plans and sections drawn for every road type; these were presented alongside photographs and house-type plans to record the character of the physical environment in different parts of the neighbourhood. This allowed for the recorded information to be related at a later stage to the lived experiences of older residents. It also allowed for analysis of different types of public space and non-residential buildings in the area to be recorded in an asset-mapping analysis. This provided a spatially located activity schedule: a vital baseline document for discussions about the role that these locations played in the lived experiences of residents and service providers, recording events and issues as well as contact and access information.

Second, interpersonal research within the project took a variety of forms, including street market stalls, organised workshops, focus groups, peer-to-peer interviews and 'participation diaries'. Each of these sources was analysed to identify specific issues related to the various domains. For example, through the medium of structured interviews, questions were asked about transportation, how people moved around the area, where they were going and what activities they undertook (and with whom). These answers were then related back to the domains of transport, outdoor space and buildings, social participation, and communication. Where answers were relevant to multiple domains, they were recorded under each. Where possible, issues were related to precise places and then located on a 'domain map' – a map specific to each age-friendly domain. These domain maps also recorded key issues discovered through spatial data analysis. This involved, for instance, presenting census data to show the location of the poorest, oldest and least mobile older residents relative to the assets identified in the outdoor space and buildings domain. The transport domain map explored this in terms of existing transport provision, while the social participation map recorded issues in relation to the same locations from the perspective of social activities.

Each of these maps identified all the issues, or determining factors of relative age-friendliness, relevant to a specific domain. These maps were subsequently brought together into a larger, community-owned action plan as a co-produced product of a longer process of analysis that had taken place through a range of stakeholder workshops. To facilitate these workshops, the domain information was presented in a manner that kept the project's analytical assumptions and findings as explicit and accessible as possible. This enabled them to be analysed both at the time and later by all stakeholders. In this way, each domain map identified key issues both in relation to the places where these issues were found to occur and in relation to any related evidence from the spatial data, interpersonal research or physical environment analysis. Each of the key issues recorded on each domain page were interrogated in terms of evidence supporting its inclusion, possible precedents for dealing with it, the impacts reported or observed and then, finally, actions to be considered in response were suggested for discussion (see, further, Hammond et al, 2012).

This approach was a deliberate attempt to retain a decision-making trail so that in the future actions could be evaluated against a specific issue and in relation to evidence identified for a particular intervention. Moreover, the spatially located domain analysis and action plan were tested and developed together with residents and other stakeholders through workshops where emerging themes on the key issues for each of the domains were discussed and agreed, possible responses explored, and, finally, sets of actual actions jointly agreed and prioritised.

This process enabled us to synthesise the analysis across and between domains, exploring the lived experience of different groups of older people relevant to an identified place. It was through this process that the project – via geographical analysis of census data – found that the socioeconomic distribution of residents in the area had led to an increase in numbers of the poorest, least mobile and oldest residents living in the most remote part of the estate. Similarly, it was through this process that the project discovered that physical boundaries on the sides of the neighbourhood – a major road next to a non-residential area and the local district centre at its eastern edge – led to a mono-directional access for services. Findings from the focus groups and walking interviews further suggested that local older people tended to travel to larger district centres in surrounding towns rather than into Manchester city centre.

Taken together, these findings challenged the project's earlier formal, representational assumptions about the relationship between the urban form of the area and the use of the transport infrastructure by residents. With this multi-faceted, interlocking approach, the project team gained insights into the complex reasons for this unexpected behaviour to create positive, collaborative, responses.

Involved design

Following the completion of environmental improvements to the gateway of Old Moat, Southway Housing Trust started to recognise that despite rejecting proposals for the installation of benches, older people in the area continued to gather at the gateway, which served as a popular stopping place for the 179 bus service. Although this service had been designed to enable the bus to stop whenever requested along its route, older residents were responding to the process of readying and waiting by gathering in particular locations. At the gateway site, people were using the walls as seats while waiting for the bus. Subsequently, in order to facilitate the informal use of these walls as seats (see Figure 10.3), the housing association arranged for a flat concrete cap to be placed over a section of castellations on the wall. These castellations (teeth-like protrusions made of brick) had previously been introduced to prevent people from sitting on the walls in the first place. Southway's continued involvement with the residents enabled it to avoid making assumptions through an abstract representation of a situation. Instead, it was now able to respond directly to evidence of the actual spatial practices of residents.

Active research and design

This section shows how the project attempted to go beyond representation and involvement to create an active increase in the capabilities of older people within the neighbourhood. A key feature of an active relationship is that older residents act to produce both knowledge of what makes an area age-(un)friendly as well as what might make it more age-friendly, acting to design and implement actions to achieve those aims. From the research perspective, the co-production of an action plan with proposals for interventions that are specific, co-produced and spatialised is discussed. From the design perspective, it demonstrates how spaces like the gateway site, which had previously been informally claimed by older people, can become actively produced and formally occupied by the older community.

Active research

The interpersonal research and the urban design analysis revealed that the 179 bus service was viewed as a vital part of the urban 'form' of the area, influencing subsequent proposals for physical improvements discussed at the workshop events. In the first instance, the service was considered important because it intersected the estate, travelling through it, rather than along its boundaries (like the more frequent bus routes into the city centre). Moreover, the project uncovered several unexpected features of the service that might be understood as enabling active ageing. Despite, for instance, being a 'hail-and-ride' service with no designated bus stops to be found along its route, residents, nevertheless, created informal 'nodes' where they were able to congregate to wait for the bus together. The bus, which only runs hourly, has been shown, in this way, to have taken on a facilitating social role because of its active and regular use by a familiar social group. In this sense, residents can be seen to have independently and creatively produced both the bus and the gathering spaces as social territories.

Active design

The gateway, where older residents had previously rejected the provision of benches before the project started, has, along with a series of other spaces along the 179 route and the main pathway into the nearest district centre, now been populated with age-friendly benches – benches that were previously seen as impossible objects in these 'unpossessed' spaces. In four other gateway sites along the route of the 179 (also used by older residents as gathering spaces), 'pocket parks' and benches have been introduced to decentralise public green spaces that are currently relatively inaccessible, as part of a broader range of suggested actions in the final action plan. Other actions have also been related to this route. The pedestrian route leading into the closest district centre has been prioritised and signposted to support further social interaction and increased mobility. These actions are part of a wide range of measures suggested across the different domains, with over 50 of 114 original items having been implemented (or in the process of being so) at the time of writing.

Active research and design

Understanding the way in which the gateway space had been appropriated by the older residents of Old Moat enabled the project to develop a co-produced action plan that sustained its meaning and relevance over time. The relatively responsive (on the part of the institutional partners) and the relatively passive interaction of the residents with city institutions in the neighbourhood around the use of the gateway space (the residents had made the spaces for waiting indirectly and not in active collaboration with the city) became more active as it became more equal. The active engagement of the older residents increased as the process undertaken by Southway Housing Trust became more collaborative. This enabled older residents and Southway Housing Trust to produce shared understandings both of what was needed (in the abstract) and what should actually be done. At the outset of the process, residents were asked to volunteer as community auditors, alongside a separate group of project champions, with members drawn from institutional bodies, service providers and politicians. By the end of the project, the action plan workshop meetings were attended by a much broader range of stakeholders and residents, making decisions together on the type and order of priority of actions to be pursued.

The example of the gateway and the age-friendly bench is important in terms of the actual potential of older residents to actively inhabit and occupy the neighbourhood. The active status of older residents is here, at least, not just a matter of participation (civic or social) but also a factor of occupation. Bus stops are used and seen as meeting and resting places, while buses become opportunities for social congregations to emerge as creative responses to existing transport and public space provision. The formal recognition of the importance of the 179 bus service as a key route for older people (in a process in which they were themselves stakeholders) led to public space projects that responded directly to the actual lived experiences of these older residents.

A series of public spaces along the route of the 179 bus (that coincided with the main pedestrian route through the estate and that led to the area of the district centre most used by older residents) were now viewed as potential resting and socialising places. These formerly static spaces were now seen as linked to the mobile social space of the bus service. Until the Old Moat residents expressed both their civic and social involvement in relation to their locality, using these spaces for these purposes had previously not been seen as possible in these terms. The development of these two kinds of community space (mobile and static) might be viewed as an example of the active production or occupation of city spaces by older residents specific to their neighbourhood and particular lived experiences. Being able to produce such formal expressions of territorial rights or claims can be considered an essential act that constitutes older people as *citizens* rather than as customers or patients. Several older people have remained involved across a range of projects and groups in the area, and while there are a variety of reasons for this (not least the continued commitment and energy of Southway Housing Trust), there is evidence that the neighbourhood space as a whole is being produced through the active involvement of older people.

Conclusion

The Age-Friendly Old Moat project offers some preliminary evidence that the parallel processes of community-led research and design can enable the creation of new places or territories for older residents to occupy, and in so doing, support the development of genuinely age-friendly neighbourhoods that increase opportunities for active ageing. This particular analysis suggests that the bar for the definition of active ageing should be set high.

The active involvement of residents in an area arguably produces an increase in capability that enables the creative self-definition or production of places or territories. In the gateway example, discussed in this chapter, this means that spaces that could previously only be occupied informally by older people (through the act of gathering together in one place) are now formally claimed (by a physical bench, formalised with the embedded logo of an age-friendly flower and constituted via a formalised relationship with relevant city institutions). In such cases, the age-friendly design 'problem' is not a problem that relates to the supply of benches, nor even their form or location. The actual age-friendly issue here is the capability of older people to influence the types of seating provided; to gain the opportunity to use them; and to express sufficient ownership over the city spaces in which they exist in order to have them maintained and protected.

Without an explicit conceptualisation of age-friendly design in the WHO AFCC guidance as a practice founded on the development of capabilities for active ageing, there remains an underlying assumption that representational or medical models of design activities still apply as the basic principles of age-friendly design. This implies in turn that social interaction and community participation are seen as independent of both built spaces and age-friendly design practice. There is a need, therefore, to extend the WHO ambition for age-friendly social policy into the realm of age-friendly design so that the essential process of resident engagement in both understanding and producing age-friendly cities is not ignored.

In this way, following the AFCC recommendations for social policy, age-friendly design should also be considered as a 'bottom-up participatory process [involving] older people in analysing and expressing their situation to inform government policies' (WHO, 2007, p 7). By considering the social and physical dimensions of the

Old Moat area in terms of older people's actual capability to analyse and express their situation, it is possible to see the way in which older residents, both through the research and design processes, have been empowered to produce and occupy physical and social environments that are able to respond to their ageing experiences. Active, in this sense, may be most productively understood as the multi-faceted capability to produce, control and occupy urban spaces.

Notes

[1] Old Moat is a politically defined area (electoral ward) of Manchester city. The area has around 14,000 people with about 13% of its population over 55 years old. While this is well below the Manchester average (circa 20%), a large student/younger population, concentrated around the district centre on the eastern edge, leads to much higher percentages of older people to the west, reaching 40% in some parts. In UK terms, residents in this area experience high levels of deprivation and life-limiting illnesses as well as low life expectancy.

[2] This work represents one of a series of projects undertaken at the Manchester School of Architecture that address spatial inclusion, in part through the pedagogy of its postgraduate architecture programme (White, 2014). The PHASE Place-Health research group has, over a 10-year period, used community-engaged architectural research techniques, and has developed partnerships with city stakeholders alongside direct engagement with local residents to explore the role of space and place in public health.

[3] Anti-social behaviour 'fears' variously involve these spaces being occupied by people who locate themselves there to drink alcohol and who may be homeless, or younger people who may congregate for informal social activities involving noise or damage, such as writing graffiti or skateboarding.

References

Boys, J. (2016) *Doing disability differently: An alternative handbook on architecture, dis/ability and designing for everyday life*, London: Routledge.

de Certeau, M. (1984) *The practice of everyday life*, Berkeley, CA: University of California Press.

Hammond, M., Phillipson, C. and White, S. (2012) *Old Moat: Age-friendly neighbourhood report*, Manchester: Southway Housing Trust, available at https://issuu.com/stefanwhite/docs/oldmoat_130301_neighbourhood_report.

Lynch, K. (1960) *The image of the city*, Cambridge, MA: MIT Press.

Nussbaum, C.M. (2011) *Creating capabilities: The human development approach*, London: Harvard University Press.

Petrescu, D. (2009) 'How to make a community as well as the space for it', available at http://seminaire.samizdat.net/IMG/pdf/Doina_Petrescu_.pdf.

Rawes, P. (ed) (2013) *Relational architectural ecologies: Architecture, nature and subjectivity*, London: Routledge.

Regnier, V. (1983) 'Urban neighbourhood cognition: relationships between functional and symbolic community elements', in R. Ohta and G. Rowles (eds) *Aging and milieu: Environmental perspectives on growing old*, New York, NY: Academic Press, pp 63-82.

Robinson, J. (2011) 'Cities in a world of cities: the comparative gesture', *International Journal of Urban and Regional Research*, 35(1): 1-23.

White, S. (2014) 'Gilles Deleuze and the project of architecture: An expressionist design-research methodology', PhD thesis, British Library.

White, S. (2017) 'Including architecture: what difference can we make?', in J. Boys (ed) *Disability, space, architecture: A reader*, London: Routledge.

World Health Organization (WHO) (2007) *Global age-friendly cities*, Geneva: WHO.

WHO (2007a) *Checklist of Essential Features of Age-friendly Cities*, Geneva: WHO.

ELEVEN

Alternative age-friendly initiatives: redefining age-friendly design

Sophie Handler

Introduction

This chapter challenges a general reluctance within the design world to engage both with the subject of ageing generally and in work to develop age-friendly environments. It identifies new and creative ways in which architects, artists and designers might be drawn into debates around age-friendly urban practice and suggests that by bringing an emerging scene of socially engaged designers into the framework of age-friendly policy, it becomes possible to both enrich current thinking and practice on age-friendly cities.

The past three years have seen increased interest in design and engineering in the dynamics of ageing and urbanisation, and the different ways in which the profession might respond to demographic trends within cities. Institutions such as the Royal Institute of British Architects (RIBA) and Arup (the global engineering firm) have started to respond to the changing demographic environment of cities, using workshops, seminars and reports to initiate a debate on their role in the creation of age-inclusive spaces. In 2013, the RIBA published its *Silver linings* report based on a series of roundtable discussions that sought to generate a series of design scenarios for the next generation of city dwelling 'third agers' (RIBA, 2013). In 2015, Arup, through its research arm, started to explore its own scenarios around urban ageing and the way in which cities are shaping the experience of growing old (Arup, 2015).

These institutional initiatives can, in some ways, be seen to run parallel to the age-friendly policy initiatives of the World Health Organization (WHO), drawing on the momentum that the field of age-friendly discussion and debate has been able to create through the WHO Global Network for Age-Friendly Cities and Communities (see Chapter Two). But, for the most part, the discourse and discussion on ageing and urbanisation within the design world has tended to stand apart from the language and thinking of age-friendly policy. It is a paradox that while policy-led discussion on age-friendly cities often focuses on issues to do with design (what cities might do to create environments that are more 'age-friendly'), within the design world itself, engagement with the idea of age-friendliness remains limited. This is particularly apparent among socially engaged design practitioners reluctant to engage with debates around population ageing and urbanisation, even as, ostensibly, these are the practitioners best placed to engage with the social policy debates around the construction of age-friendly cities (Handler, 2014).

This chapter explores how emerging definitions of age-friendly design have the potential to draw designers into a more creative engagement with current practice and debate around the construction of age-friendly cities. It describes the way in which current understandings of age-friendly design are limited and how an emerging field of socially engaged design practice can be harnessed to reinvigorate the terms of age-friendly debate and practice – drawing a new generation of designers into conversation with age-friendly policy. By redefining what we mean by age-friendly design, it becomes possible, this chapter argues, to expand and invigorate the field of age-friendly practice, enabling creative practitioners to engage with and creatively inform age-friendly policymaking.

Challenging the orthodoxies of age-friendly design

Discussions around age-friendly design have, so far, been driven by public policy, often through the initiatives of certain age-friendly cities, such as New York (Age-friendly NYC, 2009) and Philadelphia (PCA, 2011) as they advance and pilot different urban interventions. However, it might be argued that the narrative played out in these approaches tends to limit the possible ways in which age-friendly design might be understood. Age-friendly design is typically equated with the principles of universal and inclusive design. This focuses on the idea that the built environment (or any designed service or product) can be designed and/or adapted in such a way that it meets the needs of all – regardless of age or ability. Age-friendly design method is, in this way, typically understood as a process of transforming a 'resistant' environment (one that makes navigating the urban environment challenging) into one that is 'supportive', accessible and navigable to all (Kellaher et al, 2014). As a result, age-friendly design appears as a problem-solving technique: identifying environmental 'barriers' (physical barriers to mobility, for instance); identifying needs (for physical rest to better enable mobility);

designing solutions to address these barriers and needs; making design recommendations; and implementing design standards.

These design methods, and the seemingly neutral-sounding design principles that underpin them, play into popular concepts of inclusivity and universality. Even though notions of inclusivity are in many ways elusive insofar as they fail to account for difference, they have tended to persist as popular concepts in the design world nonetheless (Boys, 2014). Within discussions of age-friendly practice, these universalising notions tend to be repeated, most obviously in the popular refrain that by creating an age-friendly city we are creating cities that are 'friendly for all'. It is along these lines that Age Platform Europe (2012) has been advancing the idea of age-friendly cities as a pan-generational concept. However, recurrent use of these terms – 'universal design', 'design for all', 'inclusive design' – betray what is in many ways a partial understanding within the age-friendly movement of what design practice might involve beyond a practice focused on solving problems.

Problem-solving, utilitarian approaches manifests themselves most obviously in the standard range of age-friendly design 'products', offered up as initiatives within the domain of 'outdoor spaces and buildings' (see Chapter Two). These age-friendly design solutions, ranging from the design of discrete objects (the 'age-friendly bench' that might be slotted into any age-friendly city), to the production of universal standards, guidance and checklists, invariably tend to privilege interventions that are concrete, physical and universal in their application (IDGO, 2012). They are often standardised and standardising in their effect. In other words, they are interventions that are easy to apply in other contexts but do not necessarily account closely for the specifics of local context. An age-friendly parks checklist, for instance, might offer cities with a useful list of age-friendly items to guide them in the redevelopment of any park, but a generic checklist will fail to account for the particularities of any given park. The way in which a particular park is currently used by older people, how it might be used differently, the particular siting of the park and its broader social context all require design responses that focus on the particularities of place.

Less obviously, this problem-solving design approach tends to play into bio-medicalised models of ageing, limiting its concerns to the 'problems' of the physical body and its interaction within urban environments. This approach can be seen operating in a number of different design studies: in the identification of certain kinds of paving as a risk for falls, or the way in which access to the outdoors is promoted as a way of maximising physical health and wellbeing (IDGO, 2012).

Design is seen here as an instrumental, solely functional practice generating solutions that respond to a baseline set of physical needs, engaging with and reinforcing, in turn, a recurring set of age-related issues, primarily around mobility, access and seating (Handler, 2016).

However, in focusing on the physical body and responding primarily to the physical aspects of ageing, this approach invariably results in denying those more empowering citizenship-based models of ageing that are starting to challenge health and adult social care accounts of ageing in public discourse (Buffel et al, 2014; Buffel, 2015) (see also Chapter Twelve). So long as ageing is understood as a condition of mounting dependency and need framed around conventional, biomedical questions of functional mobility and health (Burton and Mitchell, 2006; IDGO, 2012), these conventional readings of design for ageing will fail to account for older people's agency in the production of urban space.

The socially engaged designer

There are, however, other ways of thinking about and practising design, drawing on the ideas of an emerging group of practitioners who use their design practice as a way of openly engaging with social issues (see also Chapter Ten). Design, via this approach, might, for example, be defined not by its end product, but by its ability to *co-construct* spaces that encourage the formation of local networks that foster sociability and conviviality (White et al, 2013). This might involve designing a programme, a timetabled set of possible uses for any given space, for example, rather than inserting a designed product into that space. Design practice might, for instance, be understood to enable agency – as a tool to empower users of a given space to lay claim to a particular space and to make it their own (Schneider and Till, 2009; Awan et al, 2011).

Design might also be understood as a method characterised by more open-ended creative processes. Projects that follow these approaches are typically more exploratory and less fixed on delivering a final end product. Here, engagement with the inhabitants and users of a given space starts to inform the shape of a design project and challenges the image of the designer as a figure bringing ready-made design solutions to a particular project (Awan et al, 2011). A practice such as Atelier d'Architecture Autogérée (AAA), for instance, sees design operating as, simply, an 'enabling infrastructure' within local communities (AAA, 2011). Turning leftover urban spaces into self-managed spaces, its design projects have involved a deliberately bare minimum of physical intervention. Here, its typical design process would involve: identifying an abandoned site; securing it (through planning); providing some basic physical preparation of that space (to make it useable); and then turning the focus of its practice onto building those networks and capabilities within a local community that will allow these leftover spaces to be taken over by local residents as self-managed spaces.

Socially engaged design practice has emerged, over the past decade, in response to the difficult realities of contemporary urbanisation. Its practice offers new ways of addressing a variety of urban issues: the social fragmentation that results from rapid urban development; the growing privatisation of cities; threats to public space; and the deepening trends of injustice experienced across urban neighbourhoods (Rendell, 2006; Petcou and Petrescu, 2007; Petrescu et al, 2010). In responding to these issues, the emerging figure of the socially engaged designer has evolved a different approach to practising and thinking about design. Moving design practice beyond its object-based concerns and its focus on a final product, design in this context becomes, instead, a way of generating interventions that are socially conscious and critically self-reflective (Till, 2009).

Such concerns have required designers to adopt more experimental design methods. Borrowing from the techniques of site-specific art practice (work that is intended for, and that takes its meaning from, its setting within a certain space), designers have started to explore the possibilities of socially engaged, context-specific forms of spatial practice. In effect, this has meant that designers, like site-specific artists, have started to experiment with different locations, temporalities and scales of practice. This might involve, for instance, designers devising small-scale, *temporary* interventions in specific spaces as opposed to producing permanent 'final' large-scale structures for a given site. It might involve working in locations not ordinarily considered as sites for design practice, such as those in so-called 'interstitial spaces' on the borderline of public/private grounds, which aim to explore the tensions and ambiguities in the use and ownership of urban space (Rendell, 2006).

Such designers have also started to work more closely with concepts drawn from critical geography and urban sociology, illustrated in the research of David Harvey (2008), Henri Lefebvre (1991) and Michel de Certeau (1984). Designers have started to draw on the work of these researchers in order to address issues around inclusion and exclusion in urban environments, such as the politics of ownership and reproduction of urban space, and the involvement of users and inhabitants of a space through processes of participation and collaboration.

Drawing on this alternative way of thinking about and doing design, it becomes possible to challenge the standard way in which age-friendly design is practised and understood. Broadening its remit, beyond a limited response to adapting environments to a baseline set of physical needs, this alternative picture of age-friendly design starts to open up a number of other sets of questions around what age-inclusive practice might mean. Moreover, by linking into the theoretical work of Harvey, Lefebvre and de Certeau, it becomes possible to tie age-friendly action into a more explicitly politicised and critically reflective set of discussions around older people's relationship to place. Through these theories, age-friendly design can start to address questions of inclusion and exclusion in urban environments and the politics of ownership and reproduction of urban space. It starts to advance older people's **rights to the city** and the value of public space as a shared ground, negotiated through its varied (generational) use, supporting the capacity of older people, as individuals or collective groups, to reimagine and reclaim cities for themselves in both strategic but also in small, tactical ways.

Following on from this, some questions that arise include: could design be used as a mechanism for thinking about older people as urban citizens, as social actors actively engaged in the production and reproduction of cities? (see also Buffel and Phillipson, 2016). Can design be thought of as a process where older people, like any other generational group, are able to 'lay claim' to urban space on their own terms? Is it possible to explore older people's relationship to cities and urban environments beyond 'simply' its physical impact? Beyond its effect on the ageing body? Beyond people's ability to navigate a given place? And what if inclusive design were reimagined as a practice that engages with the politics of social inclusion – and exclusion – and the ordinary everyday experience of contemporary urbanisation as much as with the physical capabilities and limits of the ageing body?

In an area where public debate has, so far, been driven largely by social policy, it becomes possible to examine, through alternative forms of creative urban practice, what an age-friendly form of spatial practice might be.

Redefining age-friendly design

Since the launch of the WHO Global Network for Age-friendly Cities and Communities in 2007, age-friendly practice has evolved steadily out of the public policy arena, filtering down through actions, strategies and initiatives developed by engaged local authorities and community groups (see Chapter Two). And yet, for the most part, designers, architects and other creative practitioners working on issues around urbanisation have shown little interest in age-friendly concepts. Even among those arguably most inclined to adopt age-friendly principles in practice (in other words, those who define themselves through the ethical framework of their socially engaged practice) there seems to have been little engagement with older people's experiences of urbanisation, and the impact that radical demographic change within cities is having on people's everyday relationship to urban space.

Table 11.1: From problem solving to alternative forms of age-friendly design

Problem-solving design approaches	Alternative design approaches
Instrumental Design approaches that are defined by their function and measured by their use value (how useful the design proves to be).	*Propositional* Design approaches that are speculative and open-ended in their nature. Function as prompts for thinking about how else a given space might be imagined and constructed.
Inclusive design A design approach that looks to adapt urban spaces to meet the needs of all, regardless of age or ability. Often universal in its application, inclusive design is not necessarily focused on the specifics of a given, spatial context.	*Relational* Design approaches that work to reveal, build on or amplify the social connections and networks that make up a given space. Necessarily context-specific.
Object-focused Design approaches focused on the production of a final designed object. Tends to privilege the 'form', aesthetic or functionality of the end product.	*Agency* Design approaches that enable people to empower themselves, or lay claim to a particular space, through the design process itself.
Solutions-driven Design approaches defined by their focus on solving a particular problem. Often focused on body-bound issues: adapting a given environment, for instance, to minimise the physical difficulties of navigating a particular place.	*Creative interventions* Experimental design actions used to transform perceptions and experiences of urban spaces. Often involves borrowing from the techniques of art practice. The final design might involve a temporary action in a given space, a film or a text.

'Age-friendliness' offers designers, artists and architects a powerful conceptual framework for developing a socially engaged urban practice. It can be seen as distinct from other policy/design concepts such as 'active design' or 'healthy cities' that carry their own focused agendas around tackling obesity and health inequalities (Sport England, 2015; WHO, 2015). Age-friendliness provides a ready-made structure endorsing citizenship–based models of ageing, where older people take on an active role in the production of the city through the participative principles of 'active ageing', challenging the biomedical health and social care accounts of ageing in cities too (see also Chapters Three and Twelve).

In these different ways, the conceptual landscape of the age-friendly city enables designers to move beyond a self-limiting focus on the contained settings of housing and age-segregated institutions out into the public space of the city. It makes it possible to shift design thinking on ageing beyond the problem-solving tradition of design practice (focused on the ageing body). It also allows designers to become involved in more experimental, participative and empowering engagement with people's possible relationships to urban space. Moreover, a more active engagement with the urban ageing agenda enables design practitioners to bring their creative methods to current thinking around age-friendly design and engage with issues that are not, as yet, common currency within the discourse of age-friendly design. In this sense, the role of the age-friendly designer starts to move beyond attempts simply to mitigate the disabling impact of the urban environment on older people (Kellaher et al, 2004).

In this way, age-friendly design promises to embrace a number of key, but often unaddressed, concerns that affect the lives of older people in different ways. It might, for instance, start to address the way in which urban environments are so often geared towards the needs of younger age groups, or the way in which their 'brand' – the image that cities project for themselves – can implicitly exclude older people from the places in which they live. It might also tackle the issue that older people are often excluded from planning and consultation processes (notably in areas undergoing regeneration), which may result in a sense of disconnectedness and exclusion from the evolving shape of the places in which they live (Smith, 2009; Buffel and Phillipson, 2016). Or it might respond to the (oft-cited) difficulties of getting out and about in older age in ways that acknowledge that these difficulties can be about more than simply the problem of the relative physical navigability of a place. Beyond mere bodily constraints, there is the physically inhibiting effect, for instance, of living in an area where the fear of crime discourages free movement outdoors (De Donder et al, 2013). There is the way too in which the loss of a partner can create an emotional unsteadiness and sense of disconnect from a surrounding environment that may inhibit mobility (Kellaher et al, 2004; Buffel et al, 2012).

In addition to the 'problems' arising from an obstructive *material* environment (linked to the WHO domain of outdoor spaces and buildings), an alternative approach to age-friendly design will, thus, also engage with the ways in which places affect older people's *identity* and *subjective* emotions, and how these may shape experiences of alienation and social exclusion. Such issues may serve as prompts for designers to work in ways that, variously, give value and weight to people's subjective perceptions of place; acknowledge the relational value of spaces, as well as the conflicts and tensions in the shared use of space; and encourage forms of practice that enable a more confident and connected sense to place. The city, in these different ways, may be viewed as a resource as much for older people as for younger people; an environment that might be laid claim to 'even in' older age.

In these different ways, the idea of age-friendly practice starts to move beyond the familiar questions of access and mobility, security and safety and the production of risk-averse design strategies (design as a practice of mitigation). It moves beyond the problem of the ageing body too, offering the urban practitioner a more critically engaged view of what age-friendly practice might be. This kind of language and these kinds of questions are not currently part of the age-friendly discourse, but they start to redefine what age-friendly design might involve, offering a new set of terms and methods for practitioners to engage with.

Expanding the field of age-friendly practice

In practice, this alternative definition of age-friendly design, as set out in this chapter, broadens out the meaning of design as design takes on different sets of characteristics. Design, here, might simply involve a temporary intervention that transforms, momentarily, people's use and perception of that place. Design might, for instance, be a participative design process that privileges processes of working with others as a way of involving non-professionals (those often left out of design processes) within the co-production of a particular space (White et al, 2013; Buffel, 2015). Or, design practice might operate 'simply' as a series of speculative 'what ifs'?, generating scenarios as a catalyst for reimagining spaces ('What if the active third age reclaimed the high street as a catalyst of new public amenity?'). Here, as one of the propositional 'what ifs?' from the RIBA's (2013) *Silver linings* report reveals, the endpoint of a design process could be a suggested future rather than a concrete output – an imagined proposition designed to provoke thought and debate.

Equally, design might be understood as a practice that, rather than creating new objects or new products, tries, instead, to make use of what already exists: retrofitting spaces as opposed to simply inserting new objects into spaces (adapting existing roadside structures, for instance, into ad hoc seats, rather than furnishing a streetscape anew with benches). There is the idea of designing for the flexible use of a given space, where the use of a space is neither fixed, designated nor pre-programmed, but that changes over time – over the course of a day, a week, or a year. Community-based design projects, such as AAA architects' ECO box project in Paris, for example, promote the idea of spaces that are self-managed by residents and are flexible and adaptive in the way that they are used in different ways over time. There is the idea, as well, of thinking about design practice as a process that makes time and space for mapping hidden experiences within the city through maps, film, and writing, for example, and using these, in turn, to inform designs and interventions that become context-specific – in other words, relevant to the desires and needs of local, often marginalised constituencies.

These alternative approaches to design practice can be seen in a number of prototypical age-friendly initiatives. Often small in scale, the end 'product' of these initiatives appears in varying forms. An age-friendly initiative in this sense may, simply, involve the production of a temporary intervention or a narrative. It may, elsewhere, involve the production of a speculative proposition or a practical action plan. They do not, however, necessarily involve the production of a physical end product. Nor do these initiatives necessarily need to be obviously functional. These are forms of practice that subvert those conventional hierarchies in thinking about older people's relationships to place. Responding less to a baseline of physical needs, they explore less tangible, less visible relationships that older people have with place. They invite critical reflection, moreover, on those changing relationships, demonstrating the way in which some designers, artists, architects and others (community engagement officers, researchers, activists) are already working in ways that, though not necessarily articulated as alternative forms of age-friendly practice are, nevertheless, initiatives that could be understood to be age-friendly in their form.

These prototypical age-friendly initiatives are each different in their approach. Some are based on the idea of challenging the generational biases implicit within the production of certain kinds of spaces. In one example, a generic multi-use games area in the London Borough of Newham for youth becomes, for one night only, an outdoor dance space for a local elders' dance club, making flexible use of spaces for older people that would carry otherwise different uses. Elsewhere, in Manchester, every couple of months a nightclub (Band on the Wall) is turned into a venue for those aged 50 plus, challenging perceptions that certain kinds of spaces might be age-specific and, in a way too, subverting the generational dynamics of Manchester's urban night-time economy and the narrative self-image of the city as youthful by association.

Some of these initiatives are based on the idea of the bare minimum of physical intervention, making use of what already exists. They adopt the practice of retrofitting where the principle of effecting 'small change' sees minimal interventions build incrementally over time. The Dutch design practice, Denoven Design, for instance, worked in this way on the age-friendly retrofitting of a streetscape as a space for impromptu exercise, designed for residents of a neighbouring sheltered housing complex. Through a series of subtle roadside modifications (a street lamp is adapted into a stretching post, a series of roadside bollards are turned into a 'slalom walking route'), Denoven provide a shared ground for exercise within the existing fabric of the streetscape.

Box 11.1: The Seatable City

In 2013, Griesheim, a small town in the west of Germany, was turned into a fully 'sittable' town for its older residents. Through the design and installation of a series of 'rapid rest stops' designed to fit on to existing items of street furniture, the Seatable City* provides a series of regularly spaced 'perches' for older residents to rest on along any given walking route. A bicycle stand is designed to double up into a new type of high stool. Add-on structures turn a roadside wall into another rest stop. The project challenges the generic form and function of the age-friendly public bench. With sitting spots provided not only in the designated, obviously public places of parks and squares but also in threshold spaces along existing walking routes, the Seatable City is able to extend the walkable reach of its older residents (based on a map produced by Griesheim's older residents).

There is a tactical economy in this project, using the existing fabric of the streetscape to create a more sittable and ultimately more walkable city where benches are seen as only a part of the solution. Operating on the principle of the bare minimum intervention – making use of what already exists (roadside walls, bicycle stands) – the project can move beyond the generic design solution (of installing benches) to provide moments for resting based on the simple principle of making, where possible, small-scale adjustments to the existing urban fabric.

Projects and initiatives like these that foreground and focus on these more ordinary uses of existing spaces identify the value of what is already there, using design simply to modify, retrofit or subtly alter what already exists – in small ways.

*The Seatable City is an initiative developed by Professor Bernhard Meyer in 2013.

Small-scale projects such as the Seatable City, which operates through a minimum of intervention, can offer creative alternatives to standardised designs that, bought off the shelf, do not necessarily meet the needs of local context. Other projects, meanwhile, demonstrate the relational possibilities of age-friendly urban practice. In a project entitled Trading Spaces, an artist's temporary appropriation of a market stall in the London Borough of Lewisham is used as a way of engaging local elderly residents in the politics of gentrification. Working with a group of local older residents, the artist, Barby Asante, sets up a temporary stall in the local marketplace as a 'space of communication', trading thoughts and views on the changing nature of the local area with market passers-by. Sited deliberately within the marketplace (a place valued for its sociability by its older residents), the project starts to acknowledge and make visible the relational significance and possibilities of spaces like these, making space for a broader set of discussions around the way in which global market forces are played out in older people's everyday lives. The temporary stall becomes the pretext for participants to trade stories on how gentrification around the marketplace is already altering the way in which they interact with others.

Elsewhere, storytelling becomes the design tool for more conventional 'age-friendly' spatial audits. In the work of Kilburn Older Voices Exchange (KOVE), for instance, narrative film is used as a way of mapping out less visible urban experiences. In 2012, working with a group of filmmakers, in collaboration with members of the Gospel Oak Older People's Network, KOVE produce Journey to a Friend, a series of eight journeys following eight older residents as they make their way around the borough. Told in the first person, these short four-minute film journeys encourage a more empathetic and contextual reading of people's ordinary experience of place. But they allow, too, through the alternative format of film for these less visible stories to be told in different emotional registers – encouraging, in the viewer, a sensitivity to changing urban experiences absent in more conventional spatial audits and mapping projects.

There are 'unrealised', speculative projects that might also be taken as illustrations of alternative forms of age-friendly design practice. These might include the imaginative constructions produced through student work (where design pedagogy offers an inventive space in which to think freely about the idea of age-friendly practice). They might refer to the kinds of scenario-based design principles that underline the production of the RIBA *Silver linings* report that think forward into possible futures for city living in the third age (the high street reimagined as a public amenity of intergenerational exchange or the city reimagined as an alternative university of the third age). Here, the fantasy construction of the city as a learning environment for older age reimagines existing urban structures and spaces as freely available platforms to support third-age learning. Cultural venues such as galleries, museums and theatres are envisioned as offering informal, open and free spaces to meet. Private businesses (cafes and restaurants) are seen opening up in the morning and afternoon trading lulls to provide sociable spaces for seminars and workshops. Transport hubs are reinvented as public spaces, accommodating lectures and lessons.

Drawing on a long tradition of propositional practice within design, initiatives like these demonstrate the way in which an age-friendly spatial practice can operate as more than simply a functional, instrumental practice engaged in solving known problems. From temporary interventions to narrative forms of mapping, projects like these redefine the possibilities of age-friendly design. Importantly, age-friendly practice starts to be described in different terms: as an empowering practice that enables older people to lay claim to cities – in different ways. It starts to suggest forms of intervention that move beyond the terms of a rights-based discourse – beyond, simply, the notion that older people have an equal right to access the resources of the city. Instead, initiatives like these begin to account for people's *desiring* relationships to place: the emotional geographies (the subjective connections, longings, fantasies) that make up people's experience of a place. No longer bound to respond simply to a baseline of 'objective' physical needs, these alternative forms of age-friendly practice start to bring a different tenor into age-friendly design. Often they demonstrate a certain amount of gentle subversion within their practice (entering a park after the gates have closed for the night, appropriating the familiar features of a street as an impromptu exercise system for older adults). Implicitly, they challenge the more heavy-weighted discourse that typically surrounds discussions of ageing and design.

Challenging the objects of age-friendly design

To talk about age-friendly design in these terms, through the active verbs of intervention – of mapping and making visible, of making flexible use of space, 'borrowing' and appropriating spaces, and talking about design in terms of collaboration – it becomes possible to move dialogue on age-friendly urban practice beyond a physical, object-based practice. Design in this framework shifts from being a product-focused discipline that might focus on the production of a generic age-friendly bench, for instance, to a process-led practice. Here, the generic bench becomes a broader project around public seating, engaging local businesses and residents in the provision of temporary, on-demand seats within local shops (as in the Take-a-Seat initiatives introduced in Manchester and New York).

Importantly, this shift away from thinking about age-friendly design as a product-focused practice involves thinking differently about the role of the designer at the same time. No longer seen through popular policy perceptions of the designer as the sole author of a single, definable end product, the work of the age-friendly designer is seen to involve, instead, the broader, integrating work of drawing together different actors as co-producers of age-friendly spaces. Here, the designer works with the shopkeeper, the older resident with the academic. An expanded definition of the age-friendly practitioner sees them as not simply a designer, artist or architect, but as a facilitator, and as a connector of people, places and things (Shalk, 2007). In this example, the figure of the age-friendly designer starts to become defined as not simply a sole practitioner but as, fundamentally, a 'relational practitioner' – someone whose design practice involves working closely in turn, with, for and by others.

To list the age-friendly urban actors involved in these emerging age-friendly initiatives is to demonstrate the importance of this relational dimension to the age-friendly designer's practice. From architects and designers, to artists, sociologists, market stallholders and nightclub owners, the range of practitioners shown working within the age-friendly field is deliberately broad. Moreover, they are given an equivalence of status within the process of design intervention. In the Take-A-Seat project, for instance, the idea of borrowing the ostensibly private business space of a high street shop – offered up as a de-commercialised public space for rest – is reliant on the shop owner's investment in this age-friendly initiative, and on the designer's and community engagement officer's willingness to engage with the shopkeeper in starting up these kind of initiatives.

Too often than not this relational dimension of design practice is hidden, subsumed within the more mainstream image of the designer as an inventive producer of objects (buildings, benches, products). But the ability to facilitate connections within a given space, to draw on a diversity of skills, know-how and influence, is, arguably, one of the primary traits of age-friendly practice if age-friendly initiatives are to endure over time, and take root within local neighbourhoods. Different actors bring different abilities, attitudes, forms of knowledge and leverage – carrying varying degrees and types of (informal) power to effect long-lasting change in different ways. There is a need to actively support the involvement of a broad cast list of urban actors within age-friendly design practice. Moreover, there is an empowering dimension to this relational aspect of age-friendly practice: drawing others into the production of urban space, enabling agency and, crucially, through practices of participation and co-production, foregrounding older people in the production of age-friendly spaces, lending older people the agency to reimagine and redesign the age-friendly city for themselves.

Older people, as these initiatives show, become involved in the co-production of an age-friendly city via different methods and routes: from co-research (Buffel, 2015) to techniques of 'walking alongside', from formal structures of civic engagement in planning processes to informal mechanisms of engagement (walking diaries and so on) (White et al, 2013). Acknowledging this variety of participatory methods is one way of acknowledging – as is now well established within the design community – the way in which processes of engagement, co-production and forms of participation are many and different (Blundell-Jones et al, 2005). Each leads to different kinds of initiatives and interventions. They involve and animate people in different ways. But they also reaffirm the fundamentally relational role of the age-friendly designer, no longer defined as a sole practitioner. As Yanki Lee notes, any 'fixation on the role of the designer as the decision-maker and the suppression of reflexivity on the designer-user relationship creates a disparity which leads to social exclusion.' (Lee, 2012, p 58) This mirrors one of the central tenets within the age-friendly cities concept, where older people are positioned as central to the process of engaging in the production of an age-friendly city (WHO, 2007).

Critical interventions in age-friendly policy

As this chapter has argued, there is a need to acknowledge this other side of design practice: moving beyond the physical focus of current conceptions of age-friendly design, drawing on the often hidden skills of the creative practitioner to rethink the role of the designer within age-friendly urban practice. Operating as a facilitator, at times as an agent provocateur of sorts, the age-friendly practitioner here appears to work along the lines of Yanki Lee's (2012) comments, as a practitioner engaged with 'reframing', challenging and questioning received ideas as opposed to solving known problems.

There is a suggestion here that the socially engaged designer, working through a set of creative methods, carries the licence to think and act differently in ways that the instrumental focus of policy-led discussions around age-friendly design do not. As Lee points out, designers trained in the arts are capable of identifying and working with phenomena that others find too ephemeral, imaginative and unstable for serious research. And crucially, as she points out, they are also trained in reframing ideas rather than solving known problems (Lee, 2012). It is this idea of reframing known problems (rather than simply problem solving) that carries a particular value for rethinking what age-friendly design might mean beyond standard perceptions of age-friendly design as a solutions-focused practice.

This last, more open-ended, dimension of design practice is an important part of that broader process of reframing received ideas around age-friendly practice. Understood as a questioning practice, age-friendly design can start to challenge assumptions and provoke critical reflection on age-friendly spatial practice. This might, for instance, involve questioning the working mechanics of the familiar age-friendly checklist and the tick-box approach to design that it fosters or it might mean placing received terminology into critical context (revealing the in-built assumptions, for instance, of well-worn terminology such as 'inclusive design' where 'needs' are understood as common and general within any 'needs' group).

Moving away from the more directive aspects of age-friendly discourse that feature in policy-led discussions around the domain of outdoor spaces and buildings, this more questioning mode of practice can start to provide an alternative, more open-ended language for thinking about age-friendly design practice. It enables designers – and others – to reflect critically on age-friendly best practice, encouraging a more self-aware and reflective reading around age-friendliness. Moreover, it challenges the heavy-weighted, body-bound discourses around ageing, offering policymakers (as well as its intended readership of designers, architects and artists) new ways of thinking about urban practice beyond the conventional set piece of age-friendly design actions: of checklists, guidance and products.

By encouraging critical reflection beyond the disciplinary boundaries of design practice, it becomes possible to open up critical debate between policymakers and design practitioners and challenge set ways of thinking around the production of age-friendly cities. It also encourages creative practices to intervene proactively into policy debates around age-friendly cities as designers start to shape, as opposed to simply react, to trends in social policy.

Conclusion

The expansion of the age-friendly movement over the past decade has coincided with an increased interest in developing age-inclusive urban initiatives within the policymaking community. But, as this chapter has argued, prevailing perceptions within this community as to what design might actually involve have, arguably, limited the creative scope of interventions within age-friendly cities.

The figure of the socially engaged designer, however, whether an architect, designer or artist, has the potential to reinvigorate the practice and debate around age-friendly design. As this chapter has argued, these practitioners offer a new design vocabulary that is starting to redefine age-friendly spatial practice. Drawing on forms of practice (such as temporary interventions and propositional modes of practice) that these practitioners have deployed elsewhere, the socially engaged designer promises to bring to the age-friendly debate forms of spatial practice that are not only engaged, politically and socially, but also more speculative, open-ended and creative – questioning prevailing ideas around design on ageing, and moving away from that tradition of design on ageing conceived of as a body-bound, instrumental and often heavy-weighted form of practice.

Still in their infancy, these alternative forms of practice are only just emerging. The general reluctance within the design world to engage with the subject of ageing more broadly and the age-friendly project specifically has hindered a more active involvement with the urban ageing agenda, though there is a clear need for more practitioners to engage with and add to the practice around age-friendly cities. And yet, within the policymaking community that is driving the age-friendly cities movement forward, there is also a clear appetite to explore these alternative forms of age-friendly design. That appetite, as this chapter argues, needs to be built on. By drawing on the spatial practices of the socially engaged designer, it becomes possible to both enrich current thinking and practice on age-friendly cities and broaden the repertoire of urban practices involved in the co-production of age-friendly cities.

References

AAA (Atelier d'Architecture Autogérée) (2011) *Making rhizome: A micro-political practice of architecture*, Paris: AAA.

Age-friendly NYC (2009) *Age-friendly NYC: Enhancing our city's livability for older New Yorkers*, New York, NY: Age-friendly NYC.

Age Platform Europe (2012) *Towards an age-friendly European Union by 2020*, Brussels: Age Platform Europe.

Arup (2015) *Shaping ageing cities: 10 European case studies*, s.l.: Arup, Help Age International, Intel, Systematica.

Awan, N., Scheider, T. and Till, J. (2011) *Spatial agency: Other ways of doing architecture*, Abingdon: Routledge.

Blundell-Jones, P., Petrescu, D. and Till, J. (eds) (2005) *Architecture and participation*, London: Spon Press.

Boys, J. (2014) *Doing disability differently: An alternative handbook on architecture, dis/ability and designing for everyday life*, Abingdon: Routledge.

Buffel, T. (2015) *Researching age-friendly communities. Stories from older people as co-investigators*, Manchester: The University of Manchester Library.

Buffel, T., McGarry P., Phillipson, C., De Donder, L., Dury, S., De Witte, N., Smetcoren, A. and Verté, D. (2014) 'Developing age-friendly cities: case studies from Brussels and Manchester and implications for policy and practice', *Journal of Aging & Social Policy*, 26(1-2): 52-72.

Buffel, T., Phillipson, C. and Scharf, T. (2012) 'Ageing in urban environments: Developing "age-friendly" cities', *Critical Social Policy*, 32(4): 597-617.

Burton, E. and Mitchell, L. (2006) *Inclusive urban design: Streets for life*, Oxford: Architectural Press.

de Certeau, M. (1984) *The practice of everyday life*, Berkeley, CA: University of California Press.

De Donder, L., Buffel, T., De Witte, N., Dury, S. and Verté, D. (2013) 'Perceptual quality of neighbourhood design and feelings of unsafety', *Ageing & Society*, 33(6): 917-37.

Handler, S. (2014) *An alternative age-friendly handbook*, Manchester: The University of Manchester Library.

Handler, S. (2016) 'Ageing, care and the practice of urban curating', in C. Bates, R. Imrie and K. Kullman (eds) *Care and design: Bodies, buildings, cities*, Chichester: Wiley-Blackwell, pp 178-97.

Harvey, D. (2008) 'The right to the city', *New Left Review*, 53 (September-October): 23-40.

IDGO (2012) 'Why does the outdoor environment matter?' available at www.idgo.ac.uk/pdf/Intro-leaflet-2012-FINAL-MC.pdf.

Kellaher, L., Peace, S.M. and Holland, C. (2004) 'Environment, identity and old age: quality of life or a life of quality?', in C. Hagan Hennessy and A. Walker (eds) *Growing older: Quality of life in old age*, Maidenhead: Open University Press, pp 35-59.

Lee, Y. (2012) *The ingenuity of ageing: For designing social innovation*, London: Department for Business, Innovation and Skills and the Royal College of Art.

Lefebvre, H. (1991) *The production of space*, Oxford: Blackwell.

Philadelphia Corporation for Aging (2011) *Laying the foundation for an age-friendly Philadelphia: A progress report*, Philadelphia, PA: Philadelphia Corporation for Aging.

Petcou, C. and Petrescu, D. (2007) 'Acting space: transversal notes, on-the-ground observations and concrete questions for us all', in AAA (ed) *Urban act*, Paris: PEPRAV, pp 319-28.

Petrescu, D., Petcou, C. and Awan, N. (eds) (2010) *Trans-local-act: Cultural practices within and across*, Paris: AAA/PEPRAV.

Rendell, J. (2006) *Art and architecture: A place between*, London: I.B. Tauris.

RIBA (Royal Institute of British Architects) (2013) *Silver linings: The Active Third Age and the City*, London: RIBA.

Schneider, T. and Till, J. (2009) 'Beyond discourse: notes on spatial agency', *Footprint*, 4 (Spring): 97-111.

Shalk, M. (2007) 'Urban curating: a critical practice towards greater "connectedness"', in D. Petrescu (ed) *Altering practices: Feminist politics and poetics of space*, London: Routledge, pp 153-65.

Sinclair, D. and Watson, J. (2014) *Making our communities ready for ageing: A call to action*, London: ILC-UK.

Smith, A. (2009) *Ageing in urban neighbourhoods: Place attachment and social exclusion*, Bristol: Policy Press.

Sport England (2015) *Active design: Planning for health and wellbeing through sport and physical activity*, London: Sport England.

Till, J. (2009) *Architecture depends*, Cambridge, MA: MIT Press.

White, S., Phillipson, C. and Hammond, M. (2013) *Old Moat: Age-friendly neighbourhood report*, Southway Housing Trust.

WHO (World Health Organization) (2015) *National healthy cities networks in the WHO European Region. Promoting health and well-being throughout Europe*, Geneva: WHO.

WHO (2007) *Global age-friendly cities: A guide*, Geneva: WHO.

TWELVE

Developing age-friendly policies for cities: strategies, challenges and reflections

Paul McGarry

Introduction

In June 2010, Manchester was formally admitted into the World Health Organization (WHO) Global Network for Age-Friendly Cities and Communities (GNAFCC), along with 13 other cities from across the world.[1] The UK's first age-friendly city, Manchester, is now one of a significant group of age-friendly cities within the UK, and only one among more than 500 across the world (see Chapter Two). Since the early 1990s, Manchester, which faces important challenges with regard to ageing inequalities, poverty, social exclusion and life expectancy, has been highly committed to improving the quality of life of its older population. Indeed, Manchester has established itself over the years as a leading authority in developing strategic policy approaches to creating age-friendly cities, both at a national and international level (Buffel et al, 2014).

This chapter charts the evolution of the Age-Friendly Manchester (AFM) programme and, more broadly, explores how the UK government's ageing policies and strategies have developed since the late 1990s, highlighting four distinctive periods of nationally led activity relating to older people. It considers how the development of the age-friendly approach in Manchester has enabled a range of actors, notably local government agencies, to develop ageing programmes in the absence of national leadership. It then focuses on the city's involvement in expanding its programme into an ambitious city-regional approach to age-friendly urban development, the first of its kind in the UK. The chapter demonstrates the potential for stimulating age-friendly initiatives at a local and regional level whilst at the same time highlighting the pressures facing urban authorities at a time of economic austerity.

The social and demographic characteristics of Manchester

Manchester: population and social dimensions

The development of the age-friendly cities and communities movement can be seen to have emerged in response to global demographic trends that show population ageing as an important feature of many urban environments. Manchester is a city, however, with a unique demographic profile. Its population of 520,000 (2014 mid-year estimate taken from Registrar General's Mid Year Estimates, ©ONS, and Manchester City Council Forecasting Model W2016) has been growing steadily since 2001 at a growth rate of nearly 2% per annum, but this growth has not been spread equally across age groups. Compared with the national age profile, Manchester has a smaller proportion of residents aged 65 and over, in other words, 10.5% in Manchester compared with 16.9% in England and Wales. Natural losses, along with a greater number of people moving out compared with a relatively small cohort of late middle-aged and older people moving into the city, has meant that in many ways Manchester bucks the trend of ageing cities. But these particular demographic trends have also meant that Manchester has had to respond to a number of city-specific challenges, especially those relating to social isolation and the experience of multiple forms of exclusion in later life.

Over the past decade, migration, particularly the selective emigration of healthier and/or affluent older people to neighbouring suburbs and beyond, combined with high immigration from abroad, has resulted in some older people being relatively isolated within certain districts in Manchester (Bullen, 2016). A study by the Audit Commission in 2008 found that, compared to those more affluent 50 and 60 year olds who have chosen to leave the city where they have spent their working lives, the remaining older population tends to be poorer, isolated and more vulnerable, with a lower life expectancy and a need for acute interventions (Audit Commission, 2008). The strong growth in Manchester's young and working-age populations over the period 2001 to 2011 will have exacerbated this pattern (Bullen, 2016).

Social exclusion, inequalities and disadvantage

Research has shown that older people in Manchester's inner-city neighbourhoods face high levels of disadvantage and social exclusion (Scharf et al, 2003; Buffel et al, 2013). People born in Manchester are more likely to die prematurely (in other words, before the age of

75) than in any other local authority in England and are therefore less likely to reach old age (Bullen et al, 2016). While the probability of surviving to age 75 has slightly increased over the past decade, rates of survival in Manchester and Greater Manchester are still lower than in England as a whole. Men and women born in Manchester have the lowest chance of survival to the age 75 of any local authority area in England and Wales. People reaching old age in Manchester are also more likely to spend a greater proportion of their remaining years living in poorer health and with greater levels of disability, and experience higher mortality rates across a range of health conditions. The age-standardised mortality rate for all causes of death in 2008-2010 among people aged 65-74 years in Manchester (2,793 per 100,000) was 64% higher than that of England as a whole (1,703 per 100,000). Bullen (2016) concludes that Manchester's older population suffers from long-term limiting illnesses at an earlier stage of life than seen nationally, placing high demands on hospital emergency services and mental health services. It is against this background that Manchester's work around age-friendly initiatives has developed.

The evolution of Age-Friendly Manchester: 1990s

Towards a citizenship-based policy approach to ageing

Manchester's work on age-friendly issues began in the early 1990s in response to the launch of the European Union's Year of Older People and Solidarity Between Generations in 1993, a year of activity encouraging member states to reflect on the implications of rapid demographic change and to explore the potential contribution of older people within those member states. In an attempt to link in with these activities, Manchester City Council created a multi-departmental Older Age and Opportunity Working Party, charged with promoting a broad range of opportunities and services for older people. The working party consisted of elected councillors and was supported by an officer group.

Working closely with the then deputy leader of the council, that group went on to develop an approach that was defined by a new, asset-based account of ageing. The approach offered an alternative view of older people's capacities to the dominant 'care model' of ageing embedded within local government and community health services. Arguing that the role of local authorities should not begin and end with its social care responsibilities (recognising that the majority of older residents are not even recipients of social care services), Manchester started to develop a narrative defined instead by the 'active involvement and contribution of older people within the city'. In a city like Manchester, where many older people face exclusion from a range of everyday services and activities, this alternative **asset-based account of ageing** represented an important shift in thinking about ageing in cities, challenging the way in which, at a local authority level, older people and the ageing agenda have traditionally been seen solely in terms of social care support to the most vulnerable and frail.

Better government for older people

In 1998, this Manchester-based work programme was consolidated further with the establishment of the Better Government for Older People (BGOP) group: a government-initiated programme of 32 'pilot' local government projects in the UK committed to developing new approaches to encourage the active engagement of older people within the community. Although Manchester was not a pilot site, the city took part in the BGOP learning network and used the emerging narrative to frame the next phase of its ageing programme.

Supported by central government in a favourable political climate, BGOP provided local authorities, such as Manchester, with vital leadership and motivation for developing their ageing strategies and enabled local authorities to develop policies for – and sometimes with – their ageing populations that aimed at going beyond seeing older people as recipients of health and care services. BGOP can, in this context, be seen as part of a broader programme of New Labour[2] public sector reform, which sought to promote citizen involvement and action in service delivery, and which was at odds with more welfarist and paternalistic forms of state provision.

Following on from the BGOP/Audit Commission report on developing ageing strategies (Audit Commission, 2008), a number of follow-on initiatives were developed. These are summarised in Table 12.1. A number of these programmes represented significant financial investment (for example, Linkage Plus and Partnership for Older People's Projects), and the mobilisation of expertise and commitment across several national and local partnerships. Many of these programmes offered models of best practice that inspired activities elsewhere.

The groundwork laid through the 1990s enabled the development of age-friendly initiatives in Manchester. These investments and programmes created a sizeable community of interest in ageing, beyond the health and care space, and a range of networks spanning sectors and disciplines. In that sense, these programmes in the 1990s and 2000s were crucial to the later development of age-friendly initiatives in Manchester, creating an alternative local government-rooted narrative of ageing, and connections into government departments and academia (McGarry and Morris, 2011).

Table 12.1: National working programmes on ageing in the UK

Sustainable Cities and the Ageing Society (Cox et al, 2004)	The Office of the Deputy Prime Minister (ODPM) commissioned this research into sustainable cities and the ageing society (conducted during 2002 and 2003) as part of its New Horizons research programme.
A Sure Start to Later Life (ODPM, 2006)	Led by the Social Exclusion Unit (which formed part of the ODPM), this initiative (ODPM, 2006) focused on 'socially excluded' older people and contained 30 government actions across a wide range of domains.
Link Age Plus (2006)	Link Age Plus, the 'delivery' arm of the Sure Start to Later Life programme, was a series of area-based pilot projects, designed to gather evidence around ageing.
Opportunity Age (DWP, 2005)	The first national cross-government ageing strategy led by the Department for Work and Pensions.
Partnerships for Older People's Projects (2006)	A Department of Health-led programme designed to reduce demands on the health and care system, promoting local preventive approaches to ageing. Manchester was one of the pilot sites.
Comprehensive Performance Assessment (2006)	A central government assessment tool for local authorities that contained a significant section on ageing.
Don't stop me now (Audit Commission, 2008)	An Audit Commission report on local government preparedness for ageing populations.
Lifetime Homes, Lifetime Neighbourhoods (DCLG, 2008)	A Department of Communities and Local Government (DCLG) strategy setting out the case for planning for ageing populations, focusing on the role of neighbourhood and home.
Beacon Council Scheme (various)	A DCLG scheme aimed at promoting best practice by local governments across a range of themes, including ageing. Manchester was successful in 1999 in this scheme.
Building a Society for All Ages (DWP, 2009) and Ageing Well (2010)	A successor strategy to Opportunity Age, with Ageing Well being the strategy's delivery project.

Valuing Older People programme: 2000s

A partnership strategy with older people and citywide stakeholders

In 2003, Manchester City Council formed the Valuing Older People (VOP) partnership. Designed to accelerate work around the ageing agenda within the local authority, VOP successfully built on the momentum that Manchester had developed through the 1990s, forming additional partnerships with older people and a variety of organisations across the city.

Most notably, VOP began to develop a comprehensive engagement programme involving older residents directly in the leadership of its work. It formed a representative older people's board ensuring that the VOP team within the council would be held accountable to a board of older volunteers. It set up a wider forum of older people's groups, ensuring that the VOP programme was informed by the views of older people from across Manchester. More broadly, the VOP programme began to commit to partnership and policy development across the council, engaging with a range of external partners (including universities and agencies representing the voluntary sector), reflecting a more strategic and ambitious framework for the delivery of its ageing initiatives. By 2010, the VOP work group, now located in the newly established Public Health Manchester service in Manchester City Council, consisted of staff from the National Health Service, local government, a housing trust, an arts agency, a national charity and a local university. During this period, the programme became well known for its annual festival of ageing, and through its Positive Images of Ageing programme. Other strong initiatives were led by leisure services and arts organisations.

Key initiatives developed in the Manchester VOP programme

As a result of its partnership strategy, the VOP programme was able to deliver a notably wide-ranging number of age-inclusive initiatives between 2003 and 2010. These included: a broad programme of healthy ageing initiatives; a sexual health programme aimed at those in mid- and later life; a training programme for frontline staff on alcohol and ageing; and initiatives aimed at increasing community-based opportunities for healthy ageing, including the introduction of free swimming for the over-60s. The programme further initiated campaigns to promote entitlement and benefit take-up and employment opportunities for older workers, and worked with the Manchester School of Architecture to explore links between design, the built environment and ageing (see also Chapter Ten). Other activities involved a community development programme (supporting older people's initiatives across the city); a small grants scheme aimed at developing these groups; an innovative communications strategy promoting positive images of ageing as a way of combating negative stereotyping of older people within Manchester; and the development of a 'cultural offer for older people' (see Box 12.1)

Box 12.1: Manchester's Cultural Offer programme

Established in 2007, the Cultural Offer programme is run by Age-Friendly Manchester (formerly known as VOP), with a working group of 19 cultural organisations from Manchester and Salford, including the Halle Orchestra, People's History Museum, Royal Exchange and the Whitworth museum. Its aim is to extend the reach of the city's world-class arts and culture to older people, and encourage arts engagement in later life, especially among those living in disadvantaged communities.

The Culture Champions scheme was launched in 2011 as part of the Cultural Offer programme. This scheme involves developing 'gatekeepers' in local communities to act as 'ambassadors' for the arts. It aims to inform elderly networks and communities about the variety of cultural events and to encourage older people to attend and try out cultural activities in Manchester.

Older people from communities throughout Manchester were invited to become 'culture champions'. Champions are given a wide range of information about cultural events in the city, receive discounted tickets, and are invited to participate in projects, for example, volunteering at the Chinese Arts Centre. Their role is then to share their experiences and knowledge of the cultural programmes in Manchester with their friends, networks and local community, and, where possible, to encourage and support visits to venues. Champions have co-programmed themed 'after-hours' events at galleries for older people, taken part in culture tours and tested experimental theatre projects.

An evaluation of the project found that involvement in the scheme had made champions feel more confident, connected, informed and inspired. They were felt to be a powerful resource for mobilising older people and stimulating interest in the cultural offer.

The innovative nature and broad scope of the VOP projects enabled the programme to advance and further promote the asset-driven and citizenship-based narrative around ageing that the city had been developing since the 1990s. It also provided opportunities for the city to deliver in practice principles that the WHO (2002) was starting to deliver through its own 'active ageing' policy framework. The latter forged a paradigm shift in the societal view of ageing which helped to reframe older people as active participants and contributors to their communities and to society at large, rather than as a social and economic 'burden' (see, further, Chapter Two).

Moreover, these VOP initiatives enabled Manchester to develop a specifically local narrative of urban ageing, complementing its strategic commitment to reducing social inequalities. A vital aspect of its work involved advancing the knowledge base around urban ageing that it had started to develop in the 1990s, especially around ageing in disadvantaged communities, built around a combination of research findings and conceptual insights. The local narrative also enabled the VOP programme to engage the city in initiatives that were able to address features of the city's older population that are atypical of older populations in most other local authority areas – notably, its lower proportions and numbers of older people; a significant proportion of black and minority ethnic elders; high levels of social exclusion and ill health; and high levels of population turnover – enabling the programme to evolve a broader narrative based around values of equality and social justice.

Between 2003 and 2010, a number of initiatives directed at a national level stimulated VOP to advance its ageing programme further. Following on from the first national strategy on ageing, Opportunity Age, in 2005, the Department for Work and Pensions commissioned its Ageing Well programme and began the coordination of a number of follow-on initiatives (see also Table 12.1): the later-life Public Service Agreement (PSA); the Link Age Plus programme of local authority-based pilot projects; the setting up of a national ageing forum; and the development of a new strategy, Building a Society for All Ages (DWP, 2009). The Manchester VOP team took part in these initiatives by presenting the Manchester approach at a range of conferences, and to government departments. During this period, the city was successful in its bid for the government-led Generations Together programme, which was designed to improve intergenerational relationships through the investment in a number of local programmes (LGA, 2009).

In all, this has meant it is possible to see through the life of the Manchester ageing programme a broad and expanding reach in its initiatives. From housing, transport, and culture and learning through to improving engagement with older people, Manchester has been highly successful in its ability to advance an unusually wide-ranging set of initiatives around ageing. In recent years, the programme has advanced Lifetime Neighbourhood initiatives to develop accessible and well-designed living environments in which residents are not excluded by age; promoted Design for Access standards in housing through extending opportunities for older people to be involved in decision making, project delivery and service design; supported employment opportunities for the over-50s; and promoted more accessible and better marketed activities within culture and learning.

Age-friendly Manchester: 2010 onwards

From 2010 onwards, the climate that supported the development of these initiatives changed radically as national leadership on the ageing agenda started to be scaled back under the new coalition government[3]. It is in this context of diminishing national leadership that the age-friendly cities movement started to gain increasing prominence within Manchester, thus providing the conceptual framework within which Manchester could further develop its work on ageing.

Age-friendly Manchester's participation in the GNAFCC

In 2009, the Manchester Ageing Strategy 2010–2020 was developed following extensive consultation with older residents, elected council members, and a panel of nationally recognised experts (Manchester City Council, 2009). The strategy mirrored many of the conceptual features outlined in the WHO guide to age-friendly cities and communities (WHO, 2007): enabling older people to be more active and engaged as urban citizens; reducing inequality; maximising access to better-quality care and support; and providing lifetime neighbourhoods with flexible, affordable housing options. One year after the publication of that strategy, Manchester joined the WHO's GNAFCC (in 2010), linking its ageing programme explicitly to the age-friendly cities movement.

Manchester's membership of the GNAFCC has meant that VOP projects were increasingly defined in relation to age-friendly principles, with the term 'age-friendly' becoming more prominent in both research and policy. For example, initiatives supported by the Manchester programme included: the Age-Friendly Old Moat neighbourhood project, a project aimed at improving the social and physical environments in which residents age (White et al, 2013; see also

Chapter Ten); the production of a research and evaluation framework for age-friendly cities for local authorities (Handler, 2014a); the publication of an alternative age-friendly handbook (Handler, 2014b; see also Chapter Eleven); and the development of a guide to working with older people as co-investigators in researching age-friendly neighbourhoods (Buffel, 2015; see also Box 12.2).

In October 2014, the VOP programme formally relaunched itself as Age-Friendly Manchester, leveraging the WHO brand to strengthen and further consolidate its programme. The term Age-Friendly Manchester has now become an umbrella term for all initiatives in the city that aim to improve older people's quality of life.

Box 12.2: Research with, not just for, older people

Age-Friendly Manchester (AFM) works closely with a range of organisations, including the Manchester Institute for Collaborative Research on Ageing (MICRA) based at the University of Manchester, to increase knowledge of how older people's quality of life in the city can be improved. This partnership is equally highly valued by the University, with a variety of researchers from different disciplines benefiting from the range of networks, support and strategic links offered by AFM.

One of the University projects supported by AFM is a study on age-friendly communities that draws on the views, concerns and expertise of older residents (Buffel, 2015). Working with targeted groups in three neighbourhoods in the south of Manchester, the project is shaped by three key characteristics:

• **Participation** – Older residents act as co-researchers at all stages of the process; including planning, design and implementation;
• **Collaboration** – a range of partners, including local government, voluntary organisations and other non-governmental organisations, act as advisers, contributing via focus groups, interviews and ongoing partnerships;
• **Action** – recommendations have been generated for urban design, regeneration, community engagement and policy implementation. A new space has been opened up allowing insights to be fed directly into ongoing programmes and initiatives in Manchester and beyond.

A diverse group of 18 adults aged between 55 and 74 were recruited and trained as co-researchers, working alongside academics, community organisations and policy-makers to improve the age-friendliness of their neighbourhood. The co-researchers took a leading role in the design of the research, implementation, analysis and dissemination of findings. The 18 co-researchers conducted 68 qualitative interviews with older residents, many of whom experienced multiple forms of social exclusion, health problems, social isolation and poverty. Older people themselves actively influenced solutions to many of the challenges experienced by older citizens living in deprived neighbourhoods. The co-researchers involved in the study have formed a permanent group to apply for funding for age-friendly projects building on study findings (see further Buffel, 2015).

Commenting upon this project, the WHO (2015, p 222) states that 'Taken as a whole, this study represents a significant methodological step forward in developing new models for community engagement. Interventions such as those used in the study represent excellent sources of data, valuable exercises in community engagement for all participants, and cost-effective mechanisms for producing informed policy in times of austerity' (see further Buffel, 2015).

Expansion of the age-friendly movement across the UK

Manchester's growing engagement with the age-friendly cities agenda was mirrored elsewhere as a number of initiatives embracing the age-friendly agenda were developed across the UK. These included the UK's first conference on age-friendly environments, the publication by the UK Urban Ageing Consortium's of a guide entitled *Creating age-friendly places* (Morris, 2013), and the establishment of the UK Network of Age-friendly Cities (a network of 12 cities from across the four UK regions sharing knowledge and best practice on age-friendly cities).

For cities like Manchester, the age-friendly movement, the GNAFCC and membership within it have offered a unifying and integrated narrative in which to advance ageing work across the council. In effect, the 'age-friendly' brand has helped to mainstream the ageing agenda, giving valuable support to the more empowering narrative developed through VOP, in other words, one that is shifting away from seeing older people as a problem, towards viewing older people as active citizens able to take part in the broader project to mobilise communities and reshape services and neighbourhoods – even within the context of economic austerity.

Implementing age-friendly policies in the context of economic austerity

The launch of Age-Friendly Manchester and other age-friendly city programmes across the UK in the wake of the global financial crisis has presented significant challenges (see also Buffel and Phillipson, 2016). Local councils have had to face significant cuts in their budgets and services, with money spent on services cut by up to 35%. For Manchester, this has meant the loss of £340 million since 2010/11, placing significant financial pressure on the types of ageing projects the city wants to deliver. In the first instance, the AFM programme has had to focus on mitigating the impact of cuts to vital services on older people. But there has also been the broader challenge of finding ways to increase investment in what might be called 'preventative' programmes (the first to be cut in the context of economic austerity) to reduce future increases in demand just at the point when available budgets are under pressure to meet existing levels of demand. Development of age-friendly initiatives in these straitened times becomes increasingly difficult. There is the constant threat that plans to promote age-friendly neighbourhoods may be compromised by budget cuts that are focused on reducing public services such as libraries, information and advice centres, and day-care facilities for older people. Moreover, these threats to cut services (libraries, lunch clubs and so on) can lead to a public perception that the age-friendly brand is unrealistic and unlikely to be implemented given restrictions on public spending.

In response, AFM has been forced to explore ways of developing initiatives, strategies and supportive networks that can sustain the programme in a difficult economic climate. The programme has had to attract, for instance, external funding to support age-friendly neighbourhood projects and the development of local networks of older people's groups. It has had to focus on building on its partnerships (with the University of Manchester, for instance) to strengthen and expand the reach of its programme within a context of economic cutbacks. In addition, AFM has sought to give older people in the city a respected and influential voice, so that key city strategies such as the 2016 Manchester Strategy refer to the age-friendly model of working amid competing agendas.

Like other global cities, Manchester experiences a range of demands to create 'world class environments that compete for investment with other national and international centres' (Buffel et al, 2014, p 67). In this environment, the idea of 'age-friendliness' has to compete with wider objectives associated with economic growth and development and, may, as a result, appear marginal to both, particularly in the context of economic austerity (Buffel and Phillipson, 2016). For a city like Manchester, one way forward could be to develop age-friendliness through a more integrated strategy: making age-friendliness a central part of policymaking with a view to promoting sustainable urban development across its broad environmental, social and economic dimensions. Successful implementation of such policies relies on the support of a range of stakeholders – including multiple levels of government; public, private and third-sector organisations; and non-governmental organisations. Reconciling the different interests and values of these groups represents one of the central challenges that the age-friendly city movement needs to address (Buffel et al, 2014).

In the variety of ways reviewed here, the WHO's unifying narrative has been a helpful advocate in promoting the age-friendly agenda within the context of austerity, providing a broader global network of support and a potent brand for selling that agenda within local authorities like Manchester. But the successful and continuing development of AFM, in spite of economic cutbacks and the scaling back of national leadership in the ageing field, owes a great deal to political leadership within Manchester. Throughout the lifetime of the programme (from VOP to AFM), there has been high-level political support from elected council members, primarily from the council's deputy leader with lead responsibility for equality strategies and the VOP lead councillor, a backbench politician who has had day-to-day contact with the VOP, now AFM, team. The encouragement and support of senior and backbench councillors has created an environment where officers feel confident in taking risks, and developing, at times, exploratory pieces of work. The support of a senior officer group, comprising the directors of housing, adult services and public health, and the deputy chief executive, has also benefited VOP and AFM, encouraging the evolution and extension of the programme beyond the city borders and raising the ambition of AFM to the broader region.

Developing city-regional approaches to age-friendliness

Responding to demographic change in the Greater Manchester region

The city-region of Greater Manchester is a conurbation of over 2.5 million people in the north-west region of the UK, comprising 10 metropolitan districts (one of which is the City of Manchester), each of which has a major town centre and outlying suburbs. The Greater Manchester Combined Authority is made up of the 10 Greater Manchester councils and mayor, working with local services, businesses, communities and other partners to improve the city-region. In recent years, population ageing has increasingly been recognised as an important part of the GM strategy with priorities for growth and reform.

The establishment of Greater Manchester (GM) priorities on ageing responds to the significant demographic changes forecast for the medium to long term. Estimates suggest that within the GM region, by 2036, 14% of the total population will be 75 and over, which is an increase of 75% from 2011 (from 221,000 to 387,000). Projections show an increase of older people living alone, and those at risk of social isolation and loneliness, with related impacts on physical and mental health and wellbeing, with people aged 75 and over at greatest risk. By 2036, one in three men aged 75 will be living alone. GM will see an 85% increase in the number of people diagnosed with some form of dementia by 2036 (to 61,000 people) (Buckner et al, 2013; Buffel et al, 2015). Evidence from the English Longitudinal Study of Ageing further suggests worsening of levels of health outcomes for younger-old cohorts in the poorest 20% of the population, with increased levels of inequalities between the richest and poorest (Nazroo, 2015).

City-regional approaches and the impact of devolution

As part of a broader national policy to devolve powers across the UK, the GM agreement granted greater powers to the Greater Manchester area in November 2015, enabling the city-region to better shape the form and direction of its regional development. In 2016, the following year, the Greater Manchester Combined Authority agreed to establish the Greater Manchester Ageing Hub, bringing together key partners to support a strategic and holistic approach to ageing. The establishment of the hub demonstrates recognition within the broader Manchester region that a narrative addressing the opportunities (thus not only the challenges) of population ageing is central to the city-region's plans for economic growth and public service reform.

This new GM-wide commitment to an asset-based ageing agenda (championed by VOP and AFM over the past decade) comes in the context of key international reports by the Organisation for Economic Co-operation and Development (OECD, 2015) and WHO (2015), both of which have called for coordinated action at city and sub-regional levels to plan for ageing populations and to take advantage of social and economic opportunities that population ageing represents. It also takes place in the context of a new five-year agreement made between the new Greater Manchester Ageing Hub and the Centre for Ageing Better, an organisation with an endowment of £50 million from the Big Lottery Fund to invest in bridging the gap between research, evidence and practice on what works for a better later life. The Centre for Ageing Better has set out an ambition to develop strategic partnerships with a small number of places, including Greater Manchester (the first to make such an agreement), to support the implementation of key priorities, in particular in the areas of economy and work, and planning, transport and housing.

Greater Manchester's Ambition for Ageing, a £10.2 million programme funded by the Big Lottery Fund's Ageing Better Programme, is aimed at creating more age-friendly places across the region. Together with the Greater Manchester hub, it provides a platform for AFM to develop further partnerships and capacity at both Greater Manchester and local levels. Salford Council, for instance, part of the GM region, has only just joined the WHO's GNFACC, building on this growing regional ambition around the urban ageing agenda.

Greater Manchester Ageing Hub

The Greater Manchester Ageing Hub is charged with two key tasks: overseeing the development of a GM strategy on ageing and coordinating the different programmes delivered by the various GM partners. Supported by a shadow steering group, the work of the GM Ageing Hub brings together Public Health England, New Economy (the GM economic think tank), GM's public service reform team, AFM (Manchester City Council), Manchester Institute for Collaborative Research on Ageing (MICRA) at the University of Manchester and the GM Centre for Voluntary Organisations (linked to the delivery of GM's Ambition for Ageing programme).

The GM Ageing Hub's vision sets out three key priorities: first, to develop GM into the UK's first age-friendly city region; second, to develop GM into a global centre of excellence for ageing; and third, to increase economic participation among the over-50s. These are now addressed in more detail.

Developing GM into the UK's first age-friendly city region

This first priority here will be supported by a number of actions including: co-producing age-friendly design to understand how urban environments can work with and for older people; investing in planning to prepare for future patterns of demographic change; supporting the development of age-friendly neighbourhoods (in other words, building on the age-friendly neighbourhoods approach to develop age-friendly districts, town centres and regional centres); considering ageing in all policy areas to identify the needs of older people in policy areas such as employment and skills, business support, transport, housing, health and spatial planning; enabling social connectedness and community asset building to address social isolation and loneliness among older people; and changing the narrative around ageing (in other words, building a positive discourse, and demonstrating the valuable contribution that older people can make as entrepreneurs, volunteers, workers and consumers to support growth and resilience).

Developing GM into a global centre of excellence for ageing

A second priority of the GM Ageing Hub is to develop GM into a global centre of excellence around ageing issues, pioneering new research, technology and solutions across a range of ageing-related domains. This will involve: using an existing evidence base to pilot new and innovative solutions to the challenges and opportunities of population ageing; drawing together and sharing best practice and learning across GM districts, and delivering at a GM level those interventions that will only work at city-regional scale; testing innovative forms of public engagement and co-production with older people; and developing national and international partnerships – to play a leading role in national networks of expertise on ageing (including supporting the evolution of the UK Network of Age-friendly Cities).

Increasing economic participation among the over-50s

The GM Ageing Hub's third priority (to promote the economic participation of those aged 50 and over) will involve an agenda aimed at: better understanding and tackling the inequalities that Greater Manchester residents face in later life; considering the culture and retail offer for older people across GM; and helping individuals and organisations in GM capitalise on the new and emerging markets for products and services being created for the older consumer. A further action will be aimed at extending healthy working years – increasing employment rates among older residents across GM, and engaging with employers to ensure that there are opportunities for older workers.

Operating through a small core team and reporting to a steering group of senior GM officials, the remit of the hub is to form strategic partnerships, identify funding opportunities, and communicate the work of the hub while coordinating and working alongside leads for a series of thematic areas. These include: economy and work; healthy ageing and lifestyles; age-friendly neighbourhoods; planning, transport and housing; technology, design and innovation; and culture and leisure.

An immediate priority of the hub includes the development of an ageing foresight report to map out the scale and nature of ageing over the next 20 years in Greater Manchester. Furthermore, workshops will be held jointly with the Centre for Ageing Better to kickstart a new project to address unemployment and social exclusion among people in mid-life. Collaborative work will also be carried following a successful bid to become a EU reference site for healthy and active ageing, supported through the creation of regional platforms promoting partnerships and innovation.

Conclusion

Over the past 15 years, Manchester's ageing agenda has evolved steadily from Valuing Older People to Age-Friendly Manchester, one of the most successful age-friendly programmes within the WHO's GNAFCC. Despite shifting political and economic ground and barriers to implementing age-friendly policies in times of austerity, Manchester has been able not just to sustain but also to *expand* and *raise* the ambition of the urban ageing agenda, further promoting its citizenship-based narrative of ageing centred around values of equality and social justice. Indeed, the city is now at the forefront of developing an ambitious city-regional approach to age-friendly urban development in Greater Manchester, the first of its kind in the UK.

The resilience of these programmes and the strength of the AFM project can, in many ways, be seen as the product of its particular efforts. During the past decade, Manchester has consistently sought to prioritise the development of neighbourhood-level initiatives, piloting innovative initiatives within local communities that recognise the centrality of older people as active citizens in developing the age-friendly approach (for example, White, 2013; Handler, 2014b; Buffel, 2015). It has been able to secure much-needed political support for the programme from the outset, harnessing leadership around the ageing agenda within the local authority, and embedding age-friendliness increasingly firmly into local authority thinking. It has been able to develop and expand its partnerships (with academic institutions and other bodies) and to extend the reach of its programme into a broader city region. It has been able, in addition, to advance an increasingly compelling, citizenship-based narrative around ageing, advanced through the WHO's age-friendly conceptual framework. These ways of working promise an agile model of local authority action that can advance age-friendly urban development from neighbourhood to city-wide to regional level.

Notes

[1] New York (US), Portland (US), Brussels (Belgium), Geneva (Switzerland), Dundalk (Ireland), Donostia-San Sebastián (Spain), Ljubljana (Slovenia), Maribor (Slovenia), Celje (Slovenia), Velenje (Slovenia), Ruše (Slovenia), Melville (Australia) and London (Canada).

[2] New Labour is a term describing the rebranded Labour Party, led in government by Tony Blair from 1997 to 2007, and by Gordon Brown from 2007 to 2010. New Labour was conceived as a more 'electable' version of the Labour Party, shifting its traditional leftist agenda to the centre-left of politics.

[3] Following the 2010 general election, a coalition government was formed to replace the defeated Labour Party, led by the Conservative Party with the Liberal Democrats. It was this coalition government that went on to implement austerity measures in response to the global financial crisis.

References

Audit Commission (2008) *Don't stop me now: Preparing for an ageing population*, London: Audit Commission.

Benington J. (ed) (2011) *New horizons for local governance*, Warwick Business School and the Local Authorities and Research Councils' Initiative.

Buckner, L., Croucher, K., Fry, G. and Jasinska, M. (2013) 'The impact of demographic change on the infrastructure for housing, health and social care in the functional economies of the North of England', *Applied Spatial Analysis and Policy*, 6(2): 123-42.

Buffel, T. (ed) (2015) *Researching age-friendly communities. Stories from older people as co-investigators*, Manchester: The University of Manchester Library.

Buffel, T. and Phillipson, C. (2016) 'Can global cities be "age-friendly cities"? Urban development and ageing populations', *Cities*, 55 (June): 94-100.

Buffel, T., Phillipson, C. and Scharf, T. (2013) 'Experiences of neighbourhood exclusion and inclusion among older people living in deprived inner-city areas in Belgium and England', *Ageing & Society*, 33(1): 89-109.

Buffel, T., McGarry P., Phillipson, C., De Donder, L., Dury, S., De Witte, N., Smetcoren, A. and Vert., D. (2014) 'Developing age-friendly cities: case studies from Brussels and Manchester and implications for policy and practice', *Journal of Aging & Social Policy*, 26(1-2): 52-72.

Buffel, T., Rémillard-Boilard, S. and Phillipson, C. (2015) *Social isolation among older people in urban areas. A review of the literature for the Ambition for Ageing Programme in Greater Manchester*, Manchester: Manchester Institute for Collaborative Research on Ageing.

Bullen, E. (2016) *Older people in Manchester: A profile of residents aged 65 and over*, Manchester: Manchester City Council.

Cox, J., Chabord, E., Griffith, S. (2004) *Sustainable Cities and the Ageing Society*, London: Office of the Deputy Prime Minister and Department for Communities and Local Government.

DCLG (Department for Communities and Local Government) (2008) *Lifetime Homes, Lifetime Neighbourhoods: A national strategy for housing in an ageing society*, London: DCLG, Department of Health, and Department for Work and Pensions.

DWP (Department for Work and Pensions) (2005) *Opportunity Age: Meeting the challenge of ageing in the 21st century*, London: DWP.

DWP (2009) *Building a Society for All Ages*, London: DWP.

Handler, S. (2014a) *A research and evaluation framework for age-friendly cities*, Manchester: Urban Ageing Consortium.

Handler, S. (2014b) *An alternative age-friendly handbook*, Manchester: The University of Manchester Library, Urban Consortium/MICRA.

LGA (Local Government Association) (2009) *Ageing Well case study: Manchester's Generations Together programme*, Manchester: LGA.

Manchester City Council (2009) *Manchester: A great place to grow older 2010–2020*, Manchester: Joint Health Unit.

McGarry, P. and Morris, J. (2011) 'A great place to grow older: a case study of how Manchester is developing an age-friendly city', *Working with Older People*, 15(1): 38-46.

Morris, J. (2013) *Creating age-friendly places*, Manchester: Beth Johnson Foundation, Keele University and Manchester City Council.

Nazroo, J. (2015) *Addressing inequalities in healthy life expectancy*, London: Government Office for Science.

OECD (Organisation for Economic Co-operation and Development) (2015) *Ageing in Cities*, Paris: OECD Publishing.

Office of the Deputy Prime Minister (ODPM) (2006) *A Sure Start to Later Life: Ending inequalities for older people,* London: Social Exclusion Unit, ODPM.

Scharf, T., Phillipson, C. and Smith, A. (2003) 'Older people's perceptions of the neighbourhood: evidence from socially deprived urban areas', *Sociological Research Online*, 8(4): n.p.

White, S., Phillipson, C. and Hammond, M. (2013) *Old Moat: Age-friendly neighbourhood report*, Manchester: Southway Housing Trust.

WHO (World Health Organistion) (2002) *Active Ageing: A Policy Framework*, Geneva: WHO.

WHO (2007) *Global age-friendly cities: A guide*, Geneva:WHO.

WHO (2015) *World Report on Ageing and Health*, Geneva: WHO.

THIRTEEN

The age-friendly community: a test for inclusivity

Sheila Peace, Jeanne Katz, Caroline Holland, Rebecca L. Jones

Introduction

The debate concerning age-friendly cities and communities (AFCC) addresses issues of demographic change at a time of continuing global urbanisation, where inequalities between people and places become central. In many economically developed countries, health and social care policy encourages older people to live in their own mainstream housing. Throughout life people may relocate, primarily to seek employment, but in later years the idea of 'staying put' as a good idea has led to discussion in the UK of the lifetime home and, subsequently, the lifetime neighbourhood (DCLG, 2008; Bevan and Croucher, 2011). Both concepts are related to the AFCC mission. Globally and nationally, moving this dynamic form of social policy forward requires recognition of the heterogeneity of the ageing population and the importance of involving people in co-design and co-production of living spaces. Yet the lives of people experiencing disadvantage and faced with long-term health conditions can challenge the positive milieu of a global social policy portrayed as inclusive, particularly when compounded by cultural, social and economic circumstances (WHO, 2007; Phillipson, 2007, 2012).

This chapter tests the inclusivity of age-friendliness for the lives of older people with sight loss living within English urban and rural communities. Vision impairment can be a lifelong experience, but often occurs in later life alongside other long-term health issues. For many people, changing sensory perception will have happened in an environment that is familiar, possibly with their disability unrecognised externally. Everyday living with its routines and activities may alter as people find new ways of coping (Wahl et al, 1999), sometimes with the support of specific social and cultural groups, sometimes through home adaptation and assistive technology, or by a combination of the two.

Yet given their changing circumstances, people may still experience forms of social exclusion in places that are not enabling.

Testing the principles of the AFCC

Since 2005, the AFCC initiative has aimed to promote active ageing 'by optimizing opportunities for health, participation, and security in order to enhance quality of life as people age' (WHO, 2016a). There are now over 500 cities and communities in 37 countries working towards being more age-friendly as part of the World Health Organization (WHO) Global Network for Age-Friendly Cities and Communities (WHO, 2016b), developing projects enabling participation across a wide range of areas (see Chapter Two, Figure 2.1). As this figure shows, the eight issues raised in terms of age-friendliness are comprehensive, and not only focus on structural aspects of the physical or material environment, but also consider social interaction and forms of participation. The underlying theme of 'active ageing' (see Chapter Two) is also an important dimension. The term 'active' in 'active ageing' relates to the opportunity for inclusion, participation and choice, whatever level of vulnerability a person may experience. In this sense, the aims are parallel to a disability rights perspective and social models of disability and health, where barriers to inclusion through broader societal influences – attitudinal, environmental, economic, social and cultural – outweigh individual difference (Marmot et al, 2012; Shakespeare, 2013). To explore how relevant this view might be for older people with sight loss, we first describe vision impairment among older people in the UK.

Sight loss in later life: the UK example

Sight loss affects people of all ages. In the UK, there are currently around two million people out of a population of 65 million who are affected by vision impairment, an impairment more likely in advanced old age, with older women and people from minority ethnic groups particularly affected.[1] Data from the Royal National Institute of Blind People (RNIB), verified within 2011 census data (ONS, 2012), shows that:

- one in five people aged 75 and over is living with sight loss;
- one in two people aged 90 and over is living with sight loss;
- nearly two-thirds of people living with sight loss are women;

- people from black and minority ethnic communities are at greater risk of some of the leading causes of sight loss;
- adults with learning difficulties are 10 times more likely to be blind or partially sighted than the general population.

The UK population has more people over the age of 60 years than under 18 years (Age UK, 2016); hence, the risk of vision impairment has become more pronounced nationally. Research continues to reveal the effects of disadvantage, with sight issues more common among people from poorer financial backgrounds (Nazroo et al, 2015).

Many people from middle age onwards begin to develop presbyopia or age-related long sight and therefore wear reading glasses. This may cause little difficulty, as reading glasses are relatively cheap and easy to access, but there may be inconveniences and additional stresses. People may become a little slower in response than they might have been and, when outdoors, less able to judge changing signs such as at countdown road crossings. These time and space issues also affect those with more complex vision impairments, who are the focus of this chapter.

In the UK, age-related macular degeneration (AMD) is the leading cause of sight impairment in adults. Other significant complaints include cataracts, glaucoma and diabetic retinopathy. Each condition presents a challenge for orientation. For example, AMD results in the loss of central vision through gradual loss of the macular so that peripheral vision is experienced. There are two types of AMD – wet and dry – with treatment currently only available in relation to wet AMD. Data shows that one in every 10 people over 65 years will have some symptoms of age-related macular degeneration increasing with age. Moreover, more than 40% of those over 75 years will develop cataracts.[2] Cataracts are due to changes in the lens of the eye, which becomes less transparent, leading to blurred or 'misty' vision. These are very common conditions and the main cause of vision impairment worldwide. Some people develop both AMD and cataracts.

Glaucoma and diabetic retinopathy are other common conditions. Diabetic retinopathy can affect people with diabetes who have high blood sugar levels, leading to damage to the retina at the back of the eye. Glaucoma develops very slowly through a build-up of pressure within the eye: the outer field of vision is first affected, working towards the centre of the eye and causing 'tunnel vision'. Currently, some 500,000 people in England and Wales have glaucoma, ranging from two in every 100 people over 40 years to five in every 100 people 80 years and older (Age UK, 2016). This variation in type of condition is not exhaustive and conditions can be experienced together.

People from black and Asian minority ethnic (BAME) groups may be more likely to have vision impairment in later life. The UK Vision Strategy (VISION2020, 2016) indicates that:

- black people under the age of 60 are more at risk of developing AMD than white or Asian people;
- in comparison to the wider community, Asian people have a great risk of developing cataracts;
- black and Asian people have a high risk of developing diabetic retinopathy;
- black people have a high risk of developing glaucoma;
- people from black and minority ethnic communities are at risk of not taking up community-based eye care services.

These basic facts about vision impairment indicate some of the issues regarding the diversity of the older population whose vision impairment experience is acknowledged here.

Stigma, sight loss and ageing: is this an excluded group?

The characteristics of vision impairment in later life and the impact of cultural difference begin to indicate the potential for multiple jeopardy and implications for social exclusion. Scharf and Keating (2012) highlight a range of definitions of social exclusion but, following their discussion, we adopt the definition given by Levitas and colleagues as 'the lack or denial of resources, rights, goods and services, and the inability to participate in the normal relationships and activities available to the majority of people in society' (Levitas et al, 2007, p 25). Is this definition supported by the literature for older people with vision impairment?

In 2002, French and Swain reviewed the field of disability studies relating to vision impairment in later life. As advocates of the social model of disability, they found little contemporary research offering anything other than an individualised view of disability to deal with issues such as health, stress and psychosocial adaptation. They concluded that those with such concerns, such as vision impaired older people, were 'neglected by society' and 'absent in the Disability Studies literature' (French and Swain, 2002, p 2). They commented that in later life sight conditions may be viewed as 'inevitable and non-urgent' with little resource spent on services. They noted that most older people are not 'registered blind' and so were not thought to be 'mobility impaired' – yet they also found more than half would never go out alone (French and Swain, 2002, p 3). Using this material, they challenged disability studies to address social exclusion from everyday society for all groups (French and Swain, 2002, p 5). Their work highlights divisions between those working with older people and those working with people with disabilities who are vision impaired.

While Zimdars and colleagues (2011) see older people with vision impairment as an under-researched group, national and international literature has developed concerning housing, living arrangements, health and wellbeing (see Peace et al, 2016). In the UK, social research funded through the Thomas Pocklington Trust (TPT) needs to be acknowledged (TPT, 2016),[3] including Hanson and colleagues' (2002) detailed study of the housing and support needs of 400 older people with vision impairment, which provides baseline data from architectural and social science perspectives. This work indicates how many vision impaired older people do not wish to leave their homes, and shows how adaptations can improve accommodation, and the importance of adequate and flexible space. Many older people with vision impairment proactively rearrange and structure their home environment in ways that enable them to retain everyday competence (Wahl et al, 1999). Hanson and colleagues' and French and Swain's studies were undertaken in parallel, but highlight the lack of communication between different research traditions.

Knowledge about the effects of vision impairment on older people's health, quality of life and wellbeing is still limited. However, research shows that there are clear risks of depression and reduced mental wellbeing for this group, which may relate, for example, to experiences such as social isolation due to difficulties in getting out of the house (McManus and Lord, 2012). The importance of social relationships is central to wellbeing. A meta-synthesis of qualitative studies of older people's emotional wellbeing and adjustment to vision loss found that an individual's ability to accept their condition and develop a positive attitude was an important factor in wellbeing, as was social support from family, friends and peers (Nyman et al, 2012). However, vision loss was not the only, or most important, factor leading to depression and low wellbeing: poor health and economic status were also important (Nyman et al, 2012, pp 971–81). Since most people in the UK in the 75-plus age group have three or more long-term health conditions (Barnett et al, 2012), the complexity of living with comorbidity is central: at least 123,000 people in the UK are thought to have both serious sight loss and dementia, with implications for housing design (TPT, 2016). There is also growing evidence that people with vision impairment are more likely to experience falls, many requiring hospital treatment (Dhital et al, 2010).

Comparable research between people with vision impairment aged 40–69 and 70–98 indicates five important common needs: daily coping skills; affordability and access to technological aids; transport; information and access to the built environment; and personal attitudes towards sight loss by all parties (Duckett et al, 2010). Older people with vision impairment may feel disempowered by well-meaning family and friends who especially fear that they will fall or injure themselves. Balance is needed between support and overprotection, and this is fundamental to discussions of inclusion and exclusion.

Researching age-friendly communities: recognising diversity

How can research concerning vision impairment in later life contribute to understanding inclusivity in AFCC? Here we consider the research methodology used for the Manchester-based age-friendly community/ neighbourhood programme (Buffel, 2015), in comparison with that of the Needs and Aspirations of Vision Impaired Older People (NAVIOP) study (Peace et al, 2016).[4] The Manchester study is a model of good practice in participatory research, '... examining how older residents, especially those in disadvantaged positions, perceive their neighbourhood (both the physical-spatial and social characteristics of their area) and how the neighbourhood influences (promotes or obstructs) active ageing' (Buffel, 2015, p 29). Yet, in aiming to address disadvantaged groups vision impairment was not a central issue.

The NAVIOP study arrived indirectly at pertinent findings for considering issues that a vision-friendly community should address. Guided by the needs of the funding body, the TPT, the research considered the following:

> How are people ageing with vision impairment able to maintain a way of life that they judge as living well? How enabling is the environment in which people live? Do people have access to the resources and information they need? What activities of daily living do people undertake/ maintain and what are their coping strategies? What are the relationships that support their wellbeing? How do people maintain their identity? (Peace et al, 2016, p 3)

A comparison of methods demonstrates fundamental differences between participatory action research (Manchester) aiming to create ongoing community development and change, and NAVIOP research, which seeks to understand the needs and aspirations of an under-researched group; the one should incorporate the other. In Manchester, location-specific research (in three wards) is qualitative, ethnographic and participatory, combining 14 focus groups with older people alongside stakeholder interviews and participant observations. The researchers recognised the need to include a wider range of participants, leading to 18 older volunteers training as co-researchers. They located and interviewed 68 'hard-to-reach' older people, including those from different ethnic groups, those who were isolated, and those experiencing health conditions and poverty. Vision impairment was not identified as a particular characteristic of this group (Buffel, personal communication, 2016). The research is supported by Manchester City Council, an active member of the WHO Global Network for Age-Friendly Cities and Communities, and used both a research advisory board with key professionals working to maintain an impact and sustainability, as well as a lay advisory committee of older people and community stakeholders to facilitate local support and communication.

In contrast, the NAVIOP study, which deliberately targeted vision impaired older people, began by contacting stakeholders in voluntary national and regional support groups for vision impaired people across England. The aim to include people from minority ethnic groups as well as people in late old age led to purposive sampling. Access was unpredictable and the final sample included people living in urban/semi-rural and rural locations from East Suffolk to Liverpool, Buckinghamshire to Coventry. In this study, the potential for disadvantage among vision impaired older people was uncertain, even if predicted by the literature. While community involvement, housing and everyday activity were central to the study, participatory action was not the aim. The project did have a research advisory group, however, including people with vision impairment and professionals from both vision impaired and ageing groups who were involved in policymaking and practice. Ideas concerning a vision-friendly community were discussed, and the research team undertook communication training for working with people with vision impairment.

In both projects, recorded in-depth interviews provided a central database. In Manchester, the co-researchers were part of the analysis and reflection process, addressing what age-friendly means to individuals and their specific neighbourhood. Issues of transportation, public toilets, community groups, social participation and safety were considered, alongside recognition of skills, knowledge and experience. In contrast, the academic team in the NAVIOP study carried out collective framework analysis for each participant, comparing findings for older people with vision impairment with those from a smaller group of family, friends and service providers. The contribution of these findings to the discussion of what is meant by an age-friendly community follows, raising methodological issues that are revisited in the conclusion of this chapter.

A profile of older participants in the NAVIOP study

The small purposive sample of 50 older people in the NAVIOP study included 36 women and 14 men living in English cities, towns and rural communities. Sight issues covered a wide range of conditions and 62% of participants – the majority with severe sight impairment – were registered with their local council. Some participants had already worn glasses for an ongoing astigmatism or presbyopia before developing further conditions. There were 17 people with AMD, 12 with multiple sight conditions (including AMD in most cases), 10 with sudden loss, trauma or illness-related sight loss, and five other conditions including glaucoma. All lived with blurred, peripheral and clouded vision that could be debilitating, often experienced alongside other health conditions such as those related to mobility (such as arthritis), heart or circulatory illness, diabetes or thyroid conditions. Four participants had had strokes and two had vascular dementia. Poor hearing was identified alongside a wide range of other ailments that could be more or less debilitating.

As noted, participants from BAME groups were over-represented in the research, although not everyone wanted to define themselves in terms of ethnicity. Of those who did self-define, 32 identified as White British, with the remaining 18 representing a wide range of ethnicities including Black British, Asian British, Black African, Asian (excluding Asian British but including Asian, Indian, East African Asian), mixed race and other (European). The diversity of cultures was reflected in the age range, with those from minority ethnic groups being younger with poorer health. The youngest participant was aged 54 (blind since birth, and from a minority ethnic group). Apart from this person, the age range was 69 to 99 years: average 79 years; median 80 years. Current marital status included 26 people widowed, 16 married, four divorced, two separated and two single. The researchers did not solicit information on sexual orientation or gender transitions and no participant talked about being non-heterosexual or transgendered.

Figure 13.1: Co-residence arrangements for participants in the NAVIOP study

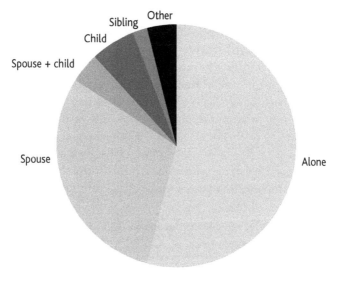

Source: Peace et al (2016, p 20)

While noting the relationship between socioeconomic status and social inclusion, the financial circumstances of these participants were hard to establish. Some did not want to discuss their finances, while the financial affairs of others were being handled by family members and people were unsure about the sources of their income. However, the researchers identified broad trends for two thirds of the sample, indicating variation between those describing themselves as 'comfortably off' or 'comfortable' and those whose incomes typically comprised state pension and pension credit who tended not to have any savings: these were primarily widowed or divorced women.

Finally, Figure.13.1 shows that over half of the participants were living alone and a further 30% with their spouse. In addition, just over two thirds were owner-occupiers and 14% social or private renters. A small number of participants were interviewed with their partner present. Respondents lived in a range of housing types from detached houses to one-bedroomed flats and most participants (64%) had lived in their present home for over 20 years. These long-term residencies are probably related to owner-occupation and have an influence on the sense of familiarity to both home and local community. The question becomes, how age and vision-friendly are these environments?

Spending the day

How may the concept of 'age-friendly' be experienced by an older person with vision impairment? Many participants in the NAVIOP study spent much of their day at home, with trips outside being either to local shops or for specific reasons – religious worship, a medical visit, or a vision impairment group meeting. 'Housing' is a central theme in the WHO AFCC programme, and the NAVIOP participants defined home as somewhere they felt secure – a place where they could do what they liked, and where they knew where everything was – in contrast to places and experiences outside the house. Home activities were markedly more safe and comfortable than community-based ones.

Vision-friendly home: adaptations and assistive technology

Over time, like most householders, participants had made changes to their environment. They had modernised kitchens and bathrooms, renewed fixtures and fittings, knocked through rooms or built conservatories to increase space. These alterations contributed to a feeling of homeliness and control rather than relating specifically to issues of sight. However, participants recognised the possibility of tripping or falling due to vision impairment. In their experience professional advice about possible adaptations was hard to access, usually triggered through recognition of a physical impairment or other health issue, and accompanied by long waiting times for occupational therapy assessments or issues concerning funding. In a few cases, the local authority had funded adaptations, but often these were self-funded or in some cases provided by a local sight-loss charity. These kinds of adaptations included stair lifts, indoor rails (particularly upstairs), ramps to front and rear doors, higher WC pans to assist sitting and rising, and bath and shower arrangements adapted to help with mobility difficulties. Some changes had been undertaken specifically for vision problems, and interviewees described kitchen improvements such as better lighting, colour contrasts and installing window blinds to reduce strong natural light. However, changes were not universal and environmental barriers were still problematic.

In contrast to these difficulties, most interviewees knew about the latest types of assistive device available, varying in sophistication and complexity. In many cases relatives or friends had searched the internet looking for devices and worked out the cost. Sometimes participants had done this themselves, or asked local vision support organisations for advice. This level of communication was essential. The most commonly used assistive devices were, in order of prevalence, various magnifiers (including Optelec for image enhancement reader devices); liquid level indicators; labels and markers on domestic equipment; specialised lighting; talking clocks; talking watches; and computers, some with special, large-character keyboards. Several respondents regularly used specialist computer software with features such as proprietary speech outputs. Other 'talking' devices and services included books/news (one using Gujerati services), microwave ovens, phones, calculators, kitchen scales and the Penfriend (audio labeller). In addition, many participants used 'everyday' technologies such as pre-set numbers on mobile phones, tape recorders and LED torches. Many also used personal alarms, and one participant with poor hearing used a vibrating pillow fire alarm. Individual participants reported using simpler kinds of aids, such as a signature guide or a monocular, and some used coloured over-glasses. However, others described how either they had tried and given up on various devices, or else had found them to become less useful as their vision deteriorated or as they developed other health issues including hearing problems.

These findings indicate how important it is for age-friendly cities and communities to embrace technological development in order to assist diversity empowerment. The prevalence and type of devices identified by participants is linked to accessibility through information sharing and communication, and this has economic implications. It is essential that older people with impaired vision have continuing support so that they know who to contact for advice in relation to housing adaptations or useful technological devices. In the NAVIOP research, cultural associations were central for vision impaired older people from BAME groups, with group leaders communicating with other voluntary bodies and statutory organisations in order to gain information and support. Some participants had particular needs due to issues such as language difficulties or social isolation. In respect of the eight dimensions in the WHO AFCC model (see Chapter Two), links between housing, communication and information, and community support and health services are essential for developing a vision-friendly home.

Of course, even with a supportive material environment, attempts to pursue an active lifestyle reflect the complexity of everyday living where vision, mobility, feelings of wellbeing and levels of social support – formal and informal – may vary. In describing their activities of daily living, research participants expressed different degrees of vulnerability. Most were able to get in and out of chairs, wash themselves, put themselves to bed and go to the toilet. A small number (*n*=6) needed support to get in and out of bed and could not carry out basic washing or showering, or needed help at particular times: "At night wife has to help me to go to the toilet" (Asian male, Coventry). In some cases, participants could undertake their own personal care, but had serious mobility difficulties within the house and used strategically placed mobility aids such as a stair lift, a wheelchair, walking sticks or a walker. Getting dressed posed difficulties for some, and several talked about choosing clothes and being unsure of whether they were clean and matching. Some had devised strategies for ensuring what they wore was appropriate, choosing particular colours or styles, yet this limited their wardrobe.

A very familiar home layout could be helpful. However, a few participants acknowledged that they still occasionally had problems. The wife of a participant from East Anglia said: "Everyone with eyesight problems gets lost even in their own home." Some participants reported that they often spent the day at home sitting in their gardens, or listening to the radio, talking books or the television. Many people sat in the same chair in their living room and had memorised how to get to and from this chair, and to, for example the bathroom, the kitchen or the 'reading' machine. An object accidentally moved from its usual place could throw a person with vision impairment into great disarray, making them feel insecure.

Meal preparation and cooking was difficult for some participants. Many employed different aids to support them with cooking: raised knobs on their cookers/microwaves to indicate temperature; strip lights over the hob; talking microwaves; talking kitchen scales; and liquid level indicators. However, experiences differed. Amy from the Midlands said, *"You can't see if it is cooked or not"*, while other participants described putting inedible things into their mouths at times. As their eyesight became poorer, many participants who lived alone had changed their eating habits. Some had completely stopped preparing food, buying ready-made meals for heating by themselves or by relatives or carers. A number of men who had cooked prior to losing their vision spoke of eating out as much as possible.

Talking about former pastimes often brought a great sense of loss. Before suffering impaired vision, several female participants had undertaken skilled craftwork (such as making porcelain dolls, greetings cards, crocheting, knitting, pottery), as well as pursuits such as doing jigsaws or gardening. Now they aimed to do other things instead, or adapted their behaviour with the support of others. For many people, talking books and the radio were an enjoyment, while changes to garden layout through infrastructure such as raised beds could maintain a long-term hobby. Daphne Palmer from Coventry said: *"Talking books are my lifeline (and the radio). I don't know what I'd do without them."* Many gained equipment through the British Wireless for the Blind Fund.

The research shows that with the support of others – family, friends, occupational therapists and especially the voluntary support organisations – these older people were finding their home environments manageable. They were able to carry out what we have called 'responsible risk-taking activities' in their own private space and voiced an acceptance of their sight loss that was perhaps more difficult to accept outside the home.

A wider vision-friendly community

There was a tension between things participants used to do and things that they now found difficult because of vision impairment, especially if this meant going out and being part of the wider community. This could feel more acute for someone going out alone rather than with a partner, family or friends. Some would not go out unaccompanied, although many of the participants had access to support groups and as such attended regular group meetings. Additional community involvement varied among the respondents.

The WHO framework identifies two areas of the material and structural environment that affect social participation in the wider community: outdoor spaces and buildings, and transportation. Some of the NAVIOP participants went out frequently, even if it meant taking taxis or asking friends for lifts, as not all visits were local. This was true for group meetings. But others, particularly participants from minority ethnic groups who had family support, went out less frequently, and when they did so it was mainly to undertake essential tasks such as attending medical appointments. Their primary social activities outside the house were to attend religious services or to attend meetings of their vision impaired groups. Mr Jamail (M) and his wife (F) from Coventry explained his regular activities:

M: "I go out on my own some days of the week. Like Friday I go to the mosque, other days I just go out to the city centre and back again. I go to the gym for the cardiac exercises once a week, so I do get out and move about."

              [...]

F: "Sometimes he goes and sits in the library."

Interviewer:	"And how do you go when you go?"
M:	"I use the bus generally."
Interviewer:	"Have you got a bus near here?"
M:	"Yes, just one, you get out of this place where the properties are, and just on the main road you can get a bus."

Some participants really missed the independence of being able to drive, and because of this public transport, especially a local bus service, was essential. Participants bemoaned the paucity of bus services, however, and the fact that many did not run at night. They also needed to know when the bus was on its way and needed help getting on board.

Figure 13.2: Demonstrating the bus hailer

Although a few participants knew about the bus 'hailer' – large flip cards indicating the desired bus number and displayed by the passenger at the bus stop (see Figure 13.2) – only one person used it.

Participants identified a need for audio announcements and somewhere comfortable to wait for public transport, as well as support from transport staff. One participant had been actively lobbying the council over bus shelters:

"They've got an older shopping area called the [...]. So they're pulling that down, rebuilding the whole area, but they haven't considered buses. Because that's the stopping place for buses to turn round and go back down into town. So there are seven routes, and the shelter they've got at the moment is a covered shelter where people can sit inside out of the rain. The proposal is cantilevered ones where there's no seats or no covering from the rain and so on."

Understanding such local plans and being informed through vision impairment groups often held at a community centre or library was important so that social relations could be maintained. Transport assistance could be a lifeline and some vision impaired participants really valued resources such as local minibuses that take people to meetings;

coach trips providing regular outings; and access to personal assistants for one-to-one shopping trips, for example.

Whether accompanied or unaccompanied, some participants found it problematic to go out walking in the wider community, and some required the use of a stick. Nine participants used ordinary walking sticks while 18 used white sticks – either a white stick or the folding 'symbol cane'. The symbol cane is used to alert others to the loss of vision and users need to have training in its use. Those participants who owned a white stick – either long or short – did not always wish to be seen using it. Did they fear being identified as having a disability?

Local journeys on foot posed considerable challenges, with narrow pedestrian walkways sometimes particularly difficult. Pavements may not exist on some stretches of road, or be wide enough for easy passing. Indeed, for many, the state of local pavements was a cause for considerable alarm as noted here:

> "It can be a little bit frightening. And pavements I find a great problem because they are uneven and I fall if I'm not careful." (Shirley from Hertfordshire)

> "The pavements are vile but I get by … the paving slabs are all crap; the council say they have no money to do repairs." (Arthur Mathieson from Coventry)

So, the local environment could be disabling. From 1995 onwards, aspects of the AFCC mission have overlapped with disability discrimination and equality legislation within the UK (see Norgate, 2012), leading to greater accessibility and visibility in public open spaces through dropped kerbs, tactile paving and audible/tactile signals at pelican crossings to control traffic flow. However, some participants were unaware of the tactile crossing signals and these were not common in all research locations. In Warwickshire, participants were especially worried (*Coventry Telegraph*, 2013) about the removal of pedestrian crossings to create 'shared spaces' for cars, bicycles and pedestrians to merge (DfT, 2011). This Department of Transport initiative has not been welcomed by older people or disabled people with severe sight impairment (Thomas, 2008).

Additionally, the lack of public toilets deterred some interviewees from going out. No audible signage in relation to public toilets for vision impaired residents was noted and some spoke of difficulties in relation to unfamiliar surroundings, for example, locking the door of a public toilet, finding the flush mechanism, or familiarising themselves with hand-washing facilities. Nevertheless, in order to preserve their independence, many participants persevered in navigating their local areas, memorising specific routes and navigable pedestrian crossings. Local shops with familiar and helpful staff were especially important, as were access to seats, and staff prepared to fetch or deliver. Other than going to the shops, participants met friends or attended clubs (not only vision impairment groups). Some found their religious faith kept them part of the wider community. Only three people, all living in rural areas, had trained guide dogs.

Nevertheless, some participants commented on exclusion resulting from vision impairment. In Milton Keynes, an active participant involved in a number of local voluntary groups commented on how a support worker could be found to help her at a meeting but not for less formal leisure activities. She said:

> "... but they can't give me anybody to walk with me if I want to walk for pleasure or help ... now U3A, you see, they have exercise groups, but if I go there they can't help me. I feel I'm barred, they don't say openly but in some way I'm not in that group, I feel an outsider because of visual impairment."

At its extreme, this feeling of exclusion was often found among those living alone without local support, who could feel lonely or socially isolated. The research indicates the importance of building confidence in older people who are becoming vision impaired to enable them to maintain and adapt their lifestyle. Talk and Support, a mutual telephone support network run through the RNIB, offers one solution.

Can the AFCC mission be socially inclusive for people with vision impairment?

To conclude, this chapter uses data from an in-depth study with older people with vision impairment to consider how their needs and aspirations can be, or are being, met in relation to the development of age-friendly cities and communities. Scharf and colleagues (2005) identified five domains of social exclusion for older people living in deprived urban communities, which we have considered here :

- material resources;
- social relations;

- civic activities;
- basic services;
- neighbourhood exclusion.

Our participants varied in the degree to which they were financially secure; had meaningful relationships with family, friends and neighbours; were able or wished to engage with 'decision-making processes' that influenced their own lives; were able to access local services; or found that their local environment enhanced their wellbeing. What they shared was the experience of vision impairment, and they bring the complexity of living with vision impaired conditions to the AFCC debate.

The familiarity of a local neighbourhood alongside adapted housing, accessibility, and the importance of maintaining social relationships were perhaps the most important issues for these participants. We acknowledge their specific profile as people linked to voluntary support groups for vision impairment, but see these associations as an asset for developing a vision-friendly community. They provide a pathway for communication, information and the opportunity to take part in community events. Here the WHO age-friendly social participation checklist (WHO 2007, p 44) provides an important tool for such groups to evaluate their accessibility, activities and affordability: if the circumstances of these participants changed, maintaining social contact could be vital for preventing isolation. Additionally, participants from BAME groups identified the importance of cultural support for gaining access to wider resources.

Each AFCC theme raises issues. Transport and the built environment are two important areas for vision impaired older people, and here the significance of more inclusive design in facilitating social inclusion is fundamental (Mahmood and Keating, 2012), both inside and outside dwellings. Our findings indicate the centrality of adaptations within the home and the ongoing development of technology to support people with degrees of sight loss. Transport, both public and private, is essential in the area of access, yet we note that issues outlined in the WHO checklist concerning transport (2007, p 20) make no mention of people with vision impairment and their needs for audible signage, or the ways in which transport and highways connect to walking routes and the crucial boundaries needed between the two to aid navigation. Through future development of assistive technology and accessible street design, people of all ages with vision impairment could feel greater integration and empowerment in their local community.

We have noted, when comparing research methods, that there is still a case to be made for targeting certain groups to make sure that their voices are heard. Participatory research methods must continue to explore diversity and draw on specialist studies when considering AFCC. The combination of vision impairment and disability in later life has been ignored, yet the diverse group of people with age-related eye conditions is increasing. For example Access Economics (2009) estimates a 184% increase in age-related macular degeneration between 2010 and 2050. At the same time, Phillipson (2012) reminds us that the growing ageing population lives in a predominantly urban world where facilities and services may change and where the local environment may become more crucial. At a time when the global AFCC mission continues to develop, albeit slowly (Tinker and Ginn, 2015), the world of vision impaired older people continues to be a test for inclusivity.

Notes

1   RNIB data from www.rnib.org.uk/ (accessed July 2016); see Peace et al, 2016.
2   See www.nhs.uk/Conditions/Visual-impairment/Pages/Introductionaspx (accessed 15 August 2016)
3   For all research and design guidance funded through the Thomas Pocklington Trust, search www.pocklington-trust.org.uk
4   The NAVIOP study was funded by the Thomas Pocklington Trust.

References

Access Economics (2009) *Future sight loss UK (1): The economic impact of partial sight and blindness in the UK Adult Population*, London: Access Economics

Age UK (2016) 'Later life in the United Kingdom', available at www.ageuk.org.uk/Documents/EN-GB/Factsheets/Later_Life_UK_factsheet.pdf?dtrk=true.

Barnett, K., Stewart, W.M., Norbury, M., Watt, G., Wyke, S. and Gutherie, B. (2012) 'Epidemiology of multimorbidity and implications for health care, research, and medical education: a cross-sectional study', *The Lancet*, 380(9836): 37-43.

Bevan, M. and Croucher, K. (2011) *Lifetime neighbourhoods*, London: HMSO.

Buffel, T. (ed) (2015) *Researching age-friendly communities. Stories from older people as co-investigators*, Manchester: The University of Manchester Library.

Coventry Telegraph (2013) 'Charities for the blind hit out over Shared Spaces in Warwick', available at www.coventrytelegraph.net/news/coventry-news/charities-blind-hit-out-over-3013043

DCLG (Department for Communities and Local Government) (2008) *Lifetime Homes, Lifetime Neighbourhoods: A national strategy*, London: DCLG, available at www.housingcare.org/information/detail-2966_lifetime_homes_lifetime_neighbourhoods_a_national_strategy.aspx.

DfT (Department for Transport) (2011) *Local Transport Note 1/11: Shared space*, London: DfT.

Dhital, A., Pey, T. and Stanford, M.R. (2010) 'Visual loss and falls: a review', *Eye*, 24(9): 1437-46.

Duckett, P., Pratt, R. and Porteous, R. (2010) *The opinions of people with sight loss on visual impairment research: Study three*, Thomas Pocklington Trust, Research Findings No. 29, London: Thomas Pocklington Trust.

French, S. and Swain, J. (2002) 'Neglected Voices in Disability Studies: the case of older visually impaired people', Paper presented at seminar on Ageing and Disability, Centre for Disability Studies (CeDR), Lancaster, available at www.lancaster.ac.uk/fass/events/disabilityconference_archive/2003/papers/french_swain2003.pdf

Hanson, J., Percival, J., Zako, R. and Johnson, M. (2002) *The housing and support needs of older people with visual impairment*, Research Findings No. 1, London: Thomas Pocklington Trust.

Levitas, R., Pantazis, C., Fahmy, E., Gordon, D., Lloyd, E. and Patsios, D. (2007) *The multi-dimensional analysis of social exclusion*, London: DCLG, Social Exclusion Unit.

Mahmood, A. and Keating, N. (2012) 'Towards inclusive built environments for older adults', in T. Scharf and N.C Keating (eds) *From exclusion to inclusion in old age: A global challenge*, Bristol: Policy Press, pp 145-62.

Marmot, M., Allen, J., Bell, R., Bloomer, E. and Goldblatt, P. (2012), 'WHO European review of social determinants of health and the health divide', *The Lancet*, 380(9846): 1011-29.

McManus, S. and Lord, C. (2012) *Circumstances of people with sight loss: Secondary analysis of Understanding Society the Life Opportunities Survey*, London: Natcen.

Nazroo, J., Whillans, J. and Mathews, K. (2015) *Changes in vision in older people: Causes and impact*, Research Findings No. 49, London: Thomas Pocklington Trust.

Norgate, S.H. (2012) 'Accessibility of urban spaces for visually impaired pedestrians', *Proceedings of the Institute of Civil Engineers: Municipal Engineer*, 65(4): 231–7.

Nyman, S.R., Dibb, B., Victor, C.R., and Gosney, M.A. (2012) 'Emotional well-being and adjustment to vision loss in later life: a meta-synthesis of qualitative studies', *Disability & Rehabilitation*, 34(12): 971-81.

ONS (2012) 'Census 2011', available at www.ons.gov.uk/ons/guide-method/census/2011/index.html?utm_source=twitterfeed&utm_medium=twitter.

Peace, S., Katz, J., Holland, C. and Jones, R. (2016) *The needs and aspirations of older people with visual impairment*, Milton Keynes/London: The Open University/Thomas Pocklington Trust.

Phillipson, C. (2007) 'The "elected" and the "excluded": sociological perpectives on the experience of place and community in old age', *Ageing & Society*, 27(3): 321-42.

Phillipson, C. (2012) *Developing age-friendly cities: Policy challenges and options*, Viewpoint 37, London: Housing Learning & Improvement Network.

Scharf, T. and Keating, N.C. (2012) 'Social exclusion in later life: a global challenge', in T. Scharf and N.C. Keating (eds) *From exclusion to inclusion in old age: A global challenge*, Bristol: Policy Press, pp 1-16.

Scharf, T., Phillipson, C. and Smith, A. (2005) 'Social exclusion of older people in deprived urban communities of England', *European Journal of Ageing*, 2(2): 76-87.

Shakespeare, T. (2013) 'The social model of disability', in L.J. Davis (ed) *The disability studies reader* (4th edn), Oxford: Routledge, pp 197-204.

Thomas, C. (2008) 'Discussion: Shared space-safe space?', *Proceedings of the Institute of Civil Engineers: Municipal Engineer*, 161(1): 59-60, available at http://dx.doi.org/10.1680/muen.2008.161.1.59.

Tinker, A. and Ginn, J. (2015) *An age friendly city – how far has London come?*, London: Kings College London.

Vision2020 (2016) *Vision2020 UK Strategy*, www.vision2020uk.org.uk

Wahl, H.-W., Oswald, F. and Zimprich, D. (1999) 'Everyday competence in visually impaired older adults: a case for person-environment perspectives', *The Gerontologist*, 39(2): 140-7.

WHO (World Health Organization) (2007) *Global age-friendly cities: A guide*, Geneva: WHO, available at www.who.int/aging/publications/Global_age_friendly_cities_Guide_English.pdf.

WHO (2016a) 'Ageing and the life course', www.who.int/ageing/active_ageing/en.

WHO (2016b) 'Checklist of essential features of age-friendly cities', www.who.int/ageing/publications/Age_friendly_cities_checklist.pdf

Zimdars, A., Nazroo, J. and Gjonca, E. (2011) 'The circumstances of older people in England with self-reported visual impairment: a secondary analysis of the English Longitudinal Study of Ageing (ELSA)', *The British Journal of Visual Impairment*, 30(1): 22–30.

FOURTEEN

Age-friendly cities and communities: a manifesto for change

Tine Buffel, Sophie Handler, Chris Phillipson

Introduction

The aim of this book has been to provide a comprehensive assessment of progress around the issue of developing age-friendly cities and communities (AFCC). Part 1 examined the origins and implementation of age-friendly policies linking these to questions surrounding changes in the nature of community life in the 21st century. A key argument in this section concerned the need to incorporate issues relating to social inequalities and exclusion as an integral part of the debate around developing AFCC. Part 2 presented empirical research drawn from case studies demonstrating the challenges and opportunities for developing age-friendly policies in communities undergoing pressures from gentrification, transnational migration and related forms of change. Part 3 identified a range of design strategies and policy initiatives aimed at improving the environments in which older people live.

Drawing on insights from the chapters in this book, this final chapter presents a 'manifesto for change', aimed at raising the aspirations of what is now a worldwide movement for improving the quality of life of older citizens. Despite the expansion of the World Health Organization (WHO) Global Network for Age-Friendly Cities and Communities (GNAFCC), challenges remain in responding to the growth of inequality and the impact of economic austerity on policies targeted at older people. Given this context, it becomes especially important to develop a framework for action that strengthens commitment to the primary goal of making environments responsive to the diverse needs of people as they age.

To assist this work, this chapter presents a 10-point manifesto for change, drawing on arguments and perspectives developed by the contributors to this book. The aim of the manifesto is to sharpen debate in the age-friendly field as well as encourage new approaches among the various stakeholders, including urban planners, community developers, health and social care professionals, policymakers, non-governmental organisations (NGOs), voluntary workers, and not least, older people themselves.

Acknowledging urban complexity

The first issue concerns applying 'age-friendliness' in a way that recognises the complexity of the global urban environment. The techniques for ensuring an age-friendly approach will vary considerably depending on the characteristics of urban change and development. While the trend towards urban living is worldwide, the pattern of urban growth demonstrates huge variation: shrinking city populations in the developed world (Europe especially), and accelerating urbanisation in Africa and Asia, with both continents demonstrating a mix of rapidly expanding cities in some cases, declining ones in others. 'Age-friendly' approaches will also vary according to the size of a city. The approach might, for example, be different in Europe, where small cities with fewer than 500,000 residents are the norm, as compared with the US where large urban agglomerations (with populations of between two and five million) are much more common. Securing 'age-friendliness' in the context of the rise of 'mega-cities' and 'hyper-cities' (the latter with populations of 20 million or more) provide another variation.

At the same time, processes for developing 'age-friendliness' will need radical adaptation, given the 'slum cities' prevalent in Southern Asia and sub-Saharan Africa. The bulk of population growth in these continents has taken place largely through the rise of vast shantytowns, many of these located on the edge of capital cities but in many cases larger in size than the urban centres to which they relate. Other developments that challenge conventional approaches to age-friendly cities include the rise of 'squatting communities' in Latin America and other parts of the world; the continued growth in inequalities in land ownership across the global north and south; the dramatic increase of global forced displacement as a result of persecution, conflict, violence or human rights violations; and the spread of homelessness across all societies – with older people living on the streets representing a major challenge to conventional approaches to developing age-friendly communities.

To these may be added the crises brought about by extreme weather linked with climate change. Events associated with hurricanes (for example, Hurricane Katrina, which hit the Gulf Coast of the US in 2005), heatwaves (such as that in Chicago in 1995) or earthquakes and tsunamis (for example, the earthquake off the Pacific Coast of

Tōhoku, Japan, in 2011) have had devastating consequences for human populations, with the evidence suggesting that older people have been among the most vulnerable in terms of loss of life, destruction of neighbourhoods, and dislodgement from their homes.

All of this underlines the need to rethink approaches to age-friendly work in the context of increasingly unequal and unstable societies, with older people displaced by the effects of war, climate change, rural decline and accelerating urban development. One issue here is the need for emergency response facilities to be seen as crucial to building age-friendly communities for the future, with these incorporating contributions from specialists in working with vulnerable older people, notably those diagnosed with dementia and related conditions, and those with physical conditions exacerbated by extreme weather. AFCC initiatives must also be linked with broader campaigns, for example, around social justice, poverty reduction and access to good quality healthcare. This will ensure that age-friendly activity is viewed as an essential element of work to improve the lives of older people across the global south and north.

Prioritising home and neighbourhood

Developing the age-friendly approach requires greater recognition of the importance of housing and neighbourhood issues in the lives of older people. Extending the range of housing options within communities should therefore be key to the development of age-friendly activity. To date, progress has been slow in increasing choice, beyond specialist provision such as retirement villages and extra-care housing. The reality, however, is that the majority of older people will continue to prefer to live in communities with a mix of ages. Interest in a greater variety of housing options (such as cooperative housing and house sharing) is likely to increase, given the growth of single-person households. Meeting this demand will require a creative partnership between older people, housing associations, building companies and other relevant groups. In many cases, groups of older people will themselves want to take control in developing new types of housing more directly tailored to the needs and aspirations they bring to daily life.

But a key constituency must also be brought into the discussion, namely, developers responsible for the regeneration of city centres and private housing builders responding to demands for new housing. There is limited evidence in the case of the former that issues connected with population ageing feature in the rebuilding of cities across Europe and elsewhere; on the contrary, in terms of their accessibility (for example, for those with mobility problems), cities represent formidable barriers in respect of encouraging social and civic participation. In terms of housing, developers and volume builders largely focus on first-time buyers, families and single professionals, an approach that will almost certainly lead to increasingly age-segregated neighbourhoods.

An alternative approach would be to encourage housing associations or similar organisations to support innovation in home adaptations, retirement housing, co-housing and similar schemes, as well as to encourage local and regional authorities to take on the development of new types of housing for later life. Along with this must come recognition that reliance on market forces alone have proved grossly inadequate for meeting housing needs in later life. This is illustrated by the narrow range of housing options in many countries – especially for those on low incomes; the patchwork provision of home adaptations; and the extent to which profit maximisation takes precedence over safety and security – as illustrated in the Grenfell Tower fire in London in 2017, where elderly people with limited mobility (along with other groups) died trapped in their homes.

Improving safety and security within neighbourhoods is also central to developing an age-friendly approach. Work is needed to ensure that groups of older people in areas of high economic deprivation have access to spaces that allow full participation within the community. In some cases, this will draw on existing resources such as libraries, community centres and colleges. Outreach activities to those in residential homes, befriending schemes for those who are housebound, and extended access to educational programmes will also be important areas for expansion within communities.

Neighbourhood support is therefore a vital part of age-friendly activity. Equally, as argued at different points in this book, it is important to address the way in which some groups may experience social exclusion and discrimination within communities. This may be especially the case with new migrant groups, older people with low incomes facing the effects of gentrification, or older people displaced through the effects of urban regeneration. The argument here is that while neighbourhoods may provide supportive structures for 'ageing in place', macro-level forces may work to undermine the stability on which vulnerable groups rely for maintaining their place in the community. Given this, assessing the extent to which resources are available to develop age-friendly work in particular neighbourhoods is essential. Equally, developing programmes of action that address economic and political inequalities as well as changes affecting communities must be a central feature of age-friendly work (see the following section).

Challenging social inequality and exclusion

The age-friendly policy debate has carried with it a strong normative message in terms of maintaining older people actively engaged in society (see Chapter Two). However, much less attention has been paid to the inequalities associated with healthy and active ageing. The experience of ageing not only differs between older women and men, between those with more versus less financial resources and between different ethnic groups, it also differs as a consequence of the unequal impact of life events, and the accumulation of advantages versus disadvantages over the life course. Various chapters in this book have illustrated the extent to which particular groups of older people can be denied access to services and opportunities. The fact that different types of exclusion (poverty, fear of crime, exclusion from civic activities) co-exist in low-income neighbourhoods, further suggests an urgent need for the coordination of policy responses to promote the social inclusion of older people.

In response to the above, the WHO has put forward the notion of 'equity' as a guiding principle in assessing the age-friendliness of cities, placing emphasis on tackling systematic disparities in health (or in the major social determinants of health) between social groups that have different levels of underlying social disadvantage or disadvantage. Increasingly, it is acknowledged that a key task for future age-friendly policies will be to increase equity of access to the basic necessities and decision-making processes of urban life, explicitly addressing persisting gender, social class, ethnic and other inequalities in the older population. However, as well as identifying and analysing inequities between different groups of older people and across various neighbourhoods, there also a need to identify viable and effective strategies, interventions and actions to tackle such disparities.

The concept of the '*right* to the city' may offer a way forward in terms of responding to the rise of inequalities and power relations affecting ageing experiences in urban settings. It builds on the idea that all urban inhabitants should have the right to contribute much more centrally to decisions that produce or transform the public spaces in their city, shifting power and control away from private capital and the market towards community residents. Ensuring older people's right to the city will be essential to achieving an age-friendly city, including the 'right' to **appropriate urban space**; the 'right' to **participate in decision**

making surrounding the production of urban space; and the 'right' to **influence strategies** for urban planning and regeneration. At the same time, recognition must also be given of the extent to which the neighbourhoods in which older people live may have been destabilised as a consequence of global economic change. Where this is the case, interventions may be required to raise the level of resources within communities before age-friendly policies can begin to be implemented.

Developing rights to the city may be especially important for older people who are reliant on their immediate environment for achieving a fulfilling existence in old age. However, the so-called 'paradox of neighbourhood participation' is particularly applicable to old age: older people tend to spend more time in their locality (*being* part of the city) compared with other age groups, but are often among the last to be engaged when it comes to decision-making processes within their neighbourhoods (*taking part* of the city). This may be especially pertinent to those living in areas characterised by intense deprivation. The fact that different types of exclusion (poverty, fear of crime, exclusion from civic activities, exclusion from decision making) coexist in such areas suggests an urgent need for the coordination of policy responses to promote the social inclusion of older people.

Actions aimed at involving older people in crime prevention projects, community development work and neighbourhood renewal schemes could offer a way forward in securing older people's right to the city. However, as suggested previously, there is no clear evidence that the needs of older people are given systematic attention in urban regeneration schemes. Policies in the field of urban and community (re)development need to be broadened to embrace the ageing agenda more effectively. The age-friendly movement has a key role to play here, by combating the way in which ageism, or age-based discrimination, may restrict older people's full 'right' to use, appropriate and shape their cities. This is especially important given the largely untapped potential in working with older people, not only as a target group, but also as key actors in neighbourhood planning and development.

Increasing diversity

One key factor concerns recognition that some groups are systematically excluded from participating in decision-making processes within urban environments. Although the age-friendly project has placed older people at the centre of various initiatives, there has been a failure within the movement to acknowledge the full diversity of ageing experiences. Examples include the marginalisation of racial and ethnic minority ethnic groups and those within the lesbian, gay, bisexual, transsexual and queer community. More generally, the social exclusion experienced by many groups in urban areas – notably migrants, refugees and those living in communities with high levels of deprivation – has been largely ignored in discussion about age-friendly policies. An important issue arising from this is the extent to which current age-friendly work tends to assimilate rather than contest the various forms of discrimination within society. Given the pressures associated with globalisation and economic recession, addressing social exclusion will be crucial to the successful development of the age-friendly cities project.

Acknowledging **social and ethnic diversity** is thus an important issue for the age-friendly movement to address. The implications are wide-ranging, including: responding to different cultural interpretations of what 'age-friendliness' might mean; shaping policies around the needs of particular groups with contrasting migration histories and life-course experiences; responding to distinctive forms of inequality experienced by particular ethnic groups, notably in areas such health, income, and housing; and understanding as well tackling the impact of racism in communities and the challenge this presents for the achievement of successful age-friendly work.

Health diversity is another concern: do age-friendly initiatives reach out to people with all types of health conditions or are they focused predominantly on the 'healthy', in other words, those involved in different forms of 'active ageing'? To date, it is probably the latter who have dominated the development of the movement. But this raises questions about whether the goal is to create '*inclusive*' rather than '*exclusive*' communities. If the former, age-friendly initiatives must have the capacity to support people diagnosed as 'frail' as well as those with particular forms of dementia and other types of conditions. This would argue against the trend of developing separate 'dementia-friendly communities' or similar. Rather, the approach should acknowledge the variety of groups for whom age-friendly issues are relevant, and build environments that support and reflect the diversity that characterises an ageing world.

Facilitating community empowerment

The diversity of groups within the older population, as highlighted in the previous section, is likely to mean that the process of developing age-friendly communities will involve reconciling conflicting interests and concerns. Following this, there is a need for methods of community development that will work with the range of concerns within and between different age groups. Such an approach faces particular challenges in terms of empowering those older people experiencing different forms of exclusion, such as those facing mobility problems, chronic poverty and different forms of discrimination. A key role for age-friendly policies and initiatives will therefore be to enhance the 'agency', 'voice' *and* 'power' of these particular groups, by expanding opportunities that facilitate their participation in identifying 'leverage points' for change in their areas. An important issue here will be to determine which interventions could afford the greatest benefits within a given local context, taking into account the diverse needs of people living in a community.

The argument of this manifesto is that 'community empowerment' should have a central place in age-friendly activities and policies. 'Community empowerment' can be defined here as the process of enabling communities to have much greater control over their environment. The goal is to facilitate community ownership, and to allow individual and groups to organise and mobilise themselves towards commonly defined goals of social and political change. Community empowerment goes much further than 'consulting', 'involving' or 'engaging' people. It implies a process of renegotiating power and building capacities to gain access, networks and/or a voice, in order to gain more control over the decisions that shape communities – whether this relates to domains of the physical environment, such as housing, transportation and public spaces, or the social environment, such as community support, health services, and social and civic participation. Existing approaches here – notably the 'Village' movement in the US and activities around co-housing – are illustrative of this process. However, these activities are often socially exclusive, with limited participation from minority groups and those living in deprived urban neighbourhoods.

Following this, there is a considerable scope for the age-friendly movement to contribute to a more equal geographical distribution of society's wants and needs, such as access to health services, community support, good air quality and inviting public spaces. Questions of accessibility, housing and transport equity and walkability can all be seen as important matters of distribution of spatial resources. However, the AFCC approach has yet to develop policies that can prevent or reduce the inequalities associated with urban living, especially as regards their impact on the neighbourhoods in which people may have spent the majority of their lives. Ensuring 'spatial justice' for different groups of older people should therefore become a crucial part of the age-friendly debate, with strategies to enable communities to increase control over the conditions that shape their lives representing a key task for public policy.

Co-producing age-friendly communities

'Co-production' represents an important way forward to ensure older people's 'right' to contribute more centrally to decisions that shape their communities. This approach aims to put the principles of 'empowerment' into practice, working 'with' communities and offering residents greater control over their environment. It builds on a partnership between older people, their families, communities, statutory and non-statutory organisations who work together to jointly develop research and a shared understanding, as well as to design, develop and deliver opportunities, projects and solutions promoting social and political change. In this sense, co-production methods are at the heart of developing age-friendly policies and initiatives: among other stakeholders, older people are recognised as key actors in developing research and action plans to improve the 'age-friendliness' of their neighbourhood.

Recognising older people as actors in the social environment is essential to creating age-friendly communities. The fundamentally subjective nature of communities, and the importance of negotiating one's local environment, make empowerment and recognition of older residents paramount to achieving age-friendliness. This implies a strong investment in working with older residents as key partners in designing policies, especially for vulnerable and isolated groups within the community. Methods of co-production and co-research have been proven useful in engaging such groups, and have gained ground in the development of health and welfare services. Such an approach provides an opportunity for older people to take a leading role in research and age-friendly work, demonstrating their competence, and contributing to the process of social change in various ways. Information and communication technologies may also support the involvement of older residents in navigating and designing their environment.

The case for co-production methods and co-research with older people in developing age-friendly cities and communities is threefold. First, the approach represents a viable method to working with older residents and mobilising their expertise, skills and knowledge to stimulate creative reform ideas and initiatives around the age-friendliness in their neighbourhood. Second, it makes older people themselves central to the creation and development of policies and age-friendly initiatives. Third, co-production offers a range of benefits to the different stakeholders involved, because it provides a forum for rich and meaningful social engagement, and mutual learning and exchange. It demonstrates that when older residents work together with community stakeholders and other partners as a team with common interests of community improvements, the resulting social process has valuable potential for enhancing the quality of life of diverse groups of older people in different types of environments.

However, despite the opportunities, there is an urgent need for more experimentation to test and learn from participatory and collaborative approaches involving older people in the co-production of community space. The ongoing development and experimentation with creative participatory methods, both in research and policy work, will be necessary to inspire new understandings and possibilities for working with older residents as key actors and leaders in developing the age-friendly agenda. The success of communities in becoming more age-friendly will, to a large extent, depend on whether older people, including those facing social exclusion, will be involved as key actors in setting the agenda for future research and policies on age-friendly developments.

Developing creative and participatory age-friendly design

Integrating principles of co-production in urban design strategies represents another key task for the age-friendly movement. Involving older people in the planning of public spaces will be especially important to ensure that neighbourhood development anticipates users with different capacities instead of designing for the mythical 'average' (that is, young) person. However, older people often remain marginalised in processes of urban development due to an underlying **ageism** that characterises much of urban planning processes where older people are easily represented as passive victims of urban change.

In this context, various contributions to this volume have made a strong case to expand current understandings of 'age-friendly design' practice, including the possibilities of what it might do. The key argument is that age-friendly practice needs to be reimagined as a fundamentally participative and empowering process that enables 'bottom-up' forms of design to be developed with local communities. Age-friendly design needs to be understood as a process that works via the principles of participation, co-production and empowerment. In this way, it becomes an empowering tool that older citizens themselves can use to produce, shape and occupy both the physical and social fabric of their surrounding urban environments, and, ultimately, exercise their right to the city.

Drawing on this alternative definition of 'age-friendly design', it becomes possible to broaden out its remit to address a whole range of questions *beyond* its response to adapting environments to a set of physical needs. Design, for example, might involve a temporary intervention in a given space – one that transforms, momentarily, older people's use and perception of that place. Design might also involve a participative process, engaging non-professionals (those often left out of design processes) in the development of spaces that encourage the formation of local social networks. It might also reflect a more politicised and critical form of intervention, addressing issues around social inclusion and exclusion and the politics of ownership and reproduction of urban space. Such conceptions of 'age-friendly design', as argued in this book, have the potential to advance older people's rights to the city and support their capacity to reimagine and reclaim cities for themselves in both strategic but also in small, tactical ways.

There is clear appetite within the policymaking community to explore such alternative understandings of age-friendly design and broaden the repertoire of urban practices involved in the co-production of age-friendly cities. But there is also an opportunity to encourage socially engaged urban practitioners (architects, designers, artists) to intervene proactively in policy debates around age-friendly cities and communities. Examples of good practice are beginning to emerge, such as students of architecture working with groups of older people to redesign their neighbourhood, aided by cooperation between housing associations and local authorities. Issues relating to ageing populations are also receiving fuller acknowledgement in the spatial frameworks developed by urban planners as well as institutions such as the engineering firm Arup and the Royal Institute of British Architects. But there is considerable scope to expand the co-production dimension in age-friendly design practice, building on partnerships between socially engaged urban practitioners (architects, designers, artists) and older people.

Encouraging multisectorial and multidisciplinary collaboration

Several chapters have demonstrated the importance of building partnerships and synergies between multiple stakeholders and sectors – professional, academic, governmental and NGOs – in developing new ways of researching and creating age-friendly environments *for*, *with* and *by* older people. The AFCC movement, in this respect, has a key role to play in breaking down silos by building on the assets and bringing together networks already present in cities and communities, as well as creating new ones – synergising those in new and creative ways to benefit older people. Given the reality of economic austerity and competing demands for resources, strategic partnerships between local authorities, public health professionals, architects, housing providers, community organisations, universities and older people may be especially crucial to achieving successes. Mobilising a range of stakeholders from different sectors and disciplines, and providing both top-down and bottom-up input in order to maximise the added value for each of the partners, will be essential for realising the potential benefits that age-friendly communities have to offer.

Within such joint efforts, political leadership and coordination by local authorities may be another critical factor in building age-friendly communities. In many of the case studies discussed in this volume, local authorities took a leading role in developing collaborative strategies for creating age-friendly communities and ensuring a positive public policy context, one in which the needs of diverse groups of older people are recognised and addressed. Local governments are in a unique position to initiate and advance age-friendly developments, as they, generally, have long been involved in the strategic planning and managing of domains such as transport, health and social care services. Linking age-friendliness to other priorities within cities, such as those linked to environmental issues, sustainable development, and accessible and affordable housing and public transport, may provide powerful synergies to help move the age-friendly agenda ahead. A major challenge for future work will be to develop co-productive and collaborative models of governance that bring together different forms of knowledge and expertise, by promoting stakeholder involvement from different sectors, including older people themselves.

A central argument of this manifesto is that AFCC policies are unlikely to be successful unless embedded in interdisciplinary networks and approaches to policy leadership, education, urban design, community engagement and evaluation. Understanding optimum environments for ageing must be seen as an interdisciplinary enterprise that will require close integration of insights from a range of disciplines. Research on environmental aspects of ageing has an impressive literature to its name. Yet, to take one example, it remains detached from analysing the impact of powerful global and economic forces transforming the physical and social context of cities. Remedying this will require close integration with insights from a range of disciplines, including urban sociology, urban economics, design, social policy and human geography. A further challenge for the AFFC programme resides in connecting this approach to broader strategies such as those relating to sustainable development, reducing inequalities and health promotion. Rethinking the way in which people build, manage, negotiate, appropriate and live in cities and communities requires cooperation with committed partners, relevant stakeholders and actors at all levels of government as well as civil society and the private sector.

Integrating research with policy

The development of the age-friendly approach has occurred at a rapid rate, notably through the stimulus of the GNAFCC. But this has been in the absence of a body of research that informs us about the effectiveness and impact of such work: for example, whether it benefits some groups rather than others; what contribution it makes to the wellbeing of older people; whether it leads to improvements in urban design; and whether it strengthens support networks within neighbourhoods. Establishing answers to these questions will be important if local and municipal authorities are to give financial support to age-friendly programmes.

Given the above, tackling the impact evaluation gap will be crucial for the next phase of developing age-friendly work. Applying mixed methods in impact evaluation will be particularly important in identifying who benefits from age-friendly initiatives and why, as well as measurement of the impact on traditionally excluded groups. An evaluation that combines qualitative (for example, longitudinal qualitative research, qualitative case study research) and quantitative (for example, randomised experiments and quasi-experimental designs) methods can generate both statistically reliable measures of the magnitude of the impact as well as a greater depth of understanding of how and why a programme was or was not effective, and how it might be adapted in future to make it more effective. In addition to measuring **outcomes** – from neighbourhood satisfaction and changes in neighbourhood networks at one end to hospital admission rates and emergency hospital visits at the other end – there is also a need for building **process** evaluation activities into programme implementation, and using these to conduct continuous quality improvement. Encouraging comparative studies examining the various approaches to building age-friendly communities in different social, political and economic contexts should also be an important element of future work.

New initiatives will be required to expand the current research base associated with age-friendly policies and initiatives. These are likely to include: developing a network, bringing together academics from existing research centres supporting age-friendly issues, to assist the work of the WHO GNAFCC; encouraging the development of doctoral and post-doctoral researchers specialising on age-friendly issues; encouraging research links with specific cities and communities; developing work on specific themes (such as the impact of gentrification and issues affecting particular migrant groups); and developing new methodological approaches for evaluating the benefits or otherwise of age-friendly interventions.

Strengthening international networking

Many of the achievements and advancements in developing age-friendly policies have been fuelled by the GNAFCC. In less than 10 years, the number of cities and communities that has committed to this agenda has expanded from a handful to over 500 (2017 figures) – reflecting the success of what now can be described as a worldwide social movement, one that advocates for the creation of environments that support the needs and aspirations of people as they age. For its members, the age-friendly movement and GNAFCC have offered a unifying and integrated narrative in which to advance ageing work at all levels of government as well as civil society and the private sector. The 'age-friendly' brand has also helped to 'mainstream' the ageing agenda into various policy fields, giving valuable support to a 'co-productive' policy design framework, one that mobilises older people's expertise, skills and knowledge to reshape services and neighbourhoods. Members have benefitted from joining the GNAFCC in various ways, through the opportunities it provides for mutual learning and sharing actions to support and enable older adults in communities; comparing strategies in creating and sustaining effective ageing policies; sharing best practice and strategies that sustain age-friendly programmes; and supporting/connecting national and international networks, organisations and partnerships with expertise on ageing issues.

However, the key question for its future development is not just how to *sustain* the network, but how to *expand* and *raise* the ambition of the age-friendly agenda in a difficult economic climate with limited funding and competing demands for resources. Four major challenges will need to be carefully addressed if the movement wants to realise its full potential. First, close consideration needs to be given to the various stages involved in social movement development, including their success factors and modes of decline, as these can teach age-friendly advocates how best to avoid the outcomes of co-optation and failure, and better position themselves for success. Second, there is an urgent need to find creative ways to mobilise new resources, in terms of knowledge, internal and external support and funding, to support the communities of practice developed through the GNAFCC. The limited resources currently available for managing and running the GNAFCC raises important concerns about the effectiveness and sustainability of the movement in the long term, especially given the rapid rise of network members and related demands and pressures. One response to this issue would be to draw on the resources of the various groups linked to the network, notably WHO Affiliated Programmes such as the AARP Network of Age-Friendly Communities (US), Age-Friendly Ireland, Age Platform Europe, the International Federation on Ageing, and the UK Network of Age-Friendly Cities. Combining and sharing the resources of these different organisations provides a platform for ensuring the long-term sustainability of the age-friendly movement.

Following the above, a third challenge for the movement will be to create much stronger linkages with academic institutions and researchers investigating the relationship between ageing and the environment from multiple disciplinary perspectives. One way forward in this respect, as suggested above, could be through the development of an international research network – pioneering new research, technology, and solutions across a range of ageing-related domains – and supporting the research side of the GNAFCC's policy work. This could involve: drawing together and sharing the existing evidence base to support the piloting of new and innovative solutions to the challenges and opportunities of population ageing; developing international collaboration in research on ageing and the environment; undertaking interdisciplinary and comparative research on the development and implementation of age-friendly programmes; testing innovative forms of public engagement and co-production/co-research with older people; and supporting early career researchers in the field. A crucial role for such a research network would be to assess and evaluate the effectiveness of age-friendly programmes in terms of improving the lives of different groups of older people and achieving community change. This will be especially important to justify future funding for new age-friendly initiatives in times of austerity where the ability to 'demonstrate impact' and realise social, health and economic benefits has become ever more important.

A fourth, and final, challenge is associated with the need for combining a strong local presence with a truly global strategy for the age-friendly movement. An important dimension of this will be to strengthen links and share networks, experiences *and* resources with cities and communities in the global south that face particular challenges in terms of acquiring the structural capacity to accommodate the needs and aspirations of their ageing populations. A global strategy also underlines the need for new models of intervention that can respond to the highly unequal contexts experienced by older people in urban as well as rural communities across the world. The key argument running through this book concerns the need for a stronger embedding of the age-friendly mission in a **citizenship-** and **rights-based** narrative of ageing, one that is centred on values of equality, community empowerment and spatial justice. Placing such values at the heart of age-friendly work will go far in meeting the goals of what is now a significant movement for social change.

Index

Note: page numbers in *italic* type refer to Figures; those in **bold** type refer to Tables.

collaboration 20
AFM (Age-Friendly Manchester) 240–1
age-friendly design 215
Fingal AFCC 155, 157
multisectoral/multidisciplinary 283–5
see also co-production of age-friendly
policies by older people; co-research;
involvement; participation
communication:
WHO checklist theme 16, *17*
communities of interest 25
community 6, 33–4, 44–5
changing views of 34–7
impact of global change 38–41
older people's engagement in 41–2, 43
policy strategies 42–4
see also neighbourhood
community empowerment:
manifesto for change 279–80
see also involvement; participation
community projects, Hong Kong 129–30
community studies 34–6, 42
limitations of network analysis 36–7
community support services:
WHO checklist theme 16, *17*
'competence-press model' 23, 52
concentration of older people, as a success
factor 24
consultation 20–1, 25, 43
Australia 179, 180
Fingal AFC (Age Friendly County)
programme 148, 152–3, 158–60,
162–3
Old Moat age-friendly project,
Manchester 195, 200–1
see also involvement; participation
core indicators 22
Coroners Ordinance, Hong Kong 136
COTA (Council of the Ageing) ACT
179–80
COTA (Council of the Ageing) Australia
176
COTA (Council of the Ageing) Victoria
176, 177
Council of Australian Governments 177
County Fingal, Ireland *see* Fingal AFC
(Age Friendly County) programme,
Ireland
Covenant on Demographic Change 19
Crabtree, S.A. 133
Creating age-friendly places (UK Urban
Ageing Consortium) 241
*Creating an age-friendly Boroondara: 2014-
2019* (City of Boroondara) 176
Crow, G. 35
cultural erasure 57
Cultural Offer programme, Manchester
237

D

Dale, Meredith 7, 75–96

Dannefer, Dale 7, 51–71, 54, 97
de Certeau, Michel 198, 215, 216
De Donder, Liesbeth 7–8, 97–118
De Witte, Nico 7–8, 97–118
Delanty, G. 39
dementia 43, 85, 126, 147, 244, 258, 275,
279
Denoven Design 221
Department of Family and Community
Studies (FACS), NSW 181
design:
universal and inclusive 212–13, 226
see also age-friendly design
Design for Access standards, UK 239
designers 9, 217, 227, 283
socially engaged 214–16, 226, 227
see also age-friendly design
Detroit, Michigan 40
diabetic retinopathy 253, 254
see also vision impairment, older people
with
disability:
and the built environment 37, 263–4,
265–77, 267
disability discrimination and equality
legislation, UK 265
social model of 252, 254–5
disability rights 252
disability studies 57, 254–5
disability threshold (WHO) **196**
disasters, and older people 122, 133,
274–5
displacement 58–9, 274
Berlin 76, 77, 90–1, 91–2
Brussels 100
see also gentrification; urban
regeneration
diversity:
Australia 169
manifesto for change 278–9
driving:
Australia 172, 173
older people with vision impairment
264
see also mobility; transportation
Dublin Declaration on Age-Friendly
Cities 150
Dundalk, County Louth, Ireland 148
Duppen, Daan 7–8, 97–118

E

earthquakes 122, 274–5
East Berlin 76
see also Berlin, Germany
ECO box project, Paris (AAA) 220
'ecological theory of ageing' 52
Economic and Social Research Council,
International Partnership and
Networking Scheme 5
economic austerity *see* austerity
economic recession 26, 28